Young People's
SCIENCE
Encyclopedia

Index by Sara Lamb
Edited by the Staff of
NATIONAL COLLEGE OF EDUCATION
Evanston, Illinois

Volume 20
Index

 CHILDRENS PRESS, CHICAGO

Photographs

Page 2:   Skylab space station (NASA)

Page 3:   *Top to Bottom:*
Wheatfield (U.S.D.A. Photo)
Technician capping Abbokinase (Abbott Laboratories)
Spider (Macmillan Science Company)
View of Earth (NASA)
Space Shuttle (NASA)
Bahama coral reef (Macmillan Science Company)

Cover: Design by Sandra Gelak
Wheat Harvester (USDA Photo)
Wood Duck (James P. Rowan)
Walking Stick (James P. Rowan)

Library of Congress Catalog Card Number: 67-17925

4 5 6 7 8 9 10 11 12 R 85 84 83 82

TABLE OF CONTENTS

YOUNG PEOPLE'S
SCIENCE ENCYCLOPEDIA

Edited by the Staff of
NATIONAL COLLEGE OF EDUCATION, Evanston, Illinois

ASSOCIATE EDITORS

HELEN J. CHALLAND, B.E., M.A., Ph.D.
  Chairman, Division of Natural Sciences
  National College of Education,
  Evanston, Illinois

DONALD A. BOYER, B.S., M.S., Ph.D.
  Science Education Consultant, Winnetka
  Public Schools, Winnetka, Illinois
  Science, National College of Education

EDITORIAL CONSULTANTS
ON THE STAFF OF NATIONAL COLLEGE OF EDUCATION

Elizabeth R. Brandt, B.A., M.Ed.
Eugene B. Cantelupe, B.A., M.F.A., Ph.D.
John H. Daugherty, B.S., M.A.
Irwin K. Feinstein, B.S., M.A., Ph.D.
Mary Gallagher, A.B., M.A., Ph.D.
Beatrice S. Garber, A.B., M.S., Ph.D.
Hal S. Galbreath, B.S. Ed., M.S.
Arthur J. Hannah, B.S., M.Ed., Ed.D.

Robert R. Kidder, A.B., M.A., Ph.D.
Jean C. Kraft, B.S., M.A., Ph.D.
Elise P. Lerman, B.A., B.F.A., M.F.A.
Mary M. Lindquist, B.A., M.A., Ph.D.
Mary-Louise Neumann, A.B., B.S.L.S.
Lavon Rasco, B.A., M.A., Ph.D.
Bruce Allen Thale, B.S.Ed., M.S.Ed.
Fred R.Wilkins, Jr., B.A., M.Ed., Ph.D.

SPECIAL SUBJECT AREA CONSULTANTS

Krafft A. Ehricke, B.A.E., H.L.D.
Benjamin M. Hair, A.B., M.D.
Charles B. Johnson, B.S., M.A., M.S.
Raymond J. Johnson, B.B.A., M.Ed.

H. Kenneth Scatliff, M.D.
Eleanor S. Segal, M.D.
Paul P. Sipiera, B.A., M.S.
Ray C. Soliday, B.A., B.S., M.A. (Deceased)

Don Dwiggins, Aviation Editor

THE STAFF

Project Director   Rudolph A. Hastedt
Project Editor   M. Frances Dyra
Editorial Assistant   Janet Zelasko

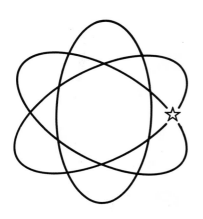

Helping Young People in Science

A message for parents and teachers . . .

Science holds more interest for more young people today than any other field of knowledge. Most parents and teachers know that motivating children to study science is hardly necessary. Not only are the things of science, such as animals, plants, astronauts, spaceships, and rocks, of interest to young people; but their natural curiosity, their tendency to question, and their habit of testing everything exemplify the ways of the scientist. Unfortunately, many children tend to lose these characteristics as they grow to maturity. Parents and teachers can help to keep them alive and vibrant by careful guidance.

Science should be an integral part of our way of life. Its processes have much to offer society and the development of personality. Increasingly and surely, science is taking the center of the stage in modern civilization, and will pervade the existence and critically affect the lives of today's children in ways the present generation cannot even imagine. Parents and teachers have an obligation to guide the learning of the rising generation so that scientific technology does not become the enslaver but the enslaved. Through the study of science men can free their minds of fear, superstition, prejudice, and ignorance. Through it men can learn a new way of thinking and a saner way of deliberating, as well as acquire a greater respect for law and order and a new chance for the development of democracy. Science can be used, however, to destroy the freedom of the mind and the freedom of the peoples. The way by which science is taught — or the way children learn it — is the key to their future.

Whether the children of today will bend technology toward the building of a happier, safer world tomorrow depends, in part, on the expectations held by parents and teachers. If they care enough about education, about honest and objective inquiry, about deliberative rather than impulsive action, and about the fulfillment of the human individual to his optimum, much of the present generation's responsibility will have been discharged.

Obviously, *example* is the best way to show expectation. Parents who provide good books in the home for their children but never open books themselves fail to inspire the child to learn. It is a good intellectual climate for a child when lively discussions and questions in the family circle lead to dictionaries, encyclopedic volumes, or other source materials which throw light on the puzzling and the unknown. The habit of such family deliberation which depends on the "look it up" technique rather than on the lazy exchange of ignorance could change significantly the direction of human affairs. It will surely improve the school achievement and the intellectual and social growth of children.

It is the obligation of every parent and teacher to help each child achieve as much as his powers permit. Excellence in education cannot be restricted to the intellectual elite in a society where enterprises are so complex as ours. All types of people are needed to perform to the maximum if the success of the whole is to be ensured. On this problem, John W. Gardner[1], President of the Carnegie Foundation, says that excellence of performance in launching a rocket missile is required of each person who has anything to do with it from the time it is designed on the drawing boards until the last minute when a mechanic adjusts the final valve

[1]John W. Gardner, *Excellence* (New York: Harper & Brothers, 1961) p. 131.

before it is blasted from its pad. A mistake anywhere along the line of production or of the launching operation could cause the rocket to blow up with a great waste of time, money, and even of human life. Therefore, it is in the interest of national survival that parents and teachers help every child to make steady progress in his education at his own best level or rate of performance.

Adequate materials which can be adapted to individual differences in ability and interest should become the possession of every home and every classroom. The encyclopedia is by far the most versatile of the source materials available. Not only is it a depository of a greater fund of information but it is, by its inherent organization, more efficient to use because of its pinpointing of individual entries arranged in alphabetical order. When the articles, such as those of the YOUNG PEOPLE'S SCIENCE ENCYCLOPEDIA, are written for a wide range of ability, the possibility is enhanced that every child may find something of value to him at his level of achievement. In the home, children of varying ages may profit from the use of such a treasury of knowledge and easy-to-do experiments.

What is science? A scientist?

Science primarily is a voyage of discovery, and a working scientist is a person in pursuit of the unknown. The pursuit is aided by increasingly better instruments, tools, and ways of thinking. To build up knowledge and to improve man's grasp or understanding of his universe home — from its very big aspects to the very little — is the aim of science.

The YOUNG PEOPLE'S SCIENCE ENCYCLOPEDIA gives to the teacher or the parent an unmatched opportunity to guide the child in using valuable information, experiments, and cross references to solve problems, to build attitudes, and to develop ways of thinking like those of the mature scientist. Let it be understood, however, that scientific thinking is not confined to scientists. The encyclopedia can be used to build the foundation for careers other than in science. All scholars, statesmen, and philosophers who achieve greatness govern their activities by such scientific attitudes and ways of thinking as:

1. Honesty in reporting about events or data
2. Maintaining healthy skepticism toward apparent facts
3. Refusing to jump to quick conclusions but preferring to hear all sides and collect all available evidence
4. Accepting the probability of change

5. Open-mindedness toward new ideas
6. Searching constantly for mistakes and omissions in one's own work
7. Cheerfully admitting one's own mistakes
8. Accepting the obligation to test one's own conclusions and to encourage others to test them.

Such attitudes or ways of thinking, which are implicit in the study of science, help to develop better personal character among today's children and youth. If science can become the partner of democracy, its effect on citizenship ultimately should contribute to a better society.

What do young people learn in science before high school? The contents of a boy's pockets or the treasure chest under his bed can give significant leads. Perhaps there are bird's eggs, a sling shot, a telescope, some rock quartz, and a pressed leaf. To the mature scientist these things can represent some of the main areas of knowledge in science: zoology, physics, astronomy, geology, and botany, respectively. But science for young people does not deal in the technical material and vocabulary of such advanced fields of science. It begins simply with something like the bird's eggs and takes the young person through a study of the familiar living things around him to the distant and the microscopic. When he reaches his first course in biology at the high school level, he is on much familiar ground.

Since science is taught in every grade level of the elementary and junior high schools, it is important for the parent as well as for the teacher to know how broadly it is based on the total content of all the sciences. In an elementary way the student is given a picture of the whole. He gets a general view of the entire universe from the extremely tiny animal under the microscope to the largest galaxy or system of stars. He is not expected to study in depth at this age, although intellectually gifted students may be encouraged to go deeper if their interest is high and other curriculum areas are not neglected. This broad picture of science as the young person views it in school has these main subdivisions:

I. The earth and its crust
    A. Rocks, minerals, and soils
    B. Erosion by wind, water, gravity, frost, and glacial action
    C. Mountain-building
    D. Earthquakes and volcanoes
    E. The continents and the seas
    F. Other land forms
II. Beyond the earth

   A. Atmosphere and weather
   B. Space
   C. Planets, stars, and galaxies
   D. Satellites: moons and man-made
   E. Air and space travel
  III. Living things
   A. Plants
   B. Animals
   C. Health and physiology
  IV. Energies and physical-chemical forces
   A. Light and color
   B. Sound
   C. Electricity and magnetism
   D. Combustion and heat
   E. Air and other gas pressures
   F. Water power
   G. Mechanics
   H. Gravity
   I. Nuclear fission and fusion
   J. Chemical change
   K. Physical change
  V. Inventions, discoveries, and great men of science

The method of discovery

One of the basic needs of children is new experiences which expand their knowledge of the world about them. They show this need constantly by the questions they ask. Their desire to explore is insatiable, as every father and mother can testify. The method of discovery is based on this need, and guides the explorations of young people so that they learn significantly from their activities of discovery.

The boy or girl whose study of science is a voyage of discovery rather than a passive absorption of content is himself a young scientist. Leaders in the academic world today are emphasizing the value of a student's learning a field of knowledge precisely the way in which the experts of that field develop and expand its facts and principles.[2] In almost every field, content is developed through research and less formal processes of discovery which reflect the attitudes and methods of the scientists. Even though knowledge in a field is known to mature scholars, teachers and parents would be advised to introduce present knowledge and all aspects of the youth's environment to him through the process of

---

[2] Jerome S. Bruner, *The Process of Education* (Cambridge: Harvard University Press, 1960) p. 20; *Strengthening Science Teaching in Elementary Schools,* Illinois Curriculum Program, Bulletin No. C-Three, 1960, p. 27.

discovery. He should be allowed to participate, to choose, to search, sometimes to launch out alone, and, above all, to have the emotional rewards of his own personal discovery or invention just as the original discoverer or inventor had. Greater interest, sustained study, and significant increments of learning result when a fact or a principle is discovered through the young person's pursuit of his own question. Giving answers is no spur to learning. Giving the young learner an opportunity to "look it up" or experiment for himself, and then asking him further questions relevant to his search so as to stimulate his curiosity to know more and grasp relationships — these are magic spurs to learning.

No one will deny that young people need an effective and usable knowledge of subject matter. The method of discovery highlights the way in which the learner acquires subject matter. It is concerned also with the attitudes the young explorer is developing in the process of learning. On this point, Jerome Bruner of Harvard University thinks the critical attitudes to be developed through the method of discovery are:

1. Open-minded inquiry
2. Intellectual courage for shrewd guessing and hunches
3. Self-reliance in learning to solve problems on one's own
4. Conviction that nature and the universe has order one can and should discover.

Bruner thinks, further, that these attitudes have to be "caught" from teachers and parents who exemplify them in their own activity. Such teachers do not teach by assertion and demonstrated proof; instead, they inject an element of excitement into the discovery situation that entices the young person to discover ideas and relationships with some of the same joy and exciting sequences of the first scientist or scholar who traveled that path.[3] This is not to say that an intelligent teacher will not occasionally resort to systematic and deductive coverage of topics which may fill in gaps or follow a series of inductive enterprises. The important thing to remember is that the over-all process should be one of discovery; however, discovery should not be used to the frustration level.

By contrast, schools which emphasize memorizing cold content through verbalizing experiences of others tend to develop in children the habits of uncritical acceptance, of dependence on the opinions of others, and of dogmatism. It is a sad picture when children constantly

[3] Bruner, *op. cit.,* pp. 20-21.

turn to the teacher or to the textbook for approved answers. Every young person needs aid in making mature responses in terms of his readiness, but this is not accomplished by "spoon feeding."

To develop intellectual self-reliance and to spur the zest for intellectual pursuit is not to give answers but to pose questions. This involves capitalizing upon, or creating, problem situations in which interesting questions arise.[4] Children are fascinated by the call of the unknown especially when a stimulating person issues the call. The enthusiasm of a teacher or a parent is contagious. Whether organized learning activities in a group convey children on a voyage of discovery or whether the individual "looks it up" at home, the same atmosphere can prevail. That atmosphere can be provided by either the teacher or the parent. Both can manage the environment so that the child's excitement about learning can be reinforced rather than ignored or discounted. Both can see that essential materials and references are available so that unnecessary frustration does not develop. Since children do not always know how or what to learn in order to solve their problems, frustration may occur if the parent or the teacher is not alert to the technical difficulties faced by children in their quests. Outside interference and too much domination of the process can dull the zest for pursuit, but parents and teachers can, nevertheless, open many doors to new learning when a moment of readiness arrives.[5]

Experiments and things to do

The YOUNG PEOPLE'S SCIENCE ENCYCLOPEDIA does not limit its presentation to information in articles, definitions, and cross references. To be sure, many interesting questions are posed in the main text of the encyclopedia. Included with many of the main articles, however, are special experiments and things to do. These are set off in a page column near the textual material in order to highlight them for easy reference. Arranged as they are in a separate "box" on the page, the more than 200 experiments and things to do can be used by the young person as if he had a separate book of experiments.

The technique of working out these experiments and things to do is a more systematic adaptation of the method of discovery. Each experiment or activity poses a question. One can find the answer only by doing the steps indicated. This is the way scientists verify their hypotheses or "hunches" about things in nature and the universe. Experimentation is a part of the scientific method and a necessary part of the job of the scientist.

---

[4] W. Ray Rucker, *Curriculum Development in the Elementary School* (New York: Harper & Brothers, 1960) p. 35.
[5] *Ibid.*, pp. 96-97.

Children have fun doing science experiments. They are like games and give added zest to learning. They teach them at the same time the discipline and order which must prevail in all scientific endeavor. Accuracy in measurement, in keeping records, and in reporting results becomes quite understandable to the child as a result of his attempts to experiment. Very often, in the beginning, the young person will fail in performing the experiment correctly because he did not take seriously enough the instructions to be exact. When he learns to be careful and accurate, his joy in performing experiments increases. The rewards are even greater. Therefore, experimenting may seem at first just like a game, but the child soon learns it is not the same as play. It can, fortunately, be more fun than play.

One concept the young person will learn early in experimenting is the concept of "control." A control in experimentation simply means that the experiment is in two parts. Not all experiments have two parts or a control, but many do, particularly when the experimenter wants to see if the new conditions to be tested are different from usual conditions. Thus, the control is the ordinary or usual way of doing things. The experimental situation has the new or different ingredients. When the experiment is concluded, the two situations are compared to see what different results occurred. If results are significantly different, the scientist may infer that the new ingredients or factors in the experimental situation were responsible for the difference.

The materials to be used in the experiments suggested in this encyclopedia are rather simple and are easy to obtain in most communities. It is important that all necessary materials are available before the experiment is attempted.

Developing critical and intuitive thinking

Critical thinking is valuable to both science and the everyday social process: Its chief characteristic probably is that it can recognize assertions lacking in substance or proof. The critical thinker is quick to recognize faults in thinking. He uses a systematic way of determining if something is true, reliable, or workable. Critical thinking is a form of scientific method or reflective thinking which ordinarily goes through, even if very quickly, these progressive steps:

1. Recognition of a problem or a question
2. Analysis of the problem, plans of attack, and the general search for information or data
3. Development of hypotheses and structure of further search for information in terms of them

4. Selection of the best solution and testing it by experimentation
5. Development of a tentative conclusion
6. Further verification of conclusions and reporting of findings to others.

Since the critical thinker is trained in thinking like the scientist, scholar, or philosopher, he realizes that even under the most controlled conditions the human mind is able to find only a *best* answer, not necessarily *the* answer. Many good answers have had to give way to others as science and technology advance. Science searches for the truth, but the quest is never ended. One can never be sure he has found the ultimate truth. The critical thinker is skeptical, therefore, when he hears others claim an indisputable truth, of having all factors under control, or of perfecting a cure-all.

The critical thinker looks also for cause and effect relationships. He wants to look beyond the symptoms of a situation, beyond even the ways in which the symptoms are affecting behavior, to the cause of the symptoms. He is more confident that a reliable solution can be worked out for problems if analysis goes down to the bedrock of cause.

If someone wants to launch out on a new enterprise with little except enthusiasm, the critical thinker is there to ask, "What are your plans?" He does not believe that things will "naturally work themselves out." He wants coordination, schedules, intermediate goals, organization of resources, and the like before he can give his approval of even the most worthy goals. He wants plans to be evolved through scientific thinking.

Intuitive thinking, on the other hand, sometimes appears to dispense with steps in definition and analysis with the related search of available data. It appears to leap immediately to a shrewd guess, to a tentative solution without the patient labor of the scientist. Although anyone may engage in intuitive thinking, it is most likely to appear in the individual with a particularly acute creative imagination. Some of the most valuable products of intuitive thinking come from advanced scholars and mature scientists whose knowledge has reached such a high state of generalization they can reach conclusions about unknowns in their own and related fields of knowledge by using the generalizations previously reached. In other words, they see *transfer* value between the familiar and the unknown. Their "hunches" often pay off because phenomena do tend to act in terms of certain broad laws. If enough of the structure or the specifics of a known situation seem to be present in the unknown situation, the creative imagination of the intuitive thinker constructs the new situation partly with the image he has already constructed of the related situation.

The chief value of intuitive thinking is that it gives us problems-with-tentative-solutions-to-be-tested. Great intuitive thinkers are the scouts of science. They forge ahead to explore what the main body of scientists should explore more systematically. Thus, intuitive thinking should be checked carefully by the above steps which characterize scientific thinking. It may result in important short cuts in the progress of science, but there is no substitute for the rigorous testing by the scientific method.

Intuitive thinking has a place in the classroom and in the parent-child discussion. The young person needs to have courage and confidence in his ability to use intuitive thinking effectively. Children who lack such confidence probably should not be encouraged to use this type of thinking initially. With most above-average and gifted youngsters, the technique can be successfully nurtured. One effective way to teach intuitive thinking is, again, by example. If teachers or parents are willing to make the best guess about an answer and then encourage young persons to join them in critical analysis to test the guess, they are more likely to encourage this kind of courage on the part of the young. Obviously, training in intuitive thinking is impossible if the adult analyzes everything in advance. The analysis comes in the discovery process when the intuitive thinker and his associates set about to "discover if I am right."

The YOUNG PEOPLE'S SCIENCE ENCYCLOPEDIA presents an excellent opportunity for the adult and the young person to engage deliberately in intuitive thinking. Suppose a generalization or scientific principle had been learned in one volume of the encyclopedia. The young person may be encouraged to think where this principle might apply elsewhere. Following up the hunches may take both on a profitable voyage of discovery in several volumes. One of the best clues to relationships to other concepts, and thus to related generalizations, is the cross reference. Cross references are marked in small capital letters in the text of articles, and at the end of articles they are indicated by "See Also:".

An example of this kind of intuitive thinking and its implications for a systematic search for proof in the encyclopedia may be seen in a young person's hunch that the force of gravity is different on each of the planets, and different on the moon from that of Earth. This leap in intuitive thinking is not a great one for an adult. For a nine-year-old child it is a substantial leap. Perhaps it was occasioned by the child's reading elementary books on space and space travel in which the reader was informed that man will weigh less on the moon than on Earth, but that if man travels to Jupiter he will weigh much more. Part of the leap in the child's thinking is made by relating weight with the force of gravity. Part of it can be accounted for in the knowledge the child has about the different sizes of the planets and the size of the moon in relation to the earth. With these relationships, the child now leaps to his hypothesis that greater size and greater force of gravity go together in the solar system. Is his guess right? It is not exactly right, but his guess will lead to a refined answer if he is encouraged to follow up his guess with systematic search of proof in the encyclopedia.

To check his guess, the young intuitive thinker may read the article on "gravity" and follow up the indicated cross references. He should be encouraged next to study more closely the characteristics of the planets and of the moon. The guiding adult may pose the questions at this point: "Are all planets composed of the same material? Does a cube of this material weigh the same on all planets? Do any planets have very light material like that of a comet?" This analysis will lead the young person to realize that size alone may not account for the differences in the force of gravitation among the planets. He will discover that the density of their matter, or the total weight of the material in the planet, has a more exact relationship with the force of gravitation on objects on or near the planetary surface.

The kind of systematic analysis and search for proof by the young person may prepare him for another intuitive leap. He has been studying about members of the solar system. His attention should be directed to the sun and its immense size and weight. Its gravitational pull on the planets keep them from flying off into space in haphazard fashion. But why does not this great attraction pull the planets into the sun itself? If the youngster has encountered the idea of regular orbits for each planet as they revolve around the sun, he is ready for his leap to a new relationship. He sees the planets arranged in a great wheel around the sun which acts as the hub. The planets move around at different speeds, but there is *order* in this difference because their speed of travel around the sun is closely related to their distance from the sun. The closest planet, Mercury, moves fastest in the shortest orbit. Venus is second in distance from the sun; it moves slower in a longer orbit. This is true of each planet in turn. Perhaps our young reader has also encountered the idea that the solar system is a part of another and greater revolving system, the Milky Way Galaxy. His intuitive hunch, then, is that *order* in the universe of heavenly bodies is based on the balance of gravitational force and the speed of revolution. As he reads about man-made satellites, he will see the connection between their speeds and their distances from the earth's surface. A satellite can be placed successfully in orbit only if the rocket which takes it aloft attains the exact speed of revolution to balance the gravitational pull of the earth. Our young reader can check his guess, in part, by referring to the article on "satellite, man-made." If he wishes to persist in this study, he may be guided to the article on "motion."

Critical and intuitive thinking should be thought of as partners in the pursuit of the unknown. Both will be employed in any skillful use of this encyclopedia. The experiments and things to do throughout the first 19 volumes are planned to give the young person a systematic approach to critical or scientific thinking. Training in intuitive thinking depends upon the teachers and parents who guide young people in the use of the set.

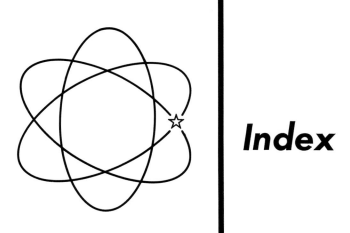

Index

HOW TO USE THIS INDEX
KINDS OF ENTRIES

Major entries are in bold print: **WEATHER**
Minor entries are in regular print: Agouti
Related entries are in italics: *Weather forecasting*

ABBREVIATIONS

Pictures are indicated by *illus.*
Experiments and Things to Do are indicated by *exp.*

NUMBERING

The *volume* number is given first, followed by
a *colon* and the *page* numbers: 2:153-155

AARDVARK 1:13
Anteater 2:113
illus. 1:13
AARDWOLF 1:13; 9:884
Abaca see **HEMP**
Abacus see **COMPUTER**
ABALONE 1:13-14
ABDOMEN 1:14
appendix 2:123
illus. 1:14
Peritoneum 13:1266-1267
Aberration of light see **STARS**
Abiogenesis see **SPONTANEOUS GENERATION**
A-Bomb see **BOMB**
ABORTION 1:14
ABRASIVES 1:14
Sand 15:1493
Abscess see **INFECTION**
Abscission layer see **LEAVES**
Absolute humidity see **HUMIDITY**
ABSOLUTE ZERO 1:15
Brownian movement 4:307
chart 1:15
Giauque, William F. 8:775
Heat 9:827
Kelvin, William Thomson, Lord 10:931
Kinetic theory 10:934
Mercury (planet) 11:1044-1046
Perpetual motion machine 13:1268
Temperature 18:1733
Temperature scales 18:1733
Thermometer 18:1743-1744
ABSORPTION OF LIGHT 1:16
exp. 1:16
ABSORPTION, PHYSIOLOGICAL 1:15
Assimilation 2:151
illus. 1:15
Acacia, illus. 14:1331
ACCELERATION 1:17
Falling bodies 7:670
Forces 8:710-711
Friction 8:731
Galileo 8:746-747
Gravity 8:795
illus. 8:711
Motion 12:1111-1112
Pendulum 13:1260-1261
Space medicine 17:1611-1617
Spectrum pollution 17:1643-1644
Velocity 19:1808-1809
ACCELERATOR 1:17
ACCELERATORS (PARTICLE) 1:17
Charged particles 4:370
circular 1:18
cyclotron 1:18
Dees 1:18
electrostatic 1:18; 6:585
linear 1:18
Neutron 12:1146
Nuclear reactor 12:1166-1168
Radioactivity 15:1422-1423
Radiation 15:1407-1409
Relativity 15:1444
Van de Graff 1:18
Acceptor atom see **ELECTRON BORROWING; ELECTRON SHARING**
ACCLIMATIZATION 1:19
ACCOMMODATION 1:19
Acetabulum see **SKELETON**
Acetate see **ACETIC ACID; SYNTHETIC FABRICS**
ACETIC ACID 1:19
Acids and bases 1:20-22
Aspirin 2:151
Film 7:681
ACETONE 1:19

ACETYLENE 1:19
torch, illus. 1:19
Acetylsalicylic acid see **ASPIRIN**
Achene 8:734
Achilles, tendon of see **FIBROUS TISSUE**
Achromatic lens see **LENS, MANMADE**
Achromycin see **ANTIBIOTICS**
ACIDS AND BASES 1:20-22
Acids: aid in digestion 1:20; carbonated drink 1:20; effect on litmus paper 1:20-21, 10:971; tooth decay 1:20
Alkali deposits 1:61
amphoterism 1:21
Anhydride 1:82
Bases: effect on litmus paper 1:20-21; hydroxyl ions 1:21; leavening 1:21
Battery 3:232-233
Citric acid 4:390
conduction of electricity 1:21
Enzymes 7:629-630
Ester 7:637
exp. 1:20
Fatty acids 7:673
Halogen 9:818
Hydrochloric acid 9:865
Hydrogen 9:866
hydrogen ion 1:21
Hydroxide 9:869
Hydroxyl 9:869
Litmus test 10:971
Lye 10:985
Neutralization 12:1145
pH acids 13:1272
Sulfuric acid 17:1685
Titration 18:1754
uses 1:21-22
ACNE 1:22
Cryotherapy 5:460
Cyst 5:474
Pimple 13:1295
Acorn see **NUTS; OAK**
Acorn worm see **PLATYHELMINTHES**
ACOUSTIC WEAPONS 1:22
ACOUSTICS 1:22-23
computation 1:23
exp., 1:23
Noise 12:1155
Sound 16:1585-1590
ACQUIRED CHARACTERISTICS 1:23-24
illus. 1:24
inheritance 1:23
Lamarck, Jean Baptiste Pierre 10:940
Acquired immunity see **IMMUNITY**
Acraniates 4:384
Acrilan see **SYNTHETIC FABRICS**
ACROMEGALY 1:24
Giant 8:775
ACTH see **CORTISONE**
ACTINIDE ELEMENTS 1:24
Berkelium 3:245
Californium 4:324-325
Curium 5:466
Einsteinium 6:562
Fermium 7:676
Mendelevium 11:1043
Plutonium 14:1340
ACTINIUM 1:24
Acupuncture 13:1235
Adam's apple see **LARYNX**
ADAPTATION 1:24-25
Acclimatazation 1:19
Acquired characteristics 1:23-24

animal: coloring 1:24-25; body structure 1:25; community living 1:25; hibernation 1:25; illus. 1:25; man 1:25; migration 1:25
Cactus 4:321
illus., examples 1:25
Physiology 13:1289-1291
Salamander 15:1489-1490
Stress 17:1677-1678
Adder see **SNAKES**
Adder's tongue fern see **WILD FLOWERS**
ADDICTION 1:25-26
Drugs 6:530
Tranquilizer 18:1766
ADDING MACHINE 1:26
Calculator 4:323-324
Computer 5:434-436
Addition see **ARITHMETIC**
Additive 7:638
ADENOIDS 1:26
Lymphatic system 10:986-987
Pharynx 13:1274
ADF see **DIRECTION FINDER**
ADHESION 1:26
Cohesion 5:420
illus. 1:26
Liquid 10:968-970
Resistance 15:1452
ADHESIVE 1:27
Mucilage 12:1117
Adiabatic cooling 14:1358
Adipose tissue see **FAT, ADIPOSE TISSUE**
Adirondacks see **NORTH AMERICA**
Adobe see **BRICK**
ADOLESCENCE 1:27
ADRENAL GLANDS 1:27
Addison's disease 1:26
Autonomic nervous system 2:190
Cortisone 5:449-450
Cushing's disease 5:471
Endocrine glands 7:610
Glandular tissue 8:781
hormones: adrenalin (epinephrine) 1:27; cortisone 1:27
illus. 1:27-28
Stress 17:1677-1678
ADRENALIN 1:27, 28
Addison's disease 1:26
Animal husbandry 1:89
Asthma 2:153
Blood pressure 3:270-271
Plants, medicinal 14:1328-1329
ADSORPTION 1:28
Colloidal state 5:421
Advanced cislunar shuttle 17:1634
Adventitious see **ROOT**
Aeration see **PURIFICATION OF WATER**
Aerial see **ANTENNA**
AEROBIC 1:28
AERODYNAMICS 1:28-29
Aeronautics 1:30-31
Air pressure 1:47
Airplane 1:52-53
Airships 1:54-55
Aviation 2:191-197
Bernoulli's principle 1:28-29
drag 1:29
gravity 1:29
high altitude flight 1:29
history 1:29
lift 1:28-29
Mechanics 11:1037-1038
slow speed flight 1:29
Streamlining 17:1677

Supersonic 17:1694-1695
supersonic flight 1:29
thrust 1:29
AERONAUTICS 1:30-31
Aerodynamics 1:28-29
Astronautics 2:157-165
Aviation 2:191-197
Compton, Arthur Holly 5:433-434
heavier-than-air craft 1:30
lighter-than-air craft 1:30
modern flight 1:31
Wright, Orville and Wilbur 19:1883
AEROSOL 1:32
AEROSPACE 1:32
Astronautics 2:157-165
AFRICA 1:32-36
animals 1:35, 9:845; illus., 1:35
birds 1:35
climate 1:34; 4:395-397
Continent 5:444
Geography 8:761-763
Geology 8:768-769
insects 1:35
land forms: Atlas Mountains 1:34;
   Lake Victoria 1:32; Nile River
   1:32; rift valley system 1:32-33;
   Sahara Desert 1:32-33
map 1:33
map, temperature and rainfall 1:34
map, vegetation 1:34
Natural resources 12:1131-1133
natural resources: bauxite 1:36;
   coal 1:36; copper 1:36; diamonds
   1:36; gold 1:36; iron ore 1:36;
   petroleum 1:36; phosphate 1:36;
   plants: flowers 1:35; jungles
   1:35; trees 1:35
rivers and drainage: Chambezi
   1:35; Congo 1:35; Laulaba 1:35;
   Niger 1:35; Nile 1:34; Zambezi
   1:35
size compared with U.S., illus. 1:32
African sleeping sickness see
   SLEEPING SICKNESS
African violet (Saintpaulia) see
   VIOLET
AFTERBURNER 1:36
Agar see **ALGAE; BACTERIOLOGY**
AGASSIZ, LOUIS 1:36
AGATE 1:37
   illus. 1:37; 14:1392
   Onyx 13:1209
   Quartz 14:1391-1392
AGERATUM 1:37
   illus. 1:37
Ages of animals see **ANIMALS, LIFE
   SPAN**
Ages of man see **EVOLUTION OF
   MAN**
Agglutination see **BLOOD TYPES**
Aggregate see **CONCRETE; FRUIT;
   ROCKS**
AGING 1:37
   Animals, life span 1:97
   Death 5:485
   signs of aging 1:37
Agouti, illus. 16:1597
AGRICULTURE 1:38-41
   Aquaculture 2:124
   Biophysics 3:255
   Botany 3:285
   Conservation of nature 5:439
   Cultivation 5:464
   Deere, John 5:490
   diversified farming 1:39
   effect of science: fertilizers
   1:38; hydroponics 1:39; improving
   plants and animals 1:39; machines
   1:38; soil 1:39

Entomology 7:628
farming practices today: inbreeding
   1:40; outbreeding 1:40
Fertilizer 7:678
Fowl 8:724-726
Gardening 8:751-753
Harvest 9:821
history 1:38
Horticulture 9:856
invention of machines 1:38
problems: pollution 1:39-40; pop-
   ulation increase 1:39-40; un-
   equal distribution of food supply
   1:39-40; upset of natural habitat
   1:39
resources: decline in soil fertil-
   ity 1:40; irrigation 1:40; soil
   erosion 1:40
Soil testing 16:1572
Topsoil 18:1760
AGRONOMY 1:42
Ailanthus see **TREE OF HEAVEN**
Aileron see **AIRPLANE**
AIR 1:42-44
   characteristics: absorption of
   water vapor 1:44; buoyancy 1:44
   composition: greenhouse effect
   1:42; mesosphere 1:43; ozone layer
   1:42; stratosphere 1:43; thermosphere 1:43; troposhere 1:43
   Dew 5:497
   exp. 1:43
   illus.: characteristics 1:44; composition 1:42
   pressure: effect of gravity 1:43;
   movement of air molecules 1:43;
   resistance 1:44
   Supersonic 17:1694-1695
Air brakes see **BRAKES**
Air column see **SOUND**
Air compressor see **COMPRESSORS**
AIR CONDITIONING 1:45
   controlling humidity 1:45
   cooling 1:45
   illus. 1:45
AIR-CUSHION VEHICLES 1:51
   Aircraft 1:48-50
   illus. 1:51
   propulsion 1:51
   uses 1:51
AIR HAMMER 1:45
AIR LOCK 1:45
   Caisson 4:322
AIR MASSES 1:46
   Air 1:42-44
   cold front 1:46
   density 1:46
   Doldrums 6:524
   High-pressure center 9:844
   Indian summer 9:876
   Low-pressure center 10:979
   Ocean 12:1188-1190
   source region 1:46
   Squall line 17:1654
   warm front 1:46
   Waterspout 19:1835
   weather 1:46; 19:1843-1846
   weather map 1:46; 19:1854-1855
   Wind 19:1874-1875
AIR POLLUTION 1:46-47
   gaseous 1:45
   particulate matter 1:47; 13:1252
   Photochemical smog 13:1277
   Pollution 14:1347-1348
AIR PRESSURE 1:47
   Air lock 1:45
   Atmosphere 2:169
   Caisson 4:322
   Compressors 5:432-433

exp. 1:47
Millibar 11:1062
Rarefied air 15:1430
AIR RESISTANCE 1:47
Air traffic control see **AVIATION**
Air transportation see **AVIATION**
AIRCRAFT 1:48-50
   Airplane 1:52-53
   Airships 1:54-55
   Autogiro 2:181
   Aviation 2:191-197
   Aerodynamics 1:28-29
   Bomb 3:279-282
   commercial airlines 1:48
   Convertiplane 5:445
   Helicopter 9:831-832
   history 1:48
   illus.: helicopter 1:50; jet 1:49;
   single-engine 1:50
   Instrument landing system 9:885
   light aircraft 1:49
   military aircraft 1:48-49
   Seaplane 16:1521-1522
   V/STOL aircraft 1:50
   Wright, Orville and Wilbur 19:1883
Aircraft carrier see **SHIPS**
Airfoil see **AIRPLANE**
Airline see **AVIATION**
AIRPLANE 1:52-53
   Aerodynamics 1:28-29
   Aeronautics 1:30-31
   aileron 1:52
   Aviation 2:191-197
   cockpit 1:53
   exp. 1:53
   Flight, principles of 7:690-691
   flying 1:53
   illus., parts 1:52
   Instrument landing system 9:885
   Instrument panel 9:886
   parts: control stick 1:53; engine
   1:52; fuselage 1:52; landing gear
   1:52; rudder pedal 1:53; tail sec-
   tion 1:52; throttle 1:53; wings 1:52
   Seaplane 16:1521-1522
   Thermal 18:1740
AIRSHIPS 1:54;55
   Aviation 2:191-197
   Balloon 3:222
   blimps 1:54
   Helium 9:833
   Hydrogen 9:866-867
   illus. 1:54
   non-rigid 1:54
   rigid 1:54
Airport see **AVIATION**
ALBATROSS 1:55
   Antarctica 2:112
ALBINO 1:55
   gene 1:55
   illus., rabbit 1:55; 14:1395
   pigment 1:55; 13:1294
   plants 1:55
   White mice 19:1868
ALBUMIN 1:56
ALCHEMY 1:56
   illus. 1:56
   Paracelsus, Philippus Aureolus
   13:1243
   Transmutation of elements 18:1769
ALCOHOL 1:56-57
   Antifreeze 2:117
   Antiseptic 2:118
   ethyl (grain) 1:56-57
   Hydroxyl 9:869
   isopropyl 1:57
   methyl (wood) 1:56
   Organic compounds 13:1222-1223
Aldebaran see **TAURUS**

Aldrin, Edwin 2:163
   illus. 2:165
ALEWIFE 1:57
   Herring 9:842
   illus. 1:57
ALFALFA 1:57
   illus. 1:57
ALGAE 1:58-59
   blue-green 1:58
   Cells 4:359
   Diatom 6:508
   economic importance 1:58
   Euglena 7:639
   Fossils 8:722
   Fungus 8:741-742
   green 1:58
   illus.: 1:58; 14:1322, 1324;
      18:1738
   intermediate forms 1:58
   Microbe 11:1054
   Oscillatoria 13:1225
   Plants, classification of 14:1322-
      1327
   red 1:59
   reproduction 1:58; 15:1445
   Seaweed 16:1523
   Spirogyra 17:1650
   yellow 1:58
ALGEBRA 1:59-60
   algebraic expression: binomial
      i :60; coefficient 1:60; monomial
      1:60; multinomial 1:60; term 1:60
   Arithmetic 2:136-137
   Equation 7:632
   exponent 1:60
   Geometry 8:770-772
   literal numbers 1:60
   Mathematics 11:1029-1030
   natural numbers 1:59
   negative integers 1:60
   Numeral systems 12:1179-1183
   positive integers 1:60
   problem solving 1:60
   rational numbers 1:60
   real numbers 1:60
   symbols 1:59
   Zero 19:1891-1892
ALIMENTARY CANAL 1:61
Alkali see **ACIDS AND BASES**
ALKALI DEPOSITS 1:61
Allegheny Mountains see **NORTH
   AMERICA**
Allele 9:839, 861
Allergen 1:61
Allergic reaction 1:161
ALLERGY 1:61-62
   allergen 1:61
   Antibiotics 2:115-116
   Antibody 2:116-117
   antigen 1:161
   Arthritis 2:140
   asthma 1:62; 2:153
   Dairy products 5:477
   delayed hypersensitivity 1:62
   Dermatitis 5:495
   Eczema 6:556
   hay fever 1:62; 9:823
   histamines 1:62
   hives 1:62; 9:849
   illus. 1:61
   immediate hypersensitivity 1:62
   pollen 1:62; 14:1346
   Ragweed 15:1425
   Skin test 16:1558
ALLIGATOR 1:62
   conservation 1:62
   illus. 1:62; 15:1449
   reproduction 1:62
   Reptilia 15:1449-1450

Allosaurus see **DINOSAUR**
ALLOY 1:62-63
   aluminum 1:68
   Bessemer Process 3:248
   Brass 3:291
   Copper 5:447
   Gold 8:785
   illus., uses 1:63
   Indium 9:876
   Metal 10:1049-1051
   Monel metal 11:1088
   Nickel 12:1148
   Palladium 13:1239
   properties 1:63
   Soldering 16:1580
   steel 1:62-63; 18:1666-1668
   true alloy 1:62
   uses 1:63
   Zinc 19:1892
ALLSPICE 1:64
   illus. 1:64
Alluvial soil see **SOIL TYPES**
ALMOND 1:64
   illus. 1:64
ALPACA 1:64; 10:975
   illus. 1:64; 16:1596
ALPHA 1:65
   Centaurus 4:363
Alpha rays see **RADIATION; RAY,
   ALPHA**
Alps Mountains see **EUROPE**
Altair see **AQUILA**
Alternating current see
   ELECTRICITY
ALTERNATION OF GENERATIONS
   1:65
   Bryophytes 4:308-309
   Club moss 5:411
   cytological 1:65
   Ferns 7:676
   Fucus 8:738
   gametophyte 1:65; 8:749
   illus. 1:65
   Kelp 10:931
   Liverworts 10:973-974
   morphological 1:65
   Moss 12:1108-1109
   Pine 13:1295-1296
   Plants, classification of
      14:1322-1327
   Spore formation 17:1653
   sporophyte 1:65; 17:1653
Alternation of host see **PARASITES**
ALTIMETER 1:66
   aneroid barometer 1:66
   Barometer 3:227
   illus. 1:66
ALTITUDE 1:66
   atmosphere 1:66
   map 1:66
   Moho 11:1080-1081
   normal lapse rate 1:66
   Rarefaction 15:1430
Alto-cumulus see **CLOUDS**
Alto-stratus see **CLOUDS**
ALUM 1:66
Alumina see **ALUMINUM; GEM;
   RUBY**
ALUMINUM 1:68
   Hall-Heroult process 9:818
   illus. 1:68
   Metal 11:1049-1051
   properties 1:68
ALYSSUM 1:69
   illus. 1:69
Amateur radio see **RADIO**
AMARYLLIS 1:69
   Century plant 4:365
   illus. 1:69; 16:1593

Amazon River see **SOUTH AMERICA**
AMBER 1:69
   Forest products 8:712
   illus. 1:69; 15:1452
   location 1:69
   uses of 1:69
Ambergris see **WHALE**
AMEBA 1:70
   Blood 3:269
   body structure 1:83
   Cell 4:359
   digestion: contractile vacuole 1:70;
   illus. 1:70; reproduction 15:1445
   locomotion: ameboid motion 1:70;
      pseudopod 1:70
   Migratory cells 11:1061
   Porifera 14:1351-1352
   Protozoa 14:1378-1379
   reproduction: binary fission 1:70;
      15:1445
   within larger organisms 1:70
Amebic dysentery see **DYSENTERY**
AMEBOID MOVEMENT 1:71
AMERICIUM 1:71
AMETHYST 1:71
   illus. 1:71; 14:1392
   Quartz 14:1391-1392
AMINO ACID 1:71
   Acids and bases 1:20-22
   animal digestion 1:86
   Assimilation 2:151
   composition 1:71
   Digestive system 6:512
   Metabolism 11:1048
   proteins 1:71; 14:1376-1377
AMMETER 1:72
   Electricity 6:566
   Galvanometer 8:748-749
   illus. 1:72
   operation 1:72
   resistance 1:72
AMMONIA 1:72
   Carbonization 4:343
   Forest products 8:713
   Haber Process 9:814
   Hydroxide 9:869
   Nitrogen 12:1150
   obtained from 1:72
   Refrigeration 15:1441-1442
   Solvay process 16:1583
   uses 1:72
Amnesia 11:1042
Amoeba see **AMEBA**
Amorphous carbon see **CARBON**
AMPERE 1:72-73
   Volt 19:1823-1824
AMPERE, ANDRE MARIE 1:73
   Ampere's law 1:73
   electricity 1:73
   electrodynamics 1:73
   illus., Ampere's law 1:73
AMPHIBIANS 1:74-75
   characteristics 1:74
   Chordata 4:384
   evolution 1:74
   Fossils 8:723
   frogs 1:74; 8:732-733
   newts 1:74; 12:1146-1147
   Respiratory system 15:1453-1455
   salamander 1:74; 15:1489-1490
   toad 1:74; 18:1755
   uses 1:75
Amphioxus see **CHORDATA**
Amphoterism see **ACIDS AND
   BASES**
Amplifier see **RADIO**
Amplitude see **SOUND**
AMUNDSEN, ROALD 1:75
   Antarctica 2:110

Arctic 2:133
Peary, Robert E. 1:75
Poles, North and South 14:1345
AMYLASE 1:75; 6:512
Anaconda see **SNAKES**
Anaesthetic see **ANESTHETIC**
Analog computer see **COMPUTER**
Analytic geometry see **GEOMETRY**
ANATOMY 1:76-78
Abdomen 1:14
Animal 1:83
Aristotle 1:76
Biology 3:253
branches: cytology 1:76; embryol-
  ogy 1:76; experimental anatomy
  1:76; histology 1:76; morphology
  1:76; physiology 1:76
Embryology 6:592-597
Galen 8:745
history 1:76
illus.: circulatory system 1:78; di-
  gestive system 1:78; musculature
  system 1:77; nervous system 1:78;
  respiratory system 1:78; skeletal
  system 1:77; skin 1:77
Leonardo da Vinci 1:76
Malpighi, Marcello 11:1010
Medicine 11:1038-1040
Morphology 11:1096
Muscle tissue 12:1122-1123
Organ 13:1222
Physiology 13:1289-1291
systems 1:76
taxonomy 1:76
Vesalius, Andreas 19:1812-1813
Zoology 19:1895-1896, 1897
Ancestral dog, illus. 6:521
ANCHOVY 1:79
Andes Mountains see **SOUTH
  AMERICA**
ANDROGEN 1:79
Estrogen 7:637
Gonad 8:787
Steroid 17:1671
ANEMIA 1:79
Blood 3:268-269
causes 1:79
Ehrlich, Paul 6:560
Jaundice 10:921
Sickle cell anemia 16:1545
symptoms 1:79
treatment 1:79
ANEMOMETER 1:79
Beaufort scale 3:238
exp. 1:80
types: hot wire 1:80; pressure plate
  1:80; Robinson 1:79
Anemone see **WILD FLOWERS**
Aneroid barometer see **BAROMETER**
ANESTHETICS 1:80-81
Chloroform 4:381
Cocaine 5:415
Ether 7:637
general: chloroform 1:81; ether
  1:81
local 1:81
Twilight sleep 18:1783
Novocaine 12:1161
Sodium pentothol 16:1571
Surgery 17:1696-1697
Angel fish, illus. 1:85
ANGIOSPERMS 1:81-82
Aspen 2:150
Calyx 4:326
Capsule 4:336
dicotyledons 1:82
Embryophyta 7:607-608
Flower 7:693-694
illus. 1:81; 14:1327

Legume 10:951
Mesozoic Era 11:1047
monocotyledons 1:81
Perennial 13:1264
photosynthesis 1:81
Plants, classification of
  14:1322-1327
reproduction 1:81
Seed 16:1524-1525
Angles see **GEOMETRY**
Angleworm see **EARTHWORM**
Angstrom see **LIGHT;
  MEASUREMENT; WAVE**
ANHYDRIDE 1:82
Hydrates 9:863
ANIMAL 1:82-87
Animals, classification of 1:91-96
Annelida 2:107-108
Arthropoda 2:140-142
Autotomy 2:190
body structure: nervous system
  1:83; organs 1:83; respiratory
  system 1:83; systems 1:83;
  one-celled 1:83;
  tissues 1:83
characteristics 1:82
digestion 1:86
excretion 1:86
food 1:83
Gland 8:780
habitat 1:82
Joints, skeletal 10:924-925
Life, characteristics of 10:958
locomotion, cilia 1:86; flagellum
  1:86; muscles 1:86; pseudopod
  1:86; 10:976
Nocturnal habits 12:1154-1155
Oral 13:1217
protection 1:87
reproduction 1:87
ANIMAL BEHAVIOR 1:88
Ethology 7:637-638
habituation 1:88
imprinting 1:88; 9:874
Insight 9:884
instinct 1:88
reflex 1:88
ANIMAL CAGES 1:88-89
exp. 1:88
ANIMAL DISEASES 1:89
Animal husbandry 1:90
Disease 6:519
Dog 6:521-523
Rabies 14:1395
types: arthropod 1:89; bacterial
  1:89; protozoan 1:89; treatment
  and prevention 1:89; worm parasites 1:89; virus 1:89
Veterinary medicine 19:1813
ANIMAL HUSBANDRY 1:89-90
Biophysics 3:255
problems 1:89
products from farm animals 1:89
ANIMAL INTELLIGENCE 1:90
Dog 6:521-523
ANIMAL TRACKS 1:90-91
exp. 1:91
illus. 1:90-91
ANIMALS, CLASSIFICATION OF
  1:91-96
Animal 1:87
Annelida 2:107-108
appendages 1:96
Arthropoda 2:140-142
body form: axis 1:94; symmetry
  1:95
body support: endoskeleton 1:95;
  exoskeleton 1:95; invertebrates
  1:95; vertebrates 1:95

Cow 5:453
Ctenophora 5:463
Dorsal 6:526
Echinodermata 6:540-550
Ectoderm 6:556
embryology 1:94; 6:592-597
Entomology 7:628
evolution 1:92; 7:647-654
Evolution of man 7:659
Exoskeleton 7:661
Flagella 7:688
illus., major phylum 1:93
Invertebrate 10:911
Linnaeus, Carolus 10:967
Mammalia 11:1011-1012
Mollusca 11:1084-1086
Morphology 11:1096
Nemathelminthes 12:1137-1138
Peripatus 13:1265
Phylogeny 13:1286
physiology 1:96
Pisces (animal) 14:1307-1308
Platyhelminthes 14:1336-1337
Porifera 14:1351-1352
Posterior 14:1353
Protozoa 14:1378-1379
Rotifera 15:1479-1480
segment 1:96; 16:1526
Skeleton 16:1552-1555
structure: analogous 1:94; homol-
  ogous 1:94
Symmetry 18:1713
Vertebrate 19:1812
Worm 19:1881-1882
ANIMALS, LIFE SPAN 1:97
Aging 1:37
Death 5:485
Dog 6:521-523
Elephant 6:591
illus. 1:97
Longevity 10:977
ANISE 2:107
Dill 6:513
Licorice 10:957
Paregoric 13:1249
Ankylosaurus 6:515
ANNEALING 2:107
ANNELIDA 2:107-108
body structure 2:107-108
Earthworm 6:548
habits 2:108
illus. 2:107; 5:471
locomotion 2:108
Nemathelminthes 12:1137-1138
Nephridia 12:1138
Peripatus 13:1265
Reproductive systems 15:1447-
  1448
Skeleton 16:1552-1555
systems 2:108
Worm 19:1881-1882
ANNUAL 2:108
Biennial 3:249
Candytuft 4:33/
Cowpea 5:454
Eggplant 6:558
Forget-me-not 8:718
Gardening 8:752
Lentil 10:954
Licorice 10:957
Perennial 13:1264
Petunia 13:1272
Plant 14:1314-1317
Scabiosa 16:1510
Shrub 17:1647
Spinach 17:1647
ANNUAL RINGS 2:109
Cambium 4:326
exp. 2:109

Perennial 13:1264
Tree-ring dating 18:1771
Vascular bundle 18:1797
Xylem 19:1884-1886
ANODE 2:109
Battery 3:232
Cathode 4:354
Electrode 6:574
Electrolysis 6:575-576
Polarization 14:1345
Anopheles see **MALARIA;
MOSQUITO**
ANTACID 2:109
Antagonist see **MUSCLE SYSTEM**
Antarctic Circle 6:543
Antarctic current see **CURRENTS,
OCEAN**
ANTARCTICA 2:110-112
Byrd, Richard Evelyn 4:319
Continent 5:444
discovery 2:110
exploration 2:110
Geography 8:761-763
geological past 2:110
Geology 8:786
importance 2:112
*International Geophysical Year:
Antarctica* 9:890; *Glaciers* 9:892-
893
land forms 2:112
map 2:111
Penguin 13:1261
plant life 2:112
seasons 2:112
shape 2:112
size 2:112
Antares see **SCORPIUS**
ANTEATER 2:113
Jungle 10:926
ANTELOPE 2:113
Cashmere 4:347
characteristics 2:113
digestive system 2:113
Gazelle 8:757
Gnu 8:784
habitat 2:113
illus. 2:113
Oryx 13:1224
Antenna (animal) see **ARTHROPODA**
ANTENNA (ELECTRONIC) 2:114
AC signal voltage 2:114
Beam 3:235
dipole 2:114
Electricity 6:571
formula for length of wire 2:114
radio waves 2:114
Television 18:1730-1732
unipole 2:114
Anterior see **ANIMALS, CLASSI-
FICATION OF**
Anthocarp 8:735
Anthracite coal see **COAL**
Anthropoid ape see **APE;
EVOLUTION**
Anthropoids 2:121
ANTHROPOLOGY 2:115
cultural 2:115
Fossils 8:719-723
history 2:115
illus. 2:115
phases of study 2:115
physical 2:115
recent discoveries 2:115
steps of man's progress 2:115
Anti-Ballistic Missile Defense System
11:1074-1075
Antiaircraft see **MISSILE**
ANTIOBIOTICS 2:115-116
anaphylaxis 2:116

Bacteriology 3:210-211
bakteriolytic 2:116
bacteriostatic 2:116
Biochemistry 3:251
broad-spectrum 2:116
Bubonic plague 4:308
chart 2:116
Domagk, Gerhard 6:525
Fleming, Sir Alexander 7:689
Impetigo 9:874
Infection 9:877-878
penicillin 2:115; 13:1261
sensitivity test 2:116
Sulfa drugs 17:1684
Surgery 17:1696-1697
synthetic 2:116
treating viruses 2:116
ANTIBODY 2:116
Allergy 1:62
antigen 2:116
Blood types 3:271
Burnet, Sir Frank MacFarlane 4:316
Gamma globulin 8:750
Globulin 8:783
immunity 2:116; 9:874
phagocytosis 2:116

Serum 16:1530
toxin 2:116
Vaccine 18:1792-1793
Anticyclone see **HIGH PRESSURE
CENTER**
ANTIDOTE 2:117
Poison 14:1342
ANTIFREEZE 2:117
Antigen see **ALLERGY; ANTIBODY**
Antihistamine see **ALLERGY**
Antiknock see **ETHYL**
ANTIMATTER 2:117
Atom 2:172-174
Matter 11:1031
ANTIMONY 2:117-118
Antineutron see **ANTIMATTER**
Antiparticle see **ANTIMATTER**
Antiproton see **ANTIMATTER**
ANTISEPTIC 2:118
exp. 2:118
Forest products 8:712
Fumigant 8:741
Lister, Joseph 10:971
sterilization 2:118
surgery 2:118; 17:1696-1697
Antitoxin see **ANTIBODY; VACCINE**
Antler see **DEER FAMILY; HORN**
ANTS 2:119-120
body structure 2:119-120
colonies 2:119-120
exp. 2:119
illus. 2:120; 9:881
reproduction 2:120
Anus see **DIGESTIVE SYSTEM**
Anvil see **EAR**
Aorta see **ARTERY; CIRCULATORY
SYSTEM**
APATITE 2:120
illus. 9:819
APE 2:121
characteristics 2:121
Chimpanzee 4:379
Gibbon 8:776
illus.: 19:1894; chimpanzee 2:121;
gibbon 2:121; gorilla 2:121; oran-
gutan 2:121; skeleton 2:121
likeness to man 2:121
Orangutan 13:1217
Primates 14:1362-1363
APHID 2:122
Bugs 4:311-312
damage 2:122

food 2:122
illus. 2:122
Parthenogenesis 13:1251-1252
reproduction 2:122
Apiculture see **BEES**
APOGEE 2:122
Orbit 13:1217-1218
Perigee 13:1265
Apollo command module 17:1633,
1634, 2635
Apollo Lunar Module 17:1635
APOPLEXY 2:122
Blood pressure 3:270-271
Appalachian Mountains see **NORTH
AMERICA**
Appendages, grouping by
illus. 1:94
APPENDIX 2:123
appendicitis 2:123
cecum 2:123
Digestive system 6:512
illus. 2:123
Inflammation 9:878-879
peritonitis 2:123; 13:1267
APPLE 2:123
food value 2:123
Orchard 13:1220
reproduction 2:123
APRICOT 2:124
Orchard 13:1220
Apthous ulcer 4:333
AQUACULTURE 2:124
advantages 2:124
illus. 2:124
Hydroponics 9:868
problems 2:124
AQUARIUM 2:124-125
animals 2:125
Guppy 9:811
illus. 2:124, 125
plants 2:125
Tropical fish 18:1772-1773
Aquarius see **WATER BEARER**
Aquatic life see **MARINE BIOLOGY**
Aqueduct see **BRIDGES;
IRRIGATION**
Aqueous humor see **EYE**
AQUILA 2:126
illus. 2:126
ARACHNIDA 2:126-127
Arthropoda 2:140-142
body structure 2:126
Daddy longlegs 5:475
exp. 2:127
habitat 2:126
illus.: garden spider 2:126
nervous system 2:126
reproduction 2:127
Scorpion 16:1515
Spiders 17:1647
Tick 18:1749
ARBORETUM 2:127-128
history of 2:127
purpose 2:127
ARBORVITAE 2:128
illus. 2:128
ARC 2:128-129
Bulb, electric 4:312
carbon arc lamps 2:128
illus.: welding 2:128
properties 2:128
uses 2:128
welding 2:128
ARCHAEOPTERYX 2:129
illus. 2:129
ARCHEOLOGY 2:129-131
artifacts 2:129, 131
carbon-14 2:131
Cave 4:357

financial support 2:131
finds 2:130-131
illus.: archeologists 2:130; arti-
  facts 2:130; dig, aerial view
  2:130; Indian burial mound 2:131;
  Indian relics 2:129; tomb of
  Rameses II 2:131
infrared spectrometry 2:131
stratigraphy 2:131
thermoluminescence 2:131
Tools 18:1757-1759
Tree-ring dating 18:1771
work of archeologists 2:130
X-ray fluorescence 2:131
ARCHEOZOIC ERA 2:132
ARCHIMEDES 2:132-133
Archimedes' principle 2:132
Buoyancy 4:315
exp. 2:132-133
Mathematics 11:1029-1030
Mechanics 11:1037-1038
Specific gravity 17:1640-1641
ARCHIPELAGO 2:133
ARCTIC 2:133-134
exploration 2:133
geographic north pole 2:133
importance 2:133
magnetic north pole 2:133
Peary, Robert Edwin 13:1257
salt lakes 2:133
tundra 2:133
Arctic Circle 6:543
Arctic fox, illus. 1:85; 14:1375
Arctic (Labrador) Current 5:470
Arctic tern, illus. 1:85
Arcturus see **BOOTES**
AREA 2:134
ARGON 2:134
ARGONAUT 2:134
illus. 2:134
ARID 2:134
ARIES 2:134
illus. 2:134
mythology 2:134
ARISTOTLE 2:135
Acceleration 1:17
anatomy, history of 1:76
philosophy 2:135
students 2:135
ARITHMETIC 2:136-137
addition 2:137
algebra 1:59
algorithms 2:137
axioms 2:137
binary operations 2:137
cardinal number 2:136
counting 2:136
division 2:137
Equation 7:632
illus.: Egyptian hieroglyphics
  2:136; Hindu digits 2:136
Mathematics 11:1029-1030
multiplication 2:137
Numeral systems 12:1179-1183
numeration: Babylonian 2:136;
  Egyptian 2:136; Hindu-Arabic
  2:136
subtraction 2:137
Zero 19:1891-1892
ARMADILLO 2:138
illus. 2:138
Jungle 10:926
Armament see **MISSILE; ROCKET;
  WEAPONS**
ARMATURE 2:138
alternating current generator 2:138
direct current generator 2:138
Dynamo 6:537
Generator 8:760

illus. 2:138
Motor 12:1114-1116
Armstrong, Neil A. 2:163
illus. 2:165
ARNICA 2:138
ARROWROOT 2:138
Arroyo 11:1046
ARSENIC 2:138
Poison 14:1342
Arterioles 4:335
ARTERIOSCLEROSIS 2:139
Fatty acids 7:673
Gangrene 8:750
Sclerosis 16:1515
ARTERY 2:139
aorta 2:139
Arteriosclerosis 2:139
Capillary 4:335
Circulatory system 4:387
Gangrene 8:750
Heart 9:825
Histology 9:846-849
illus. 2:139
pulmonary 2:139
pulse 2:139
structure 2:139
Vein 19:1808-1809
Artesian well see **WELL**
ARTHRITIS 2:139-140
Gout 8:789
Hench, Philip 9:834-835
rheumatoid 2:140
symptom of other diseases 2:139
ARTHROPODA 2:140-142
Arachnida 2:125-127
Beetles 3:242-243
body structure 2:141
Centipede 4:363
characteristics 2:140
Cockroach 5:415
Crab 5:454
Crayfish 5:456
exoskeleton 2:141
Eye, simple 7:668
Fly 7:696-697
habitat 2:140
illus.: 2:141; American locust
  2:142; centipede 2:142; crab
  2:142; honey bee 2:142; katydid
  2:140; tarantula 2:140
Insecta 9:880-882
Joints, skeletal 10:924-925
Lobster 10:976
locomotion 2:142
Molting 11:1087
Muscle system 12:1120-1122
nervous system 2:142
Peripatus 13:1265
reproduction 2:142; 15:1447-1448
respiratory system 2:142;15:1453-
  1455
Skeleton 16:1522
ARTICHOKE 2:143
Artificial immunity 3:211
ARTIFICIAL RESPIRATION 2:143;
  10:915
cardiopulmonary resuscitation
  2:143
Drowning 6:528
Heimlich Choke Maneuver 2:143;
  9:831
illus. 2:143
mouth-to-mouth 2:143
ARTIODACTYLA 2:144
Deer family 5:489-490
Herbivore 9:837
Hippopotamus 9:845
Hoof 9:852
Horse 9:854-855

Mammalia 11:1011-1012
Oxen 13:1231
Pig 13:1293
Ruminants 15:1483
Sheep 16:1534
Ungulata 18:1785
Yak 19:1887
ASBESTOS 2:144
ASCARIS 2:144
illus. 12:1137
in humans 2:144
prevention 2:144
Ascorbic acid see **VITAMIN**
Aseptic 2:118
ASH 2:144-145
illus. 2:144
ASIA 2:145-149
climate: 2:146; continental 2:148;
  monsoon 2:146; subtropical
  2:147; tropical 2:148; 4:395-397
Continent 5:444
Geography 8:761-763
Geology 8:768-769
illus.: giant panda 2:149; ibex
  2:148; Marco Polo's sheep 2:148;
  seladang 2:146; sloth bear 2:146;
  takin 2:146
Jungle 10:926-927
land forms: Anatolian plateau
  2:146; Arabian plateau 2:146;
  Dekkan plateau 2:146; Himalayas
  2:146; Iranian plateau 2:146;
  Karakoram 2:146; Pamirs 2:146;
  Tibetan plateau 2:146
map: 2:146; temperature and rainfall 2:145; vegetation 2:145
Monsoon 11:1091
natural resources: coal 2:149; manganese 2:149; natural gas 2:149;
  oil 2:149; precious minerals 2:149;
  tin 2:149; 12:1131-1133
plants and animals 2:148-149
rivers and drainage: Brahmaputra
  2:148; Ganges 2:148; Hwang Ho
  2:148; Indus 2:148; Irawaddy
  2:148; Lena 2:148; Mekong 2:148;
  Ob 2:148; Si 2:148; Yangtze
  2:148; Yensei 2:148
Steppe 17:1670
taiga 2:147
Asp see **SNAKES**
ASPARAGUS 2:150
ASPEN 2:150
illus. 2:150
ASPHALT 2:150
illus. 2:150
Macadam 10:988
ASPHYXIA 2:150-151
Asphyxiation see **ASPHYXIA; FIRST
  AID**
ASPIRIN 2:151
Acetic acid 1:19
composition 2:151
Drugs 6:530
Pharmacology 13:1273
preparation 2:151
uses 2:151
Asexual reproduction see **REPRO-
  DUCTION, ASEXUAL**
ASSAYING 2:151
fire process 2:151
wet process 2:151
ASSIMILATION 2:151
ASTATINE 2:152
ASTER 2:152
Daisy 5:477
illus. 2:152
ASTEROID 2:152
Bode's Law 2:152

Ceres 2:152
Comet 5:426
illus., Ceres 2:152
Meteor 11:1053
Vesta 2:152
ASTHMA 2:153
aerosol 1:32
causes 2:153
Hay fever 9:823
symptoms 2:153
treatment 2:153
ASTIGMATISM 2:153-154
Eye 7:664-667
illus. 2:153:154
Optometry 13:1215-1217
ASTRAGALUS 2:154
ASTRINGENT 2:154
ASTROLABE 2:154
Celestial navigation 4:358
illus. 5:407
ASTROLOGY 2:154
Astronomy 2:166-167
history 2:154
ASTRONAUT 2:155-156
Astronautics 2:157-165
chart 2:156
G 8:744
history 2:155
illus. 2:155, 156
missions 2:155
National Aeronautics and Space
  Administration 2:156
Rarefied air 15:1430
Shepard, Alan B. 16:1535
Space medicine 17:1611-1616
Space pilot 17:1616-1617
training 2:156
ASTRONAUTICS 2:157-165
advanced manned space programs
  2:164
Aeronautics 1:31
Apollo 2:163
Astronaut 2:155-156
Astronomy 2:167
Aviation 2:191-197
Balloon 3:333
Cape Canaveral 4:334
Ehricke, Krafft A. 6:560
general principles of spacecraft
  in motion: escape velocity 2:158;
  hazards in space 2:158; orbital
  velocity 2:158
illus.: Apollo Command Module
  2:163; Apollo 18 2:161; Aldrin,
  Edwin 2:165; Armstrong, Neil
  2:165; astronauts 2:165; Lunar
  Roving Vehicle 2:163; Lunar Mod-
  ule, close-up 2:165; moon 2:162,
  165; Saturn V 2:157; Space
  Shuttle 2:164; spacecraft 2:158;
  surveyor 2:161
launch vehicles 2:159, chart 2:161
Lunar base 10:980-983
lunar exploration 2:162
manned space flight 2:162
Missile 11:1071-1075
moon probes, chart 2:161
National Aeronautics and Space
  Administration 2:157
Navigation 12:1134-1135
Robotics 15:1461
Rocket engine 15:1463-1467
Satellite, man-made 16:1507-1508
satellites, chart 2:159
scientific satellites and inter-
  planetary spacecraft: applications satellites 2:160; LAND-
  SAT program navigation aids
  2:160; weather satellites 2:160

Space 17:1607-1611
space probes 2:160-162
Space Shuttle Orbiter 17:1618-
  1619
Space station 17:1620-1621
Space travel 17:1622
Space vehicles 17:1624-1637
Sputnik I 2:157, 159
Viking Project 19:1814
ASTRONOMY 2:166-167
astrolabe 2:154
Eclipse 6:551
Equator 7:632
Galileo 8:746-747
Halley, Edmund 9:817
history 2:166-167
illus.: solar eclipse 2:167;
  radio telescope 2:166
Infrared Astronomical Satellite
  9:879
instruments: Hale reflector 2:167;
  radio telescope 2:167; spectro-
  scopes 2:167
Jupiter 10:929
Kepler, Johannes 10:931
Mechanics 11:1037-1038
Mercury (planet) 11:1044-1046
Milky Way 11:1062
Observatory 12:1187
Ptolemy 14:1382-1383
Radio telescope 15:1419
Solar system 16:1575-1578
Solstice 16:1581
space probes 2:167
space travel 2:167
Stars 17:1660-1662
Telescope 18:1728-1730
ASTROPHYSICS 2:167
Asymmetry see **ANIMALS, CLAS-
  SIFICATION OF; PROTOZOA**
ATAVISM 2:167
ATHLETE'S FOOT 2:168
Ringworm 15:1459
Atlantic Ocean see
  OCEANOGRAPHY
Atlas see **ROCKET**
ATMOSPHERE 2:169-171
Air 1:42-43
Altimeter 1:66
Altitude 3:227
Barometer 3:227
Calm, regions of 4:325
Carbon life 4:342
components, chart 2:168
composition 2:168-169
Convection 5:445
Earth 6:543
Gravity 8:794-795
Greenhouse effect 8:797
illus.: air currents 2:168; atmo-
  spheric layers 2:170; 19:1844
International Geophysical Year:
  Atmosphere 9:891-892
Jet stream 10:924
layers: 2:171; exosphere 2:171;
  mesosphere 2:170-171; ozono-
  sphere 2:171; stratosphere
  2:170-171; thermosphere
  2:170-171; troposphere
  2:170-171
Lightning 10:963-964
Mercury (planet) 11:1044-1046
Moon 11:1092-1094
origin 2:169-170
Oxygen 13:1232-1233
Ozone 13:1234
Rarefied air 15:1430
Rarefaction 15:1430
Short wave radio 16:1540-1541

Sky 16:1559
Water vapor 19:1834
Waterspout 19:1835
Weather 19:1843
ATOLL 2:172
Coelenterata 5:417-419
Coral 5:448
illus.: 2:172
Reef 15:1440
ATOM 2:172-174
Alchemy 1:56
Aluminum 1:68
Americium 1:71
Antimatter 2:117
Antimony 2:117-118
Argon 2:134
Arsenic 2:138
atomic number 2:173
atomic weight 2:173-174
Berkelium 3:245
Beryllium 3:247
Bismuth 3:264
Bohr theory 3:278
Boron 3:283
Bromine 3:297
Cadmium 4:322
Californium 4:324-325
Carbon 4:337-338
Charged particles 4:370
Chemical change 4:371-372
Chemistry 4:374
Cobalt 5:415
Copper 5:447
Dalton, John 5:478
Dysprosium 6:537
Electricity 6:563-572
Electronics 6:581-585
Elements 6:586-589
Erbium 7:634
Europium 7:646
Fermium 7:676
Gadolinium 8:744
Gold 8:786
half-life 2:173
Holmium 9:850
Hydrogen 9:866
illus. 2:173
ion 2:173
Ionization 10:912
isotope 2:173-174
Lanthanum 10:942
Lutetium 10:985
Magnesium 10:995
Manganese 11:1013
Matter 11:1031
Mendeleev's Periodic Table
  11:1042-1043
Mendelevium 11:1043
Mercury (element) 11:1044
Microscope, electron 11:1057
Molecular theory 11:1083
Molecular weight 11:1083
Molybdenum 11:1087
Neodymium 12:1138
Neon 12:1138
neutron 2:172, 173
Nickel 12:1148
Nobelium 12:1154
Nuclear particles 12:1164-1165
nuclei 2:173
orbitals 2:173
Palladium 13:1239
Phosphorus 13:1276-1277
Physical states and changes
  13:1286-1287
Platinum 14:1335-1336
Proton (elementary particle)
  14:1377
protons 2:172, 173

radioactivity 2:173
Rhenium 15:1456-1457
Rhodium 15:1458
Rubidium 15:1483
Samarium 15:1493
Scandium 16:1511
Silver 16:1549
Sodium 16:1571
Strontium 17:1679
structure 2:172
Sulfur 17:1684-1685
Thallium 18:1737
Thulium 18:1747
Titanium 18:1754
Xenon 19:1884
Yttrium 19:1890
Zinc 10:1892
Zirconium 19:1893
Atom smasher see **ACCELERATORS**
Atomic bomb see **BOMB**
Atomic energy see **NUCLEAR
ENERGY**
Atomic number see **ATOM;
ELEMENTS**
ATROPHY 2:174
Muscular dystrophy 12:1123
ATROPINE 2:174; 14:1328
Attar see **PERFUME**
AUDUBON, JOHN JAMES 2:175
AUK 2:175
illus.: 2:175; puffin 2:175
Murre 12:1119
Aureomycin see **ANTIBIOTICS**
Auricle see **HEART**
AURIGA 2:176
illus. 2:176
mythology 2:176
AURORA BOREALIS 2:176
Atmosphere 2:171
illus. 2:176
*International Geophysical Year:
Atmosphere* 9:891-892
Sun 17:1686-1691
AUSTRALIA 2:177-181
aborigines 2:177
Birds, flightless 3:261
climate: Mediterranean subtrop-
ical 2:180; temperate marine
2:180; Victoria Desert 2:178-179;
4:394-397
Coelenterata 5:417-419
Continent 5:444
Dingo 6:513
Eucalyptus 7:638-639
Geography 8:763
Geology 8:769
illus.: bandicoot 2:177; black swan
2:177; cockatiel 2:180; common
heath 2:180; dingo 2:177; duckbill platypus 2:177; kangaroo
2:177; koala 2:181; kung-gai-
chase 2:177; waratah 2:177;
wombat 2:180
Koala 10:936
land forms: Arnheim Land 2:178;
Great Australian Bight 2:178;
Great Barrier Reef 2:178; Great
Dividing Range 2:178; Gulf of
Carpentaria 2:178; Yorke
Peninsula 2:178
map: 2:178; temperature and rainfall 2:178; vegetation 2:178
Marsupial 11:1026
natural resources 2:181; 12:1131-
1133
plants and animals: duckbill 2:180;
eucalyptus 2:180; kangaroo
2:180; koala 2:181; wallaby 2:181
Reef 15:1440

rivers and drainage: Coral Sea
2:180; Murray-Darling 2:180
Tasman Sea 2:180
Wallaby 19:1827
Wombat 19:1879
AUTOGIRO 2:181
Aircraft 1:50
Helicopter 9:831-832
Automatic pilot see **INSTRUMENT
PANEL**
Automatic sprinkler see **FIRE
EXTINGUISHERS**
Automatic rifle, illus. 19:1839
AUTOMATION 2:182-183
automatic control: closed-loop con-
trol 2:183; open-loop control
2:182; hunting 2:183
Automobile 2:184-189
electronics 2:183
history: automobile 2:182; cotton
gin 2:182; computers 2:182;
reaper 2:182; steam engine 2:182
illus. 2:182-183; weather fore-
casting 19:1851
Machinery 10:989-991
Missile 11:1071-1075
Photoelectricity 13:1278-1280
Solenoid 16:1581
Thermostat 18:1744-1745
AUTOMOBILE 2:184-188
Accelerator 1:17
Battery 3:232-233
body 2:188-189
brake systems 2:188
Carburetor 4:343
Differential 6:509
engine: cooling system 2:186; fuel
system 2:186; ignition system
2:186; internal-combustion 2:184;
lubricating system 2:186; 7:619-
623
Ethyl 7:638
illus.: anti-pollution device 2:186;
antique 2:185; brake system
2:187; engine 2:184; front wheel
suspension 2:189; manufac-
turing 2:188; modern 2:184;
steering system 2:187; transmission 2:187
Machinery 10:989-991
Motor 12:1114-1116
steering systems 2:187-188
suspension systems 2:188-189
Thermodynamics 18:1741-1742
transmission: automatic 2:187;
clutch 2:186; differential 2:186,
187; drive shaft 2:187
AUTONOMIC NERVOUS SYSTEM
2:189-190
Anatomy 1:76
Atropine 2:174
Biofeedback 3:252
Blood pressure 3:270-271
Blushing 3:274
Brain 3:288-289
exp. 2:189
hormones 2:190
Hypothalamus 9:872
Medulla oblongata 11:1041
Muscle tissue 12:1122-1123
Nervous system 12:1141-1145
parasympathetic 2:190
sympathetic 2:190
AUTOTOMY 2:190
Regeneration 15:1442-1443
Walking stick 19:1827
Autumn see **SEASONS**
AUTUMNAL EQUINOX 2:190
Auxin see **HORMONES, PLANT**

AVALANCHE 2:190
Aves see **BIRD**
AVIATION 2:191-197
Aircraft 1:48-50
Airplane 1:52-53
Balloon 3:222
Beacon 3:235
Dirigible 6:518
early history 2:191-192
future 2:196-197
general 2:194
government control and regula-
tions 2:195
illus.: bi-plane hang-glider 2:191;
Black Bart 2:196; cockpit of B-1
2:194; DC-10 2:192; early de-
sign 2:191; history 2:193; SST
Concorde 2:194; 707 2:191; Whit-
comb Winglet 2:196; X-15 2:195
Jet propulsion 10:923
military 2:192, 194
post World War I 2:192
research and development 2:195
SST 2:194
turbo jet engine 2:192
World War I 2:192
World War II 2:192
Wright, Orville and Wilbur 19:1883
AVOCADO 2:197
Laurel 10:945
AVOCET 2:197
illus. 2:197
Avogadro's Law see **GAS**
Avoirdupois system see
MEASUREMENT; WEIGHT
Axillary see **BUD**
Axle see **MACHINES, SIMPLE**
Axon see **NERVE CELL**
Aye-aye 14:1363
AZALEA 2:197
illus. 16:1545
BABY ANIMALS 3:207-208
Animal behavior 1:88
fertilization 3:207
gestation 3:207
illus.: lion 3:207; owl 3:207; pig
3:207; snake 3:207 larvae 3:207
BABY'S TEARS 3:208
illus. 3:208
BACHELOR'S BUTTON 3:208
illus. 3:208
Bacilli 3:209
BACON, FRANCIS 3:209
Bacon, Roger 1:30-31, 56
BACTERIA 3:209
Acne 1:22
Agriculture 1:41
Antibiotic 2:115
Antibody 2:116-117
Bacteriology 3:210-211
characteristics 3:209
Decomposer organism 5:486
energy sources 3:209
exp. 3:211
Fermentation 7:675
Fossils 8:722
Fungus 8:741-742
Germ theory 8:773
helpful 3:211
illus.: 3:209-210; 14:1322,
1325; 18:1739
Impetigo 9:874
Infection 9:877
Leeuwenhoek, Anton Van 10:950
Meningitis 11:1043
Nemathelminthes 12:1137-1138
Nitrogen cycle 12:1150-1151
nitrogen fixation 1:57; 3:211
Parasites 13:1247-1249

Penicillin 13:1261
Pimple 13:1295
Plant diseases 14:1318-1319
Plants, classification of 14:1322-1327
reproduction 3:209
Rot 15:1479
BACTERIOLOGY 3:210-211
artificial immunity 3:210
Bacteria 3:209
Germ theory 8:773
Koch, Robert 10:936
Leeuwenhoek, Anton van 10:950
Medicine 11:1038-1040
Microbe 11:1054
Microorganism 11:1054
Pasteurization 11:1253
Penicillin 13:1261-1262
pure culture 3:210
Sewage disposal 16:1530-1531
Spirochetes 17:1650
techniques of study: electron microscope 3:211; hybridization 3:211; infrared photography 3:211
Vaccine 18:1793
BADGER 3:212
characteristics 3:212
illus. 3:212; 7:643
odor communication 3:212
reproduction 3:212
usefulness 3:212
Weasel 19:1841-1842
BAER, KARL ERNST VON 3:212
BAIRD, JOHN LOGIE 3:212
Baking soda see **SODIUM BICARBONATE**
BALANCE 3:123
analytical 3:213
beam scale 3:213
equal arm 3:213
illus. 3:213
spring scale 3:213
torsion 5:453
BALANCE OF NATURE 3:214-221
Acclimatization 1:19
Biome 3:254
Botany 3:284-285
Carbon cycle 4:339
carnivores 3:216
causes of upset: agriculture 3:215; careless lumbering practices 3:215; introduction of foreign life 3:216; pollution 3:215; raising domesticated animals 3:215; removal of a kind of animal or plant from region 3:215
Chaparral 4:369
Climax community 4:397
commensalism 3:218
Conservation of nature 5:439-441
Crustacea 5:459
Demography 5:492
Ecology 6:552-553
Ecosystem 6:555
effect of plants 3:217
Environment 7:628
examples of balanced communities: arctic regions 3:221; climax community 3:215; lake 3:220; land 3:220-221; ocean 3:220; pond 3:219; savanna 3:221
factors of control: climate 3:214; destructive external forces 3:215; dominant vegetation 3:215; plant life 3:215; topography of land 3:214; type of soil 3:214-215
food-chain 3:217
food pyramid 3:217
Gregarious 8:797

Habitat 9:814
herbivores 3:216; 9:837
illus.: arctic animals 3:219; bracket fungus 3:220; cardinal 3:214; caribou 3:216; cat 3:219; communities 3:217; deer 3:218; fox 3:218; lamprey eel 3:220; life cycle 3:221; mouse 3:218; ocean environments 3:214; penguin 3:214; polar bear 3:216; raccoon 3:218; squirrel 3:218; symbiosis 3:220; tapeworm 3:220; walrus 3:216; water cycle 3:221
International Control of Natural Resources 9:889
members of a balanced community 3:216-219
mutualism 3:218
Ocean 12:1188-1190
omnivores 3:216; 13:1209
Paleontology 13:1238
parasites 3:218-219; 13:1249
Predator-prey 14:1358-1359
protection 3:216
relationships within community 3:218
scavengers 3:216
Terrarium 18:1735-1736
Tundra 18:1778
symbiosis 3:218
Weed control 19:1858-1859
Wilderness 19:1871, 1874
Balanced forces see **FORCES**
Bald eagle see **BIRDS OF PREY; EAGLE**
Ball-and-socket see **JOINTS, SKELETAL**
Ball bearing see **BEARING**
BALLISTICS 3:221
BALLOON 3:222
Aeronautics 1:30
Buoyancy 4:315
Dirigible 6:518
history 3:222
illus. 1:30; 3:222
Parachute 13:1244
Radiosonde 15:1424
uses today 3:222
BALSA 3:222
illus. 16:1593
BALSAM FIR 3:223
illus. 3:223
BAMBOO 3:223
illus. 3:223; 16:1593
BANANA 3:222
illus. 1:81; 3:223
Bantam see **CHICKEN**
BANTING, FREDERICK GRANT 3:224
Insulin 9:887
BANYAN 3:224
illus. 3:224
Barbary ape see **MONKEY**
BARBERRY 3:224
illus. 3:224
BARBITURATE 3:225
uses 3:225
BARIUM 3:225
uses 3:225
BARK 3:225
illus.: American beech 3:225; cross-section 3:225; paper birch 3:225; pine 3:225; shagbark hickory 3:225; sugar maple 3:225; sycamore 3:225
BARLEY 3:226
Cereal grains 4:366
illus. 3:226
BARNACLE 3:226

BARNARD, EDWARD EMERSON 3:226
Crux 5:460
illus.: dark nebula 3:226
Barndoor skate, illus. 15:1432
BAROMETER 3:227-228
aneroid 3:228
exp. 3:227
illus. 3:227-228
Millibar 11:1062
Pressure 14:1361
Pressure gauge 14:1361
Standard pressure 17:1657-1658
Barometric altimeter 1:66
BARRACUDA 3:228
characteristics 3:228
illus. 3:228
Basal metabolism rate see **METABOLISM**
Basalt see **ROCKS**
Base see **ACIDS AND BASES**
BASIL 3:228
illus. 3:228
BASS 3:229
Grouper 9:808
illus. 3:229
BAT 3:229-230
characteristics 3:229
food 3:230
habitat 3:230
illus. 3:229-230
locomotion 3:229-230
Nocturnal habits 12:1154-1155
reproduction 3:230
Bathyscaphe 3:230-231
BATHYSPHERE AND BATHYSCAPHE 3:230-231
Beebe, Charles William 3:241
Deep-sea diving 5:488-489
illus. 3:231
maneuverability 3:230-231
Piccard, Auguste 13:1292
Trieste 3:230
uses 3:231
BATTERY 3:223-233
Automobile 2:186
Condenser 5:438
dry cell 3:232
Electricity 6:563-572
Electrochemistry 6:573
Electrode 6:574
Electromagnet 6:577
electromagnetive force 3:233
exp. 3:233
Fuel 8:738-740
fuel cell 3:233
galvanic cell 3:232
illus.: chart 3:232; storage battery 3:233
internal resistance 3:233
polarization 3:233
primary 3:233
secondary 3:233
Volt 19:1823-1824
Volta, Alessandro 19:1824
BAUXITE 3:234
Africa 1:36
Aluminum 1:68
Europe 7:645
illus. 3:234
BAY 3:234
Gulf 9:809
illus. 3:234
Bay scallop, illus. 11:1085
BAYBERRY 3:234
illus. 3:234
BEACH 3:234
BEACON 3:235
BEAK 3:235

Beam see **BEACON; INSTRUMENT LANDING SYSTEM**
BEAM ANTENNA 3:235
  Antenna (electronic) 2:114
  illus. 3:235
  structure 3:235
  uses 3:235
Bean see **LEGUME**
BEAR 3:236
  American: black 3:236; brown (kodiak) 3:236; grizzly 3:236; polar 3:236
  characteristics 3:236
  illus.: Alaskan brown 3:236; black 3:236; polar 3:236; locomotion 3:236
BEARING 3:237
  ball 3:237
  Diamond 6:507
  early uses 3:237
  Friction 8:731
  illus. 3:237
  Indium 9:876
  roller 3:237
  sleeve 3:237
  spiral 3:237
BEAUFORT SCALE 3:238
  Gale 8:745
  illus., chart 3:238
BEAVER 3:238-239
  dam 3:239
  illus. 1:84; 12:1159; 3:239
  Rodent 15:1474-1475
BECQUEREL, ANTOINE HENRI 3:239
Bedbug see **BUGS**
BEE 3:239-240
  bumblebees 3:240
  food 1:86
  Frisch, Karl von 8:732
  honeybees 3:240
  illus.: bumblebee 3:239; honey 3:240; loaded with pollen 3:240; pupae 3:240; worker and drone 3:240
  Larva 3:240
  Parthenogenesis 13:1252
  Poison gland 14:1343
  Pollination 14:1346-1347
  protection 1:87
  reproduction 3:239-240
  social 3:240
  solitary 3:239-240
  stingless 3:240
BEEBE, CHARLES WILLIAM 3:241
  Bathysphere and bathyscaphe 3:230-231
BEECH 3:241
  Hardwood 9:820
  illus. 3:241
BEET 3:241
  illus. 3:241
BEETLES 3:242-243
  Animals, classification of 1:95
  body structure 3:242
  Bugs 4:312
  characteristics 3:243
  exp. 3:242
  grub 3:242
  illus.: Japanese beetle 9:881
  larva 3:242; 10:943
  life cycle 3:243
  Mealworm 11:1032
  Metamorphosis 11:1052
  Photochemistry 13:1278
  varieties: glow worm 3:243; tiger 3:243; water 3:243

BEGONIA 3:244
  illus. 3:244
BELL, ALEXANDER GRAHAM 3:244
  Decibel 5:486
  illus. 18:1726
  Telephone 18:1726-1727
Belladonna see **ATROPINE**
BENDS 3:245
  Caisson 4:322
  Decompression 5:487
  Raptures of the deep 15:1429
Beneficiation 10:914
Beneguela Current 5:470
BENZENE 3:245
Berberis, illus. 16:1545
Beriberi see **VITAMIN DEFICIENCY**
BERKELIUM 3:245
Berm 3:234
BERNOULLI, DANIEL 3:245-246
  Mechanics 11:1037-1038
Bernoulli's principle 3:246
  exp. 3:245
BERRY 3:246
  Fruit 8:736
BERYL 3:246
  Gem 8:759
BERYLLIUM 3:247
  Woehler, Friedrich 19:1878
BERZELIUS, JONS JACOB 3:247
BESSEMER PROCESS 3:247-248
  addition of carbon 3:248
  basic oxygen furnace 3:247
  illus. 3:247
  Iron 10:913-915
  Kelly, William 3:247
  Open hearth process 13:1210-1212
  oxidation 3:248
  Steel 17:1666-1668
Bessemer, Sir Henry 3:247
Beta Centauri 4:363
Beta ray see **RAY, BETA**
Betatron see **NUCLEAR REACTORS**
BETELGEUSE 3:248
  Canis Major and Canis Minor 4:333
  Orion 13:1224
Bicarbonate of soda see **SODIUM BICARBONATE**
Biceps see **MUSCLE SYSTEM**
Bicuspid see **TEETH**
BICYCLE 3:249
  brake 3:291
  history 3:249
  illus. 3:249; pump 14:1385
  Machinery 10:989-991
  structure 3:249
BIENNIAL 3:249
  Boysenberry 3:287
  Cambium 4:326
  Forget-me-not 8:718
  Foxglove 8:727
  Gardening 8:752
  illus. 3:249
  Perennial 13:1264
  Pineapple 13:1296-1297
  Plant 14:1314-1317
BIG AND LITTLE DIPPERS 3:250
  illus. 3:250
  Polaris 14:1344
  Ursa Major and Minor 18:1791
  Bilateral symmetry 4:385
BILE 3:250; 6:512-513
  Gallbladder 8:747
Bill see **BEAK**
Binary fission 1:70
BINOCULARS 3:250-251
  illus. 3:251; 13:1215
  Lens, man-made 10:952-953

  opera glass 3:250
  Optical instruments 13:1214-1215
  prism 3:250-251
Binomial 1:60
BIOCHEMISTRY 3:251
  Biophysics 3:255
  Chemistry 4:377
  Zoology 19:1895-1896, 1897
BIOCIDES 3:252
  illus. 3:252
BIODEGRADABLE 3:252
  Detergent 5:496
BIOFEEDBACK 3:252
  Autonomic nervous system 2:189
  conditioning 3:252
  psychosomatic illness 3:252
Biogeography 3:254; 8:762, 763
BIOLOGICAL CLOCK 3:254
  Circadian rhythm 4:386
BIOLOGICAL CLOCK 3:254
  Circadian rhythm 4:386
BIOLOGY 3:253-254
  Aristotle 2:135
  Biophysics 3:255
  branches: anatomy 3:253; biogeography 3:254; botany 3:253; ecology 3:253; economic botany 3:253; economic zoology 3:254; embryology 3:254; eugenics 3:253; evolution 3:245; genetics 3:253; paleontology 3:253; pathology 3:254; psychology 3:254; sociology 3:253; taxonomy 3:253; teratology 3:254; veterinary medicine 3:254; zoology 3:253
  Dissection 6:520
  Ecology 6:552
  Fission 7:688
  Flagella 7:688
  illus.: branches 3:253; brown bear 3:254
  Lamarck, Jean Baptiste Pierre 10:940
  Limnology 10:965-966
  Locus 10:977
  Morphology 11:1096
  Nuclear science 12:1170-1175
  Ocean 12:1188-1190
BIOMASS 3:254
  Eutrophication 7:646
  Succession 17:1682-1683
BIOME 3:254
  Agriculture 1:39
  Biosphere 3:255
  Chaparral 4:369
  Ecosystem 6:555
  illus. 3:254
  Prairie 14:1355; 1356
  Savanna 16:1510
  Tundra 18:1778
BIOMETRY 3:254
BIOPHYSICS 3:255
  applications 3:255
  bionics 3:255
  illus.: electron microscope 3:255
  Physics 13:1287-1288
BIOSPHERE 3:255
Biota 6:552
BIRCH 3:255
  illus. 3:255
  varieties 3:255
BIRD 3:256-257
  Birds, flightless 3:261
  characteristics 3:256
  Chordata 4:383-385
  Crop 5:458
  endangered 3:257
  extinct 3:257
  Feather 7:673-674

flying 3:256
Fowl 8:724-726
Gizzard 8:778
illus.: feet 3:256; large land birds 3:257
migration 3:257; 11:1059-1061
Nocturnal habits 12:1154-1155
protection 1:87
Pterodactyl 14:1382
See also individual bird names
BIRD FEEDERS 3:258
illus. 3:258
BIRD HOUSES 3:257-259
Bluebird 3:273
design 3:259
illus. 3:258-259
Bird migration see **MIGRATION**
BIRD NESTS 3:259-260
Bittern 3:264
Catbird 4:353
cowbird 3:259; 5:454
cuckoo 3:259
dove 3:259
eagle 3:260; 6:538
Eggs 6:559
hummingbird 3:259
illus. 18:1708; bittern 3:259; brown towhee 3:260; catbird 3:259; kill-deer 3:259; osprey 3:260; tern 3:260; vireo 3:260; woodpecker 3:260
killdeer 3:260
kingfisher 3:260
lining 3:260
location 3:260
Meadowlark 11:1032
Nutcracker 12:1183
oriole 3:259
osprey 3:260
woodpecker 3:260
Bird of paradise 14:1330
BIRDS, FLIGHTLESS 3:261
Bird 3:256-257
Dodo 6:521
illus.: ostrich 3:261; rhea 3:261
Kiwi 10:935
Ostrich 13:1228
prehistoric 3:261
present day: cassowary 3:261; emu 3:261; kiwi 3:261; ostrich 3:261; penguin 3:261; rhea 3:261
BIRDS OF PREY 3:262-263
characteristics 3:262
Claw 4:392
Cormorant 5:448
diurnal 3:262
eagle 3:262; 6:538
falcon 3:262; 7:669
hawk 3:263; 9:822
illus.: eagle 3:262; osprey 3:263; screech owl 3:263; shrike 3:263; vulture 3:263
Kite 10:935
nocturnal 3:262
Nocturnal habits 12:1154-1155
Osprey 13:1227
owl 3:263
Shrike 16:1542
vulture 3:263
BIRTH 3:264
Parturition 13:1252
BIRTHMARK 3:264
Wart 19:1829
BISMUTH 3:264
Bison, illus. 7:643
BITTERN 3:264
Heron 9:841-842
illus.: 3:259; 3:264; 14:1375
nests 3:259

BITTERROOT 3:264
illus. 3:264
BITTERSWEET 3:265
illus. 3:265
Bituminous coal see **COAL**
Bivalve see **MOLLUSCA**
BLACK DEATH 3:265
bubonic plague 3:265; 4:308
diphtheria 3:265; 6:517
Epidemic 7:630-631
smallpox 3:265; 16:1561-1562
Black-eyed Susan see **WILD FLOWERS**
Black snake see **SNAKES**
Black tar 10:988
Black-tailed deer, illus. 5:489
Black walnut, illus. 9:820
Black widow spider see **SPIDERS**
BLACKBERRY 3:265
illus. 3:265
BLACKBIRD 2:266
illus. 3:266
BLADDER, URINARY 3:266
Blastula see **CLEAVAGE**
Blast furnace 10:914
BLAZING STAR 3:266
illus. 3:266
BLEACHING AGENTS 3:266
chlorine 3:266
ozone 3:266
sodium chlorite 3:266
sodium perborate 3:266
tennant 3:266
BLEEDING HEART 3:267
illus. 3:267
Plants, tropical 14:1329-1330
BLIGHT 3:267
Cineraria 4:386
Parasites 13:1249
Blimp see **AIRSHIPS; DIRIGIBLE**
BLINDNESS 3:267
causes 3:267
optic nerve 3:267
retina 3:267
Blips 10:908
Blister see **BURNS**
BLIZZARD 3:267
Block and tackle see **MACHINES, SIMPLE**
BLOOD 3:268-269
albumin 3:269
Anemia 1:79
Blue baby 3:272
Blushing 3:274
Circulatory system 4:387-389
clots 3:269
Coagulant 5:412
Connective tissue 5:439
Diastole 6:508
fibrinogen 3:269
function of 3:268
globulin 3:269; 8:750, 783
Heart 9:823-825
hemoglobin 3:268
Hemophilia 9:834
Histology 9:848
illus.: cells 3:268, 269
Infection 9:877-878
Leukemia 10:956
Lymphatic system 10:986-987
Malpighi, Marcello 11:1010
Medicine 11:1038-1040
Mononucleosis 11:1090
plasma 3:268, 269
platelets 3:269
red blood cells 3:268
Rh factor 15:1456
Scab 16:1510
Serum 16:1530

Spleen 17:1650-1651
thrombin 3:269
Thrombosis 18:1746
thromboplastin 3:269
Transfusion 18:1766-1767
Vein 19:1808-1809
Vitamin 19:1817-1818
white blood cells 3:269
BLOOD COUNT 3:270
BLOOD PRESSURE 3:270-271
Biofeedback 3:252
diastolic 3:270; 6:508
Faint 7:669
Headache 9:823
heart 3:270; 9:823-825
hypertension 3:270; 9:871
hypotension 3:271; 9:872
illus.: sphygmomanometer 3:270
sphygmomanometer 3:270
systolic 3:270
BLOOD TYPES 3:271
agglutination 3:271
antibodies 3:271
antigens 3:271
Hemophilia 9:834
illus.: four blood groups 3:271
Rh factor 15:1456
Spleen 17:1650-1651
Transfusion 18:1766-1767
Blood vessels 4:387-389
Blossom see **FLOWER**
BLUE BABY 3:272
cause 3:272
treatment 3:272
Blue-eyed grass, illus. 7:694
BLUE JAY 3:272
illus. 3:272
Blue mussel, illus. 11:1085
Blue whale see **WHALE**
BLUEBELL 3:272
illus. 3:272
BLUEBERRY 3:272-273
illus. 3:273
BLUEBIRD 3:273
Bird houses 3:258
illus. 3:273
BLUEFISH 3:273
illus. 3:273
BLUEGILL 3:273
illus. 3:273
Sunfish 17:1693
Bluegrass see **GRASSES**
BLUEPRINT 3:274
exp. 3:274
illus. 3:274
Photochemistry 13:1277-1278
BLUSHING 3:274
Boa see **SNAKES**
Boar see **PIG**
BOATS 3:275-276
illus. 275, 276
oar-propelled 3:276
paddle-propelled 3:276
power-propelled 3:276
wind- and sail-propelled 3:276
Bobcat see **CAT FAMILY**
BOBOLINK 3:277
illus. 3:277
BOBWHITE 3:277
illus. 3:277
Quail 14:1390
Boeing 707, illus. 1:31
BOG 3:277
Cranberry 5:455
formation 3:277
illus.: orchid 3:277
succession 3:277
BOHR THEORY 3:278
Atom 2:173

Chemistry 4:373-377
Electron 6:579
Rutherford, Ernest 15:1486-1487
BOILING POINT 3:278
  Centrigrade or Celsius 4:363
  effect of air pressure 3:278
  exp. 3:278
  Gas 8:755
  Heat of vaporization 9:830
  Liquid 10:968-970
Boll weevil, illus. 14:1319
BOMB 3:279-282
  armor-piercing 3:280
  ballistics 3:221
  casing 3:279
  chemical 3:281
  Chemical warfare 4:373
  Cobalt 5:415
  demolition 3:280
  depth 3:281
  detonation 3:279
  explosive charge 3:280
  Explosives 7:663
  Fallout 7:670
  fins 3:279
  fragmentation 3:280
  fuse 3:279
  guided 3:281
  illus.: atomic bomb 3:279; fragmen-
    tation 3:281; general purpose
    3:280; incendiary 3:281
  incendiary 3:281
  nuclear: atomic (fission) 3:281-
    282; effect of 3:282; hydrogen
    (fusion) 3:282; neutron 3:282
  Nuclear energy 12:1162-1164
  Nuclear science 12:1170-1175
  Weapons 19:1838-1841
BONE 3:282-283
  cartilage 3:282
  Connective tissue 5:439
  dermal 3:282
  illus. 3:282
  Joints, skeletal 10:924-925
  marrow 3:282
  Ossification 13:1228
  Skeleton 16:1555
Boobies 8:750
BOOTES 3:283
  illus. 3:283
  Virgo 19:1816
BORAX 3:283
BORIC ACID 3:283
BORON 3:283
Boston terrier, illus. 6:523
Botanical garden see **ARBORETUM;**
  CONSERVATORY
BOTANY 3:284-285
  Biology 3:253-254
  branches of: agriculture 3:285;
    cytology 3:284; ecology 3:285;
    economic botany 3:285; histology
    3:284; pathology 3:285; physi-
    ology 3:284; taxonomy 3:285
  Bud 4:309-310
  Deliquescence 5:492
  Efflorescence 6:558
  illus. 3:284, 285
  Rot 15:1479
BOTULISM 2:286
BOUGAINVILLEA 3:286
  illus. 14:1331
  Plants, tropical 14:1329-1331
BOX ELDER 3:286
  illus. 3:286
BOYLE, SIR ROBERT 3:286
  Atmosphere 2:169
  Bernoulli, Daniel 3:246
  Elements 6:586-589

BOYLE'S LAW 3:287
  Boyle, Sir Robert 3:286
  Expansion 7:661-662
  exp. 3:287
  Gay-Lussac's Gas Law 8:757
BOYSENBERRY 3:287
  illus. 3:287
BRAIN 3:288-289
  cerebellum 3:289
  Cerebral palsy 4:366
  cerebrum 3:288-289; 4:367
  Concussion 5:437
  Cranium 5:455
  Ear 6:538-540
  electrical current 3:289
  electroencephalograph 3:289;
    6:574-575
  epilepsy 3:289
  Hypothalamus 9:872
  illus.: animal 3:289; human 3:288
  medulla oblongata 3:289; 11:1041
  Meninges 11:1043
  Multiple sclerosis 12:1119
  Mumps 12:1119
  Nervous system 12:1141-1145
  Paralysis 13:1245
  Pineal gland 13:1296
  Pituitary gland 14:1310
  vertebrate 3:289
  waves 6:574
BRAKE 3:290-291
  Automobile 2:188
  band 3:291
  disc 3:291
  double block 3:290
  external shoe 3:291
  illus.: band 3:291; double block
    3:290; external shoe 3:290;
    internal shoe 3:290; single
    block 3:290
  internal shoe 3:291
  prony 3:291
  single block 3:290
Bramble see **BRIAR**
BRASS 3:291
  illus. 3:291
BRAUN, WERNHER VON 3:292
  illus. 3:292
  National Aeronautics and Space
    Administration 3:292
Brazil Current 5:470
Brazil nut see **NUTS**
Brazilian tapir, illus. 16:1596
Breadfruit 14:1330
  illus. 14:1331
BREAST 3:292
Breathing see **RESPIRATORY**
  SYSTEM
BREEDING 3:293
  Cow 5:453
  Dog 6:521-523
  Fowl 8:724-726
  Heredity 9:837-841
  Horticulture 9:856-857
  hybridization 3:293; 9:861-862
  illus.: Brahman cattle 3:293
  mutations 3:293
  Pedigree 13:1258
BRIAR 3:293
BRICK 3:293
  composition 3:293
  illus. 3:293
  varieties 3:293
Brick top, illus. 12:1124
Bridal wreath see **SPIREA**
BRIDGES 3:294-296
  Cables 4:320
  construction 3:294
  fixed: arch 3:295; beam 3:295;

    cantilever 3:295; continuous
    3:295; plate-girder 3:295; sus-
    pension 3:295; truss 3:295
  illus.: bascule 3:295; continuous
    3:295; single arch 3:296; sus-
    pension 3:294; transporter 3:296;
    Verrazano-Narrows Bridge 3:296
  moveable: bascule 3:296; pontoon
    3:296; draw 3:296; vertical lift
    3:296
  notable: Brooklyn Bridge 3:296;
    Golden Gate 3:296 Straits of
    Mackinac 3:296; Verrazano-
    Narrows 3:296
  transporter 3:296
BRINE 3:296
  Pickling 13:1292
Brimstone see **SULFUR**
BRITISH THERMAL UNIT 3:296-297
  Calorie 4:325
  Heat 9:826
  Heat of vaporization 9:830
  illus. 3:297; 9:827
  therms 3:297
Brittle star see **ECHINODERMATA**
BROCCOLI 3:297
  illus. 3:297
BROMIDE 3:297
BROMINE 3:297
  Bromide 3:297
Bronchi see **LUNG**
BRONCHITIS 3:297
  Lung 10:983-984
Brontosaurus see **DINOSAURS**
Bronze see **ALLOYS**
BROWNIAN MOVEMENT 4:307
  illus. 4:307
  Kinetic Molecular Theory 4:307
  Kinetic theory 10:934
  Molecular theory 11:1083
  Molecule 11:1084
Brussels sprouts see **CABBAGE**
BRYOPHYTES 4:307-308
  Embryophyta 7:608
  evolution 4:308
  gametophytes 4:308
  illus.: hornworts 4:308; liverworts
    4:308; mosses 4:308
  liverworts 4:308; 10:974
  moss 4:308; 12:1108-1109
  spores 4:308
Bubble chamber 8:781
BUBONIC PLAGUE 4:308
  Black Death 3:265
  cause 4:308
  symptoms 4:308
  treatment 4:308
BUCKEYE 4:309
  illus. 4:309
BUCKWHEAT 4:309
  illus. 4:309
BUD 4:309-310
  Calyx 4:326
  illus. 4:309-310
  internode 4:309
  leaf axils 4:309
  Leaves 10:949
  node 4:309; 12:1155
  Stem 17:1668
  terminal 4:309
Budding see **REPRODUCTION,**
  ASEXUAL
BUFFALO 4:310
  characteristics 4:310
  food 4:310
  habitat 4:310
  illus.: American bison 4:310;
    11:1011; water buffalo 4:310
  reproduction 4:310

Buffalo treehopper, illus. 14:1375
BUGS 4:311-312
  aquatic 4:311
  assassin bugs 4:312
  bedbugs 4:312
  characteristics 4:311
  chinch bugs 4:312
  cone-nosed 4:312
  illus.: waterbug 4:312
  lace bugs 4:312
  red bugs 4:312
  squash bugs 4:312
  stinkbugs 4:311
BULBS 4:314
  Bud 4:309-310
  Corm 5:448
  Daffodil 5:475
  exp. presence of sugar 4:314
  Gardening 8:752
  Garlic 8:753
  Lily 10:964
  Perennial 13:1264
  Stem, underground 17:1668, 1669
BULB, ELECTRIC 4:312-313
  arc lamp 4:312
  Edison, Thomas Alva 4:312; 6:557
  exp. 4:313
  fluorescent 4:313
  illus.: Edison's original 4:313
  incandescent lamp 4:312-313
  Lamp 10:941
  mercury 4:313
  Phosphorescence 13:1276
  sodium 4:313
  vapor lamp 4:313
Bull moose, illus. 5:490
Bullet see **PROJECTILES;**
  WEAPONS
Bullhead see **CATFISH**
Bundle of His 9:825
BUNSEN, ROBERT WILHELM 4:314
BUNSEN BURNER 4:314
BUNTING 4:314
  illus. 4:314
BUOY 4:315
  illus. 4:315
BUOYANCY 4:315
  Air 1:44
  Archimedes' principle 4:315
  Dirigible 6:518
  Equilibrium 7:633
  exp. 4:315
  Specific gravity 17:1640-1641
  Submarine 17:1680-1681
BURBANK, LUTHER 4:316
  Daisy 5:477
  illus. 4:316
BURNET, SIR FRANK
  MACFARLANE 4:316
BURNS 4:316
  first-degree 4:316
  second-degree 4:316
  third-degree 4:316
  treatment 4:316
BURRO 4:316-317
  Donkey 6:525
  illus. 4:317
BURSITIS 4:317
  acute 4:317
  chronic 4:317
  treatment 4:317
Bush katydid 14:1375
Bushmaster see **SNAKES**
BUTANE 4:317
  isomers 4:317
Butte 11:1046
Butter-and-eggs, illus. 7:694
BUTTERCUP 4:317
  illus. 4:317

BUTTERFLIES 4:317-319
  chrysalis 4:317
  exp. 4:318
  illus.: aphrodite fritillary 4:319;
    black swallowtail 4:318; cabbage
    butterfly 4:319; cosmopolite
    4:318; meadow fritillary 4:319;
    monarch 4:319; orange sulphur
    4:318; pearl crescent 4:319;
    Western swallowtail 4:319
  Larva 10:943
  life cycle 4:317
  Metamorphosis 11:1052
  Moths 12:1108-1109
  Protective coloration
    14:1375-1376
  varieties: buckeyes 4:317; fritil-
    laries 4:318; monarch 4:318;
    swallowtail 4:318
BYRD, RICHARD EVELYN 4:319
  Antarctica 2:110
  illus. 2:110; 4:319
  Poles, North and South 14:1345
CABBAGE 4:320
  Cauliflower 4:356
  illus. 4:320
  Kohlrabi 10:936
  Mustard 12:1127-1128
CABLES 4:320
  Coaxial cable 5:415
  Fibrous tissue 7:679
  illus. 4:320
  submarine 4:320
  underground 4:320
Cacao see **COCOA**
CACTUS 4:321
  characteristics 4:321
  illus.: barrel 4:321; flower
    4:321; saguaro 4:321
  Plants, succulent 14:1329
  water storage 4:321
CADDIS FLY 4:321
  illus. 4:321
CADMIUM 4:322
CAFFEINE 4:322
  Coffee 5:419
  Plants, medicinal 14:1328-1329
Cafe coronary 9:831
CAISSON 4:322
  airlocks 4:322
  box 4:322
  bridges 3:294-296
  illus. 4:322
  open 4:322
  pneumatic 4:322
  sandhogs 4:322
Caisson disease see **BENDS**
CALABASH 4:323
CALADIUM 4:323
  illus. 4:323
CALAMINE 4:323
Calcite see **ROCKS**
CALCIUM 4:323
CALCIUM CARBONATE 4:323
  Coral 5:448
CALCULATOR 4:323-324
  Computer 5:434-436
  illus. 4:324
  Slide rule 16:1560
Calculus see **MATHEMATICS**
CALENDAR 4:324
  Astronomy 2:166-167
  Gregorian 4:324
  Julian 4:324
  leap year 4:324
  Measurement 11:1033-1036
  Roman 4:324
  Time zones 18:1751-1752
  United Nations new world 4:324

CALENDULA 4:324
California Current 5:470
CALIFORNIUM 4:324-325
CALIPER 4:325
  illus. 4:325
  Measurement 11:1033-1036
Callicarpa, illus. 16:1545
CALM, REGIONS OF 4:325
CALORIE 4:325
  British Thermal Unit 3:297
  Energy 7:612-617
  Fahrenheit 7:669
  Freezing point 8:728
  Heat 9:826
  Heat of fusion 9:828-829
  Heat of vaporization 9:830
  illus. 9:827
  Specific heat 17:1641
Calorimeter 4:325
  British Thermal Unit 3:297
  Heat of reaction 9:829
  illus. 9:829
  Thermochemistry 18:1740
CALORIMETRY 4:325-326
  bomb calorimeter 4:326
  Calorie 4:325
  calorimeter 4:325
  specific heat 4:326
Caloris Basin 11:1046
CALYX 4:326
CAMBIUM 4:326
  Annual rings 2:109
  Grafting 8:790
  Plant 14:1314-1317
CAMEL 4:326-327
  Alpaca 1:64
  Bactrian 4:326-327
  characteristics 4:327
  dromedary (Arabian) camel
    4:326-327
  food 4:327
  habitat 4:327
  illus.: Bactrian 4:327; dromedary
    (Arabian) 4:327
  Llama 10:975
  uses 4:327
CAMELLIA 4:327
  illus. 4:327
  Tea 18:1721-1722
CAMERA 4:328-329
  box 4:328
  double lens reflex 4:329
  effect of light 4:328
  exp.: construction 4:328; how a
    camera works 4:328
  illus.: 13:1215; TV 4:329
  Land, Edwin Herbert 10:941
  movie 4:329
  110-cartridge 4:328
  126-cartridge 4:328
  Optical instruments 13:1214-1215
  parts: diaphragm 4:329; lens 4:329;
    shutter 4:329
  Photography 13:281-1282
  self-printing 4:329
  television 4:329
  35mm single lens reflex 4:328
  35mm viewfinder 4:328
CAMOMILE 4:329
CAMOUFLAGE 4:329
  chameleon 4:329
  Giraffe 8:778
  Illus.: American lizard 4:329; whip-
    poorwill 4:329
  polar bear 4:329
  Protective coloration 14:1375-1376
  zebra 4:329
CAMPHOR 4:330
Canadian lynx, illus. 1:85

CANAL 4:330
history 4:330
illus.: lock-type 4:330
Isthmus 10:919
lock 4:330
well-known canals: Panama 4:330; Suez 4:330
CANARY 4:330
Animals, classification of 1:94
illus. 4:330
Canary Current 5:469
CANCER (CONSTELLATION) 4:331
illus. 4:331
mythology 4:331
CANCER (DISEASE) 4:331
Aerosol 1:32
benign tumor 4:331
Carcinogen 4:344
carcinoma 4:331
causes 4:331
characteristics of cancer cells: lactic acid 4:331; no control over multiplying 4:331; invasion of neighboring structures 4:331; require less oxygen 4:331; size of nuclei 4:331
Chemotherapy 4:377
Drugs 6:528-530
epithelial cell 4:331
Fibiger, Johannes Andreas 7:679
illus.: cells 4:331
Leukemia 10:956
malignant tumor 4:331; 11:1009
Pleurisy 14:1337
Radiation, uses of 15:1414-1515
treatment 4:331
Tumor 18:1777
Cancerroot, illus. 13:1247
CANDELA 4:332
foot-candle 4:332
illumination 4:332
illus. 4:332
Light 10:959-963
luminous intensity 4:332
lux 4:332
CANDYTUFT 4:332
illus. 4:332
CANIS MAJOR AND CANIS MINOR 4:333
illus. 4:333
mythology 4:333
Sirius 16:1551
CANKER SORE 4:333
apthous ulcer 4:333
cause of 4:333
CANKER WORM 4:333
Canna see **PLANTS, TROPICAL**
CANNED HEAT 4:333
Cannibal fish see **TROPICAL FISH**
Canning see **FOOD PRESERVATION**
Cannon see **WEAPONS**
Cantaloupe see **MELONS**
Cantilever see **BRIDGES**
CANYON 4:334
Mesa 11:1046
trenches 4:334
Capacitator see **CONDENSER**
CAPE 4:334
CAPE CANAVERAL 4:334
Cape Kennedy 4:334
Capella see **AURIGA**
CAPER 4:334
CAPILLARITY 4:334-335
adhesion 4:334
cohesion 4:334
exp. 4:335
factors affecting 4:334
Liquid 10:968-970
Surface tension 17:1695

CAPILLARY 4:335
arterioles 4:335
functions 4:335
illus. 4:335
sinusoids 4:335
Vein 19:1808-1809
venules 4:335
CAPRICORNUS 4:336
illus. 4:336
Capsium see **CAYENNE**
CAPSULE 4:336; 8:735
Seed 16:1524-1525
Syringa 18:1714
CAPYBARA 4:336
illus. 15:1475; 16:1596
CARAT 4:336
CARAWAY 4:336
illus. 4:336
CARBOHYDRATES 4:337
animal digestion 1:86
Cellulose 4:361
changing to acids 1:20
Chitin 4:380
Digestive system 6:512
Elements in the human body 6:590
Fat 7:672
Gum 9:810
Haworth, Sir Walter 9:822
illus.: digestion 4:337
in animals 4:337
in plants 4:337
Metabolism 11:1048
Protein 14:1376-1377
Sugar 17:1683
CARBOLIC ACID 4:337
CARBON 4:337-338
Biochemistry 3:251
carbon-12 4:338
Coal 5:412
Diamond 6:507
exp. 4:338
forms: coal 4:338; coke 4:388; charcoal 4:338; diamond 4:337; graphite 4:338; lampblack 4:338
Hydrocarbon 9:684
Lampblack 10:941
necessity 4:338
Nitrogen cycle 12:1150-1151
organic chemistry 3:338
Organic compounds 13:1222
Protein 14:1376-1377
CARBON CYCLE 4:339
Carbon 4:337-338
Carbon dioxide 4:340
Chlorophyll 4:382
Decomposer organism 5:486
Decomposition 5:486-487
illus. 4:339
Nitrogen cycle 12:1050-1051
Photosynthesis 13:1285
CARBON DIOXIDE 4:340
Carbon cycle 3:339
Chlorophyll 4:381
exp. 4:340
Lung 10:984
uses: carbonated drink 1:20; 4:340; dry ice 4:340; fire extinguisher 4:340; leavening 4:340
CARBON LIFE 4:341-342
Balance of nature 3:214-221
Carbon 4:337-338
Carbon cycle 4:339
plants 4:341-342
animals 4:341
resisting poison 4:341
Silicon life 16:1546-1547
CARBON MONOXIDE 4:342; 10:913-914
Asphyxia 2:151

Gas 8:755
White damp 19:1867
CARBON TETRACHLORIDE 4:342
Chlorine 4:381
exp. 4:324
uses 4:342
Carbonated drink 1:20; 4:340
CARBONATES 4:343
properties 4:343
uses 4:343
Carbonic acid 1:20
Carboniferous age see **GEOLOGIC TIME TABLE**
CARBONIZATION 4:343
Carbon 4:338
CARBURETOR 4:343
Accelerator 1:17
illus. 4:343
CARCINOGEN 4:344
Carcinoma see **CANCER (DISEASE)**
Cardiac valve 6:511
CARDINAL 4:344
Grosbeak 9:807
illus. 1:82; 4:344
CARDINAL CLIMBER 4:344
illus. 4:344
Cardiograph see **ELECTRO-CARDIOGRAPH**
Cardiovascular system see **CIRCULATORY SYSTEM**
Caribou see **DEER FAMILY**
Caries see **TOOTH DECAY**
CARNATION 4:344
Carnauba wax palm, illus. 16:1593
CARNIVORE 4:345; 3:216
Bear 3:236
characteristics 4:345
Hyena 9:869
teeth 4:345
Cat family 4:348-351
Herbivore 9:837
illus.: skulls 4:345
Mammalia 11:1011-1012
Mongoose 11:1089
Pike 13:1294
CARNOTITE 4:345
Carotene see **VITAMIN**
Carotid artery see **CIRCULATORY SYSTEM**
CARP 4:345
illus. 4:345
Carpil see **PISTIL**
CARRIER WAVE 4:345
Oscillator 13:1224-1225
CARRIERS 4:345
CARROT 4:346
Dill 6:513
illus. 4:346
CARTILAGE TISSUE 4:346
Connective tissue 5:439
Ear 6:538
Histology 9:846-849
Lamprey 10:941
Ossification 13:1228
matrix 4:346
types: collagenous 4:346; elastic 4:346; fibrocartilage 4:346
CARTOGRAPHY 4:346
illus. 4:346
CARVER, GEORGE WASHINGTON 4:346-347
Caryopsis 8:735,793
Casein see **DAIRY PRODUCTS; PAINTS**
Cashew see **NUTS**
CASHMERE 4:347
Cassava, illus. 16:1593
Cassia see **CINNAMON**
CASSIOPEIA 4:347

Cassiterite see **TIN**
Cassowary 3:261
Cast iron see **IRON**
Casters 3:237
CASTOR OIL 4:347
CAT FAMILY 4:348-351
  characteristics: claws 4:348; loco-
    motion 4:348; hunting 4:348-349;
    purring 4:349; vision 4:348
  Civet 4:391
  Claw 4:392
  illus.: Angora 4:349; black leopard
    4:351; bobcat 4:351; claws 4:348;
    eyes 4:348; jaguarundi 4:351;
    lion 4:351; manx 4:349; ocelot
    4:351; puma 4:351; Siamese
    4:349; skeleton 4:348; snow leo-
    pard 4:351; tabby 4:349; tiger
    4:350
  varieties: bobcat 4:351; cheetah
    4:350; house cats 4:349; jaguar
    4:350; leopard 4:350-351; lion
    4:351; lynx 4:351; miacis 4:350;
    ocelot 4:351; tiger 4:351; puma
    4:350
Catabolism see **METABOLISM**
CATALPA 4:352
  illus. 4:352
CATALYST 4:352
  exp. 4:353
  Haber Process 9:814
  Manganese 11:1013
  types 4:352
  uses 4:352
CATARACT 4:353
  Blindness 3:267
  degenerative 4:353
  developmental 4:353
  Eye 7:664-667
  senile 4:353
  traumatic 4:353
CATBIRD 4:353
  illus. 4:353
CATERPILLAR 4:353
  Butterflies 4:317
  Cocoon 5:417
  Cutworm 5:471
  illus.: 4:35•; 9:881; 14:1319
  Metamorphosis 11:1052
  Moths 12:1110
CATFISH 4:354
CATHODE 4:354
  Anode 2:109
  Battery 3:232
  Electrode 6:574
  Electrolysis 6:576
  Photoelectricity 13:1278-1280
  Polarization 14:1345
  Vacuum tube 18:1793-1794
CATHODE RAY 4:354-355
  Cathode-ray tube 4:355
  illus.: demonstrations 4:355
  Oscilloscope 13:1225
CATHODE-RAY TUBE 4:355
  Cathode 4:354
  Electronics 6:583
  Illus. 4:355
  Oscilloscope 13:1225
  parts: electron gun 4:355; envelope
    4:355; phosphor screen 4:355
  Television 18:1730-1732
  types: kinescope 4:355; oscil-
    loscope 4:355
CATKIN 4:356
CATNIP 4:356
  Mint 11:1070
CATTAIL 4:356
  illus. 4:356
Cattle see **COW; OXEN; UNGULATA**

Caucasoid see **EVOLUTION OF MAN**
CAULIFLOWER 4:356
  Cabbage 4:320
  illus. 4:356
CAUSTIC 4:356
CAVE 4:356-357
  caverns: Carlsbad Cavern 4:357;
    Cathedral Caverns 4:357; Mam-
    moth Cave 4:356; Wind Cave
    4:357; Wyandotte Cave 4:357
  formation 4:356
  illus.: Cathedral Caverns 4:357
  lava 4:357
  Sinkhole 16:1550
  Speleology 17:1644
  Stalagmite and stalactite 17:1657
  value 4:357
CAVIAR 4:357
Cavity see **TOOTH DECAY**
Cavy see **GUINEA PIG**
CAYENNE 4:357
  Pepper 13:1263
Cecum 6:512
CEDAR 4:357
  Arborvitae 2:128
  eastern red 4:357
  illus.: red cedar 4:357
  incense 4:357
  southern white 4:357
  Spanish 4:357
  western red 4:357
CELERY 4:358
  illus. 4:358
CELESTIAL NAVIGATION 4:358
  Constellation 5:442
  illus. 4:358
  Navigation 12:1134-1135
  tools: chronometer 4:358; Nautical
    Almanac 4:358; sextant 4:358
CELLOPHANE 4:358
CELLS 4:359-360
  Anatomy 1:76
  Animals, classification of 1:91-96
  Blood 3:268-269
  Corpuscle 5:449
  Division of labor 6:521
  Embryology 6:592-597
  Epithelial tissue 7:632
  Gene 8:760
  Glandular tissue 8:781
  Heredity 9:837-841
  Homeostasis 9:851
  illus.: bacteria 4:360; bone 4:359;
    cork 4:360; diagrammatic general-
    ized 4:360; gland 4:359; involun-
    tary muscle 4:359; leaf 4:360;
    lymph 4:359; nerve 4:359; onion
    4:360; red blood 4:359; skin
    4:359; voluntary muscle 4:359
  Metabolism 11:1048
  Mitosis and meiosis 11:1076-1078
  Nerve cell 12:1141
  Nervous system 12:1141-1145
  Nucleic acid 12:1178
  parts: centriole 4:360; cytoplasm
    4:360; golgi bodies 4:360; mito-
    chondria 4:360; nucleus 4:360;
    plastids 4:360; vacuoles 4:360
  Plant 14:1314-1317
  plasma membrane 4:360
  protoplasm 4:359, 360
  Protozoa 14:1378-1379
  Schultze, Max 16:1513
  Schwann, Theodor 16:1513
  Specialization 17:1640
  tissue 4:359
Cells in series and parallel see
  BATTERY; ELECTRICITY
CELLULOID 4:361

CELLULOSE 4:361
  Cellophane 4:358
  Cells 4:360
  Celluloid 4:361
  Forest products 8:713
  Plant 14:1314-1317
  Plaster 13:1332
  Plastics 14:1332-1334
  Rayon 15:1436
  Sugar 17:1683
Celsius see **CENTIGRADE**
CEMENT 4:361
  illus. 4:361
  Sand 15:1493
CENEZOIC ERA 4:361-362
  fossils 4:361
  Geologic time table 8:765
  Glacial ages 8:779
  illus.: map 4:362
  Mesozoic Era 11:1047
  Prehistoric mammals 14:1359-
  Quaternary period: Pleistocene
    epoch 4:362; Recent epoch 4:362;
    Eocene epoch 4:361
  Tertiary period: Miocene epoch
    4:362; Oligocene epoch 4:361;
    Paleocene epoch 4:361; Plio-
    cene epoch 4:362
CENTAURUS 4:363
  Alpha Centauri 4:363
  Beta Centauri 4:363
  illus. 4:363
  Proxima Centauri 4:363
CENTIGRADE OR CELSIUS 4:363
  Degree 5:491
CENTIPEDE 4:363
  illus. 4:363
**CENTRIFUGAL AND CENTRIPETAL
  FORCES** 4:364
  Earth 6:541
  exp. 4:364
  Rotation 15:1479
Centrifugal pump, illus. 14:1385
CENTRIFUGE 4:365
  *Centrifugal and centripetal
    forces* 4:364
  illus. 4:365
  uses 4:365
Centriole see **CELLS**
Centripetal see **CENTRIFUGAL AND
  CENTRIPETAL FORCES**
CENTURY PLANT 4:365
  illus. 4:365
CEPHEUS 4:365
  illus. 4:365
  mythology 4:365
CEREAL GRAINS 4:366
  Barley 3:226
  Corn 5:449
  Flour 7:693
  Gluten 8:783
  Grasses 8:792-793
  illus. 4:366
  Rice 15:1458-1459
  Rye 15:1487
  Seed 16:1524-1525
  Sorghum 16:1584
  Wheat 19:1866
CEREBELLUM 4:366
  Brain 3:289
  Cells 4:366
  characteristics 4:366
  function 4:366
  illus. 4:366
CEREBRAL PALSY 4:366
  causes 4:366
  symptoms 4:366
  treatment 4:366
Cerebro Vascular Accident 2:122

CEREBRUM 4:367
Brain 3:288
Cerebral palsy 4:366
functions 4:367
illus. 4:367
structure: cortex 4:367; frontal
lobe 4:367; occipital lobe 4:367;
parietal lobe 4:367; temporal
lobe 4:367
Cereus, night-blooming see
NIGHT-BLOOMING PLANTS
CERIUM 4:368
CESIUM 4:368
CETACEA 4:368
adaptations 4:368
breathing 4:368
Dolphin 6:524
illus.: dolphin 4:368; Greenland
whale 4:368
locomotion 4:368
Mammalia 11:1011-1012
porpoise 4:368; 14:1352
whale 4:368; 19:1864-1865
CHAIN REACTION 4:368
Bomb 3:282
Chalcedony see **QUARTZ**
CHALK 4:369
illus. 4:369
Putty 14:1388
CHAMELEON 4:369; 4:329
illus. 14:1375
Lizard 10:975
protection 1:87
Chamois, illus. 7:643
Changes of state see **PHYSICAL
STATES AND CHANGES; SUB-
STANCES, PROPERTIES OF**
CHANNEL 4:369
Lagoon 10:939
CHAPARRAL 4:369
CHARCOAL 4:370
Carbon 4:338
Carbonization 4:343
Coke 5:420
exp. 4:370
Filter 7:681
Forest products 8:712
Chard see **SWISS CHARD**
Charge see **BATTERY;
ELECTRICITY**
CHARGED PARTICLES 4:370
basic atomic particles 4:370
Millikan's electronic charge
11:1063
Charioteer see **AURIGA**
CHARLES' LAW 4:370-371
Boyle's Law 3:287
Gay-Lussac's Gas Law 8:757
CHAT 4:371
illus. 4:371
Cheese see **DAIRY PRODUCTS**
Cheetah see **CAT FAMILY**
Chemical bond 4:375
CHEMICAL CHANGE 4:371-372
alteration of electron 4:372
Camera 4:328
Carbon life 4:341
chemical bonds 4:372
Electrochemistry 6:573
endothermic 4:372
exp. 4:371
Matter 11:1031
Mixture 11:1079
Physical states and changes
13:1286-1287
Reagent 15:1437
types: combination 4:372; decom-
position 4:372; double replace-
ment 4:372; replacement 4:372

Chemical equations 4:375-376
Chemical laws see **CHEMISTRY**
Chemical reaction 4:375
CHEMICAL WARFARE 4:372-373
chlorine 4:373
fire 4:373
history 4:372
illus. 4:373
mustard gas 4:373
Poison 14:1342
protection from 4:373
smoke screens 4:373
CHEMISTRY 4:373-377
Acids and bases 1:20-22
Alchemy 1:56
arrangement of electrons 4:374
Atom 2:127-174
basic operations: crystallization
4:376; quantitative combustion
4:376; solution 4:376; distillation 4:376;
Boyle, Sir Robert 3:286
branches: analytical 4:377; biochemistry 4:377; chemical education 4:377; chemical engineering
4:377; general (inorganic) 4:377;
geochemistry 4:377; industrial
chemistry 4:377; organic 4:377;
pharmaceutical 4:377; physical
4:377
chart: chemical compounds
4:376; elements 4:374; metals
and nonmetals 4:375
chemical bond 4:375
Chemical change 4:371-372
chemical equations 4:375
chemical reaction 4:375-376
Crystal 5:460-461
Deliquescence 5:492
Dissociation 6:520
elements 4:374; 6:586-589
Filter 7:681
history 4:373
Hydrocarbons 9:864
Hydrogen 9:867
illus.: laboratory 4:377
Ion 10:911-912
Laboratory 10:938
Lavoisier, Antoine Laurent 10:946
Limnology 10:965-966
Matter 11:1031
Mendeleev's Periodic Table
11:1042-1043
metals 4:375; 11:1049-1051
Mixture 11:1079
modern 4:373-377
molecular compound 4:375
molecular crystal compound 4:375
Molecular weight 11:1083
Neutralization 12:1145
nonmetals 4:375
Nuclear science 12:1170-1175
Organic compounds 13:1222-1223
Physical states and changes
13:1286-1287
Physiology 13:1289-1292
Polymer 14:1348
Precipitation (chemical) 14:1357
Radical, chemical 15:1416
Reagent 15:1437
Salt 15:1492
structural formulas 4:375
Sublimation 17:1680
Symbol, chemical 18:1713
Thermochemistry 18:1740
Chemosynthetics 3:209
CHEMOTHERAPY 4:377
Cancer (disease) 4:331
Disease 6:519

Ehrlich, Paul 6:560
Fungicides 8:741
Leukemia 10:956
CHERRY 4:377
Orchard 13:1220
Chert see **ROCKS**
Chestnut see **NUTS**
Chestnut tree, illus. 7:644
Chewing gum 4:378
CHICKADEE 4:377
Bird houses 3:258
illus. 4:377
CHICKEN 4:378
exp., embryo development 6:596
Fowl 8:724
illus.: domestic 4:378; embryo
6:593, 597; wild 4:378
varieties 4:378
CHICKEN POX 4:378
symptoms 4:378
CHICLE 4:378
Forest products 8:713
CHICORY 4:378
illus. 4:379; 5:431
Chigger see **MITE**
Chihuahua, illus. 6:523
CHIMPANZEE 4:379
Ape 2:121
characteristics 4:379
diet 4:379
Gorilla 8:789
habitat 4:379
illus. 4:379; 14:1381
Primates 14:1362-1363
similarity to man 4:379
CHINCHILLA 4:379
Chinch bug see **BUGS**
CHINOOK WIND 4:379
CHIPMUNK 4:380
illus. 1:84; 4:380; 12:1159
Chiroptera 3:229; 11:1012
CHITIN 4:380
Animals, classification of 1:95
Arthropoda 2:141
Cell 4:360
chemical composition 4:380
Crab 5:454
Crayfish 5:456
Crustacea 5:459
Exoskeleton 7:661
CHITON 4:380
illus. 4:380; 11:1085
CHLORIDE 4:380-381
uses 4:381
Chlorination see **CHLORINE;
WATER**
CHLORINE 4:381
Bleaching agents 3:266
Chemical warfare 4:373
Chloride 4:380
Gas 8:756
uses: bleaching agent 4:381; germ
killer 4:381; manufacture of
other chemicals 4:381
CHLOROFORM 4:381
Anesthetics 1:81
Chlorine 4:381
Lanolin 10:942
Chloromycetin see **ANTIBIOTICS**
CHLOROPHYLL 4:382
albino plants 1:55
Algae 1:58
Angiosperm 1:81
Carbon cycle 4:339
Cells 4:360
Fischer, Hans 7:686
Photosynthesis 13:1285
Plant 14:1314-1317
Plastid 14:1334

Chlorophyta 18:1739
Chloroplasts 4: 382
Chocolate see **COCOA**
CHOLERA 4:382
 cause 4:382
 symptoms 4:382
 treatment 4:382
CHOLESTEROL 4:382-383
 abnormal amounts in the body
  4:384
 Arteriosclerosis 2:139
 Lanolin 10:942
 sources 4:382-383
 Steroid 17:1671
 uses 4:383
CHORDATA 4:383-385
 Animals, classification of 1:95
 Bird 3:256-257
 chordates with skulls: fish 4:384;
  tetrapods 4:385
 chordates without skulls: acorn
  worm 4:384; amphioxus 4:384;
  tunicates 4:384
 illus.: amphioxus 4:383; verte-
  brates 4:384
 Invertebrates 10:911
 nervous system 4:384
 Notochord 12:1161
 Reptilia 15:1449-1450
 respiratory system 4:384
 Skeleton 16:1552-1555
 Snakes 16:1564-1566
Choroid coat see **EYE**
CHROMATOPHORES 4:385
CHROMIUM 4:385
CHROMOSOMES 4:385
 Acquired characteristics 1:23
 Alternation of generations 1:65
 Clubfoot 5:412
 Fruit fly 8:737
 Gene 8:760
 Heredity 9:838
 histones 4:385
 illus. 4:385
 Locus 10:977
 Mitosis and meiosis 11:1076-1078
 Mongolism 11:1088-1089
 Mutation 12:1128
 Nucleic acid 12:1178
 nucleotides 4:385
 Reproduction, asexual 15:1445
 Zygote 19:1896
Chronometer see **CLOCKS**
Chyme 6:511
Chrysalis see **METAMORPHOSIS**
CHRYSANTHEMUM 4:386
 illus. 4:386
Chrysophyta 18:1738
Cicada see **BUGS; INSECTA**
Cinchona, illus. 14:1328
CILIA 4:386
 Stentor 17:1670
CINERARIA 4:386
 illus. 4:386
CINNABAR 4:386
 Mercury (element) 11:1044
CINNAMON 4:386
 Laurel 10:945
Cion 8:790
CIRCADIAN RHYTHM 4:386
Circle see **EARTH; GEOMETRY**
Circuits see **ELECTRICITY**
CIRCULATORY SYSTEM 4:387-389
 Anatomy 1:76
 Animal 1:82-87
 Arteriosclerosis 2:139
 Artery 2:139
 Blood 3:268-269
 Blood pressure 3:270-271

Blue baby 3:272
Crayfish 4:388
 Digestive system 6:510
 earthworm 4:388
 Electrocardiograph 6:573
 Embryology 6:592-597
 evolution 4:387-389
 exp., dissection of heart 4:388
 fish 4:388
 frog 4:388-389
 Galen 8:745
 Glandular tissue 8:781
 grasshopper 4:387-388
 Harvey, William 9:821
 Heart 9:823-825; four-chambered
  4:389; three-chambered 4:389
 Heart murmur 9:826
 Heartbeat 9:826
 illus.: crayfish 4:387; frog 4:387;
  grasshopper 4:387; human 4:389
 Histology 9:849
 Lung 10:983-984
 Lymphatic system 10:986-987
 parts: arteries 4:387; heart 4:387;
  veins 4:387
 Physiology 13:1289-1291
 Respiratory system 15:1453-1455
 Spleen 17:1651
 Thrombosis 18:1746
 Valves, circulatory 18:1795
 Vein 19:1808-1809
Circumpolar star see **CONSTEL-
 LATION; POLARIS**
CIRRHOSIS 4:390
 biliary 4:390
 portal 4:390
Cirro-cumulus see **CLOUDS**
Cirro-stratus see **CLOUDS**
Cirrus see **CLOUDS**
Cislunar space 17:1608
CITRIC ACID 4:390
Citrine, illus. 14:1392
Citron see **CITRUS FRUITS**
CITRONELLA 4:390
CITRUS FRUITS 4:390-391
 Berry 3:246
 Citric acid 4:390
 Citron 4:391
 Fruit 8:736
 grapefruit 4:391
 Horticulture 9:856-857
 illus.: oranges growing 4:391
 kumquat 4:391
 lemon 4:390
 lime 4:391
 orange 4:390-391
CIVET 4:391
CLAM 4:392
 illus. 4:392
 locomotion 1:86
Clamworm, illus. 19:1881
Class see **ANIMALS, CLASSI-
 FICATION OF; PLANTS,
 CLASSIFICATION OF**
CLAW 4:392
 Cat family 4:348
 illus. 4:392
CLAY 4:392
 Feldspar 7:674
 Loam 10:975
 illus.: uses 4:392
 Mineral 11:1065-1067
 properties 4:392
 types 4:392
CLEAVAGE 4:393
 blastula 4:393
 ectoderm 4:393; 6:556
 embryos, characteristics of 4:393-
  394; 6:594-595

 endoderm 4:393; 7:610
 gastrula 4:393
 illus. 4:393; starfish 6:594
 mesoderm 4:393
CLEFT PALATE 4:394r
 Harelip *9:821*
CLEMATIS 4:394
 illus. 4:394
 Plants, tropical *14:1329-1331*
CLIFF 4:394
 illus. 4:394
CLIMATE 4:395-397
 classification: dry 4:397; warm
  temperate 4:397; polar 4:397;
  snow 4:397; tropical rainy 4:397
 controls: altitude 4:397-395;
  cyclonic fronts 4:394; land masses
  4:394-395; latitude 4:394-395;
  mountain barriers 4:394-396;
  ocean currents 4:394-396; sea-
  sonal highs and lows 4:394-395;
  winds 4:394-396
 Europe 7:645
 Geography 8:762
 illus.: wind over mountains 4:396
 International Geophysical Year:
  Glaciers 9:892-893
 Isothermal lines 10:918
 maps 4:395, 396
 Mistral 11:1075
 Monsoon 11:1091
 Natural resources 12:1131-1133
 notations 4:397
 Paleontology 13:1237-1238
 Steppe 17:1670
 subdivisions 4:397
CLIMAX COMMUNITY 3:215; 4:397
 Ecology 6:552-553
 Ecosystem 6:555
Climbing pothos 14:1331
CLOACA 4:397
CLOCKS 5:407-408
 Astronomy 2:166-167
 electrical 5:408
 gears: 5:407
 illus. 5:407, 408
 Measurement 11:1033-1036
 mechanism 5:407
 pendulum 5:408; 13:1260-1261
 standard for time measurement
  5:407
 Sundial 17:1692
Closed-circuit television see
 TELEVISION
Clotting see **BLOOD**
CLOUD CHAMBER 5:408
 types 5:408
 uses 5:408
 vapor trails 5:408
CLOUDS 5:409-410
 cloud burst 5:410
 cloud seeding 5:410
 Colloidal state 5:421
 exp. 5:409
 Hail 9:816
 illus. 5:410; 19:1845
 Lightning 10:963-964
 Precipitation (weather) 14:1358
 Rain making 15:1426-1427
 Tornado 18:1761
 types: cirrus 5:409-410; cumulus
  409-410; stratus 5:409-410
 Weather 19:1843-1846
CLOVER 5:411
 Alfalfa 1:57
 illus. 5:411
CLOVES 5:411
 illus. 5:411; 7:607
CLUBFOOT 5:412

Clutch see **AUTOMOBILE**
COACERVATE 5:412
COAGULANT 5:412
COAL 5:412-413
  Africa 1:36
  anthracite 5:412-413
  bituminous 5:413
  Carbon 4:338
  Carbon cycle 4:339
  Carbonization 4:343
  Combustion 5:425
  Europe 7:645
  Forest products 8:713
  formation 5:412
  Fossil fuels 8:719
  Geologic time table 8:765
  illus.: Coal Age Swamp 5:412; products 5:414; shaft mine 5:413; strip mining 5:413; types of coal 5:412
  lignite 5:413
  mines: shaft 5:413; strip 5:413
  Natural resources 12:1131-1133
  Open pit mine 13:1212
  Organic rock 13:1223
  peat 5:413
  Smoke 16:1563
  uses 5:413
COAL GAS 5:414
  Gas 8:754-756
Coal products, illus. 5:414
COAL TAR 5:414
  Dye 6:534-535
  exp. 5:414
  Lampblack 10:941
  Synthetic fabrics 18:1714
  Tar 18:1717
  uses 5:414
COAXIAL CABLE 5:415
COBALT 5:415
Cobalt bomb see **BOMB**
Cobra see **SNAKES**
COCAINE 5:415; 14:1329
Cocci see **BACTERIA**
Coccyx see **SKELETON**
Cochlea see **EAR**
Cockatoo see **PARROT**
COCKLE 5:415
  illus. 5:415
Cocklebur see **SEED DISPERSAL**
COCKROACH 5:415
  illus. 5:415; 9:881
COCOA 5:416
  illus., cacao bean 5:416
COCONUT 5:416
  coir 5:416
  copra 5:416
  Drupe 6:530
  illus. 5:416
  uses 5:416
COCOON 5:417
  illus. 5:417
  Metamorphosis 11:1052
  Moths 12:1110
COD 5:417
  illus. 5:417
Codeine see **OPIUM**
Codling moth see **MOTHS**
Coefficient 1:60
COELACANTH 5:417
  illus. 5:417
COELENTERATA 5:417-418
  body structure 5:418
  Coral 5:448
  digestive system 5:418-419; 6:510
  Eye, simple 7:668
  feeding 5:418
  Gastrovascular cavity 8:756
  Hydra 9:862
  Hydroid colony 9:867

  illus. 5:418
  Jellyfish 10:921
  Man-of-war, Portuguese 11:1014
  Marine biology 11:1019-1021
  medusa stage 5:418
  Nematocyst 12:1138
  Polyps 14:1348
  Reef 15:1440
  reproduction 5:418
  Sea anemone 16:1516
  Skeleton 16:1552
  Tentacle 18:1734
  types 5:419
COELOM 5:419
COFFEE 5:419
  Caffeine 4:322
  illus. 5:419; 14:1328
COGWHEEL 5:419
COHESION 5:420
  Adhesion 1:26-27
  Resistance 15:1452
COKE 5:420
  Carbon 4:338
  Coal gas 5:414
  Coal tar 5:414
  Forest products 8:713
COLA 5:420
  illus. 5:420
COLD 5:420
  cause 5:420
  cold sore 5:420
  cure 5:420
  symptoms 5:420
Coldframe 8:797
COLEUS 5:421
  illus. 5:421
Collarbone see **SKELETON**
Collard see **MUSTARD**
Collared lizard, illus. 10:975
Collie, illus. 6:522
Colloid see **COLLOIDAL STATE**
COLLOIDAL STATE 5:421
  colloidal suspension 5:421
  illus. 5:421
  properties 5:421
  Tyndall effect 18:1783
Colon see **DIGESTIVE SYSTEM**
COLOR 1:16; 5:422-423
  Absorption of light 1:16
  achromatic 5:423
  chromatic 5:423
  classic color triangle 5:423
  complementary 5:423
  composition of black 5:423
  composition of white 5:423
  exp.: in a beam of sunlight, 5:422; mixing colored lights 5:423; white 5:422
  infrared 5:423
  Iridescence 10:912
  Measurement 11:1033-1036
  nanometers 5:423
  Photometer 13:1284
  Pigment 13:1294
  Spectroscope 17:1642-1643
  spectrum 5:422; 17:1643
  Staining 17:1656
  wavelengths of the spectrum 5:423
  White light 10:1867
COLOR BLINDNESS 5:424
  Dalton, John 5:478
  Eye 7:664-667
  Heredity 9:840
  illus. 5:424
  safety problems 5:424
  testing 5:424
Colorado desert 5:496
COLORIMETER 5:424
  illus. 5:424

Colt patent, illus. 19:1839
COLUMBINE 5:424-425
Columnar tissue see **EPITHELIAL TISSUE**
COMA 5:425
  Diabetes 5:497
Comb jellies see **CTENOPHORA**
COMBUSTIBLE 5:425
COMBUSTION 5:425
  Combustible 5:425
  conditions of 5:425
  explosives 5:425
  Fire 7:683
  Fuel 8:738
  Kindling temperature 10:933
  Oxygen 13:1232-1233
  spontaneous 5:425; 17:1651
COMET 5:426
  chart 5:426
  composition 5:426
  ellipse 5:426
  Halley's comet 5:426; 9:817
  illus. 5:426
  Saturn 16:1509-1510
  solar wind 5:426
Commensalism see **BALANCE OF NATURE**
COMMUNICABLE DISEASES 5:426
COMMUNICATION 5:427-429
  attenuation 5:428
  bits 5:427
  channel capacity 5:427
  coder 5:427-428
  communication channel 5:427
  decoder 4:427, 429
  Edison, Thomas Alva 6:556-557
  electromagnetic waves 5:427
  illus.: printing press 5:429; radio sound waves 5:429; satellites 5:428 telegraph 5:427; television 5:428; telephone 5:428
  information 5:427
  meanings 5:429
  noise 5:482
  Printing 14:1364-1370
  signal 5:428
  signal-to-noise ratio 5:428
  telephone 5:429; 18:1726-1727
Community see **BALANCE OF NATURE**
COMMUTATOR 5:429
  Dynamo 6:537
  Motor 12:1114-1116
Comparator 11:1036
COMPASS 5:430
  agonic line 5:430
  exp. 5:430
  gyrocompasses 5:430
  illus. 5:430
  Magnet 10:996
  magnetic North Pole 5:430
  variation 5:430
Complementary color see **COLOR**
COMPOSITE FLOWER 5:431
  Ageratum 1:37
  Aster 2:152
  Chrysanthemum 4:386
  Daisy 5:477
  Flower 7:693
  Gaillardia 8:744
  illus. 5:431
  Sunflower 17:1693
  Zinnia 19:1892
COMPOST 5:431
COMPOUND 5:431-432
  Carbonates 4:343
  Chemistry 4:373-377
  Chloride 4:381
  classification 5:432

Compounds, stability of 5:432
Dalton, John 5:478
Decomposition 5:486
Dissociation 6:520
Electron 6:579
Electron borrowing 6:580
electron microscope 5:432
Electron sharing 6:580-581
Elements in the human body 6:590
illus. 5:431
Mendeleev's Periodic Table
  11:1042-1043
Mixture 11:1079
Molecular theory 11:1083
COMPOUNDS, STABILITY OF 5:432
chemical bond 5:432
Decomposition 5:486-487
Dissociation 6:520
effect of temperature 5:432
Electron borrowing 6:580
Mendeleev's Periodic Table
  11:1042-1043
Compression see **ENGINE**
COMPRESSORS 5:432-433
illus. 432-433
Refrigeration 15:1441-1442
Turbine 18:1778-1779
types: centrifugal 5:433; recipro-
  cating-piston 5:433
COMPTON, ARTHUR HOLLY 5:433-
  434
illus. 5:434
science and religion 5:434
COMPUTER 5:434-436
Adding machine 1:26
analog 5:434
bit 5:436
Calculator 4:323-324
data processing 5:436
digital 5:434
effect of electronics 5:434
history 5:434
illus. 5:435, 436; weather fore-
  casting 19:1851
input 5:434
language 5:436
memory 5:436
Missile 11:1071-1075
output 5:434
programming 5:436
Slide rule 16:1560
Concave see **LENS, MAN-MADE**
Conception see **PREGNANCY**
CONCH 5:437
illus. 5:437
CONCRETE 5:437
Gravel 8:793
CONCUSSION 5:437
CONDENSATION 5:437
Clouds 5:409
Dew 5:497
Distillation 6:520
Dry ice 6:530-531
exp. 5:437
Humidity 9:858-859
Liquid 10:970
Rain making 15:1426-1427
Water cycle 19:1832-1833
CONDENSER 5:438
illus. 5:438
Condor see **BIRDS OF PREY**
CONDUCTION 5:438
Heat barrier 9:828
CONDUCTOR 5:439
Lye 10:985
CONDUIT 5:439
CONE 5:439
Conifer 5:439
illus. 5:439

CONGENITAL 5:439
Clubfoot 5:412
Conglomerate see **ROCKS**
CONIFER 5:439
Forestry 8:716
Softwood 16:1571-1572
Conjugation see **PARAMECIUM;**
  REPRODUCTION, SEXUAL
CONJUNCTIVITIS 5:439
CONNECTIVE TISSUE 5:439
Animals, classification of 1:95
Edema 6:556
Fat, adipose tissue 7:672
Fiber 7:678
Fibrous tissue 7:679
Histology 9:846-849
Muscle tissue 12:1122-1123
Ossification 13:1228
Skin 16:1556-1557
Conservation of energy see **ENERGY**
CONSERVATION OF NATURE
  5:439-441
Agriculture 1:40
air 5:439
animal life 5:440-441
Erosion 7:635-636
Forestry 8:716-717
illus. 5:440-441
International Control of Natural
  Resources 9:889
minerals 5:441
Natural resources 12:1131-1133
plant life 5:440
Pollution 14:1347-1348
Preserve 14:1361
soil 5:440
Strip mining 17:1678
water 5:440
CONSERVATORY 5:441
Greenhouse 8:797
CONSTELLATION 5:442-443
Alpha 1:65
Aquila 2:126
Aries 2:134
Auriga 2:176
Big and Little Dippers 3:250
Bootes 3:283
Cancer (constellation) 4:330-331
Canis Major and Canis Minor 4:333
Capricornus 4:336
Cassiopeia 4:347
Centaurus 4:363
Cepheus 4:365
chart 5:443
circumpolar 5:443
Crux 5:460
Cygnus 5:474
Draco 6:526-527
Gemini 8:760
Hercules 9:837
Leo 10:954
Libra 10:956-957
Magnitude 11:1008
mythology 5:442
Orion 13:1224
Pegasus 13:1259
Perseus 13:1269
Polaris 14:1344
Sagittarius 15:1488-1489
Scorpius 16:1515-1516
sky chart 5:442
Solar system 16:1575-1578
Star, double 17:1658-1659
Star, variable 17:1659
Stars 17:1660-1662
Taurus 18:1719
Ursa Major and Minor 18:1791
usefulness 5:442
Virgo 19:1816

Water Bearer 19:1831
Zodiac 19:1893
CONSTIPATION 5:443
Constrictor, boa see **SNAKES**
Contact lenses see **LENS, MAN-**
  MADE
CONTINENT 5:444
Africa 1:32-36
Antarctica 2:110
Asia 2:145-149
Australia 2:177-181
Europe 7:640-645
Grand Banks 8:791
Island 10:917
map 5:444
Moho 11:1080-1081
North America 12:1156-1160
South America 16:1593-1597
CONTINENTAL DIVIDE 5:444
Watershed 19:1835
CONTINENTAL DRIFT 5:444
convection current 5:444
Earth, early development of 6:545-
  547
evolution of earth 5:444
fault zone 5:444
Glomar Challenger 8:783
Mid-Atlantic Ridge 11:1058
Mountains 12:1116-1117
Ocean 12:1188-1190
plate tectonics 5:444; 14:1334-
  1335
Rift valley 15:1459
Trench, deep-ocean 18:1771
Contour farming, illus. 1:41
Contractile vacuole see **AMEBA**
CONVECTION 5:445
exp. 5:445
Heat barrier 9:828
Conversion factors to metric
  measurement 1:98
CONVERTER 5:445
CONVERTIPLANE 5:445
design 5:445
CONVEYOR BELT 5:446
Convex see **LENS, MAN-MADE**
CONVULSION 5:446
causes 5:446
Epilepsy 7:631
treatment 5:446
Cook, James 2:110
Cooper, L. Gordon see **SPACE**
  TRAVEL
COOT 5:446
illus. 5:446
COPEPOD 5:446
COPERNICUS, NICOLAUS 5:446-
  447
Astronomy 2:166-167
Galileo 8:747
illus. 5:447
Kepler, Johannes 10:931
opposition to Ptolemy 5:446
Ptolemy 14:1382-1383
science and religion 5:446
Revolution 15:1456
COPPER 5:447
illus. 5:447
Metal 11:1049-1051
Mineral 11:1065
Mineralogy 11:1067-1069
Monel metal 11:1088
Open-pit mine 13:1212
properties 5:447
world supply 5:447
Copperhead see **SNAKES**
Copra see **COCONUT**
Copulation see **REPRODUCTION,**
  SEXUAL

CORAL 5:448
Atoll 2:172
Coelenterata 5:418
illus. 5:418; 5:448
Reef 15:1440
Coral snake see **SNAKES**
Coreopsis, illus. 5:431
CORI, CARL F. AND GERTY T. 5:448
CORK 5:448
Bark 3:225
CORM 5:448
Banana 3:223-224
Gardening 8:751-753
Gladiolus 8:780
Stem, undergound 17:1668-1669
CORMORANT 5:448
illus. 5:448
CORN 5:449
Cereal grains 4:366
illus. 1:81; 5:449; 6:554; 18:1763
Popcorn 14:1349
Corn borer, illus. 14:1320
Cornea see **EYE**
Corona see **SUN**
Coronary see **HEART;
THROMBOSIS**
CORPUSCLE 5:449
CORPUSCULAR THEORY 5:449
CORROSION 5:449
Metal 11:1049-1051
CORTEX 5:449
CORTISONE 5:449-450
Addison's Disease 1:26
Adrenal glands 1:27-28
Arthritis 2:140
Asthma 2:153
Cushing's disease 5:471
effect of 5:449
functions 5:450
Hench, Philip 9:834
CORUNDUM 5:450
Aluminum 1:68
illus. 5:450; 9:819
Sapphire 15:1496
COSMOLOGY 5:450
COSMONAUT 5:450-451
Astronaut 2:155-156
Astronautics 2:157-165
chart 5:451
extra-vehicular activity 5:450
flights with dogs 5:450
Gagarin, Yuri 5:450
Lunar base 10:980-983
rendezvous 5:451
Titov, Gherman 5:450
COSMOS 5:451
COTTON 5:452
growing 5:452
illus. 5:452
picking 5:452
textiles 5:452
Whitney, Eli 19:1869
Cottonmouth see **SNAKES**
Cottonwood see **POPLAR**
COTYLEDON 5:452
illus. 5:452
Dicotyledon 6:508
Monocotyledon 11:1090
Polycotyledon 14:1348
COULOMB 5:453
Ampere 1:72
Electricity 6:566
COULOMB, CHARLES AUGUSTIN
6:453
Electrostatics 6:585
torsion balance 5:453
Coupling see **TRAIN; RAILROAD**
COW 5:453
breeds 5:453

characteristics 5:453
digestive system 1:83; 5:453
illus.: 1:89; 5:453; digestive
system 1:83
Leather 10:947
usefulness 5:453
COWBIRD 5:454
Bird nests 3:259
illus. 5:454
COYOTE 5:454
illus. 1:84; 5:454
COWPEA 5:454
CRAB 5:454
Chitin 4:380
Crustacea 5:459
illus. 5:454
CRAB APPLE 5:455
illus. 5:455
Crab, the see **CANCER
(CONSTELLATION)**
CRANBERRY 5:455
illus. 5:455
CRANE 5:455
Egret 6:560
illus. 5:455
Crane fly see **DADDY LONGLEGS;
FLY**
Craniata 4:384
CRANIUM 5:455
CRAPPIE 5:455
illus. 5:455
Sunfish 17:1693
CRATER 5:456
Meteor 11:1052-1053
CRAYFISH 5:456:15:1443
Crustacea 5:459
Cuticle 5:471
Exoskeleton 7:661
illus.: 5:456; reproductive system
15:1448
Lobster 10:976
Marine biology 11:1019
Cream see **DAIRY PRODUCTS**
CREOSOTE 5:456
Cress see **WATERCRESS**
CRETIN 5:456
cause 5:456
Midget 11:1059
Myxedema 12:1128
symptoms 5:456
Thyroid 18:1749
treatment 5:456
CREVICE 5:457
CRICKET 5:457
food 1:83
illus. 5:457
CRINOID 5:457
Cro-Magnon man see **EVOLUTION
OF MAN**
CROCODILE 5:457
Alligator 1:62
characteristics 5:457
diet 5:457
habitat 5:457
illus. 5:457
CROCUS 5:457-458
Cromwell Current 5:470
CROP 5:458
Crop rotation see **AGRICULTURE;
NITROGEN CYCLE**
Cross-breeding see **HYBRID-
IZATION**
CROSS-EYES 5:458
CROSSBILL 5:458
CROTON 5:458
CROW 5:458
Blue jay 3:272
illus. 5:458
Raven 15:1431

CRUSTACEA 5:459
Arthropoda 2:140-142
Autotomy 2:190
Copepod 5:466
Crab 5:454
Daphnia 5:481
habitat 5:459
illus. 5:459
Larva 10:943
Lobster 10:976
Marine biology 11:1019-1021
Shrimp 16:1542-1543
CRUX 5:460
Centaurus 4:363
Cygnus 5:474
illus. 5:460
CRYOGENICS 5:460; 8:775
CRYOTHERAPY 3:264; 5:460
CRYSTAL 5:460-461
Calamine 4:323
Carbon 4:337
Chemistry 4:375
Cholesterol 4:382
Diamond 6:507
Efflorescence 6:558
exp. 5:461
formation 5:461
Gem 8:759
Germanium 8:773
Goldschmidt, Victor Moritz
8:787
Hematite 9:833
Hydrates 9:863
Ice 9:873
illus. 5:460-461; 11:1068
Mineral 11:1065-1067
Mineralogy 11:1067-1069
rate of growth 5:461
shapes 5:460-461
Tourmaline 18:1762
CRYSTAL RADIO SET 5:462
construction 5:462
Crystal 5:460-461
exp. 5:462
Galena 8:746
parts 5:462
Crystallization see **CHEMISTRY**
CRYSTALLOGRAPHY 5:462-463
CTENOPHORA 5:463
digestive system 5:463
illus. 5:463
locomotion 5:463
reproduction 5:463
Cube see **GEOMETRY**
Cuboidal tissue see **EPITHELIAL
TISSUE**
CUCKOO 5:463
Bird nests 3:259
illus. 5:463
CUCUMBER 5:464
illus. 5:464
Cuesta 7:636
Cugnot, Nicola 2:189
CULTIVATION 5:464
Fallow 7:670
Gardening 8:751-753
illus. 6:464
Cumulo-nimbus see **CLOUDS**
Cumulo-stratus see **CLOUDS**
CURARE 5:464-465
history 5:464
illus. 5:464
uses 5:464-465
CURIE, PIERRE AND MARIE 5:465-
466
illus. 5:465
Pitchblende 14:1309
Radioactivity 15:1422-1423
Radium 15:1424-1425

Rutherford, Ernest 15:1486-1487
Uranium 18:1788-1789
CURIUM 5:466
 illus. 5:466
CURLEW 5:467
 illus. 5:467
CURRANT 5:467
 illus. 5:467
Current, air see **AIR; AIR MASSES; CLIMATE**
CURRENTS, OCEAN 5:467-471
 Antarctic 5:470
 Arctic (Labrador) 5:470
 Benguela 5:470
 Brazil 5:470
 California 5:470
 Canary 5:470
 causes: heat of sun 5:468; prevailing winds 5:468; rotation of earth 5:468; salinity 5:468
 Cromwell 5:470
 equatorial countercurrent 5:470
 exp. 5:468
 functions: affect weather 5:471; equalize earth temperature 5:471; provide food 5:471
 Grand Banks 8:791
 Gulf Stream Countercurrent 5:470; 9:809-810
 illus. 5:469; 5:470
 International Geophysical Year 5:470
 Japanese (Kurashio) 5:470
 North Atlantic Drift 5:469; 12:1160
 North Equatorial 5:469
 Ocean 12:1188-1190
 Oceanography 12:1190-1195
 Oyashio 5:470
 Pelagic 13:1259
 Peru (Humboldt) 5:470
 Sargassum 15:1497
 Sea level 16:1517
 Sea water 16:1519-1520
 Water 19:1830-1831
 Wave 19:1836-1837
 West Wind Drift 19:1863
 zones: Indian Ocean 5:469; North America 5:469; North Pacific 5:469; polar 5:469; South Atlantic 5:469; South Pacific 5:469
CUSHING'S DISEASE 5:471
 cause 5:471
 symptoms 5:471
 treatment 5:471
CUTICLE 5:471
 illus. 5:471
Cuttings see **PROPAGATION**
CUTTLEFISH 5:471
 illus. 5:471
 Mollusca 11:1084-1086
CUTWORM 5:471
CUVIER, GEORGES 5:472
CYANIDE 5:472
 Cyanophyta 18:1738
CYCAD 5:473
 Gynosperm 9:812
 illus. 9:812; 18:1763
CYCLAMATES 5:473
CYCLAMEN 5:473
CYCLE 5:473
CYCLONE 5:473
 Air masses 1:46
 High-pressure center 9:844

Hurricane 9:859-860
 illus. 5:473
 Low-pressure center 10:979
 Wind 19:1874-1875
Cyclotron see **ACCELERATORS (PARTICLE); NUCLEAR REACTORS**
CYGNUS 5:474
 illus. 5:474
 mythology 5:474
Cylinder see **ENGINE, GEOMETRY**
Cynosure see **URSA MAJOR AND URSA MINOR**
CYPRESS 5:474
 illus. 5:474
CYST 5:474
CYTOLOGY 5:474
 Anatomy 1:76
 Botany 3:284
 Dachshund, illus. 6:523
DADDY LONGLEGS 5:475
 illus. 5:475
DAFFODIL 5:475
 illus. 5:475
 Stem, underground 17:1668-1669
Daguerrotype see **PHOTOGRAPHY**
DAHLIA 5:475
 illus. 5:475
Dairy cattle see **COW**
DAIRY PRODUCTS 5:476-477
 Animal husbandry 1:89-90
 butter 5:477
 casein 5:477
 cheese: hard 5:477; manufacture 5:477; soft 5:477
 ice cream 5:477
 illus. 5:476
 milk: allergic reaction 5:477; buttermilk 5:477; condensed 5:476; cream 5:476; evaporated 5:476; skimmed 5:476; whole 5:476; 11:1061
 Pasteurization 13:1253
DAISY 5:477
 illus. 5:477
DALE, SIR HENRY H. 5:478
DALTON, JOHN 5:478
 Bernoulli's principle 3:246
 Joule, James Prescott 10:925
DAM 5:479-480
 arch 5:480
 Bridges 3:294-296
 buttress 5:479-480
 embankments 5:480
 Flood 7:692
 gravity: solid 5:479
 Hydroelectric power 9:865-866
 illus.: buttress 5:479; earthfill 5:480; hydroelectric power 9:865; power dam 7:614; solid gravity 5:479
 Irrigation 10:916
 Levee 10:956
 River 15:1459-1460
 solid gravity 5:479
 timber 5:480
 uses 5:480
 Waterfall 19:1834-1835
Dandelion see **WILD FLOWERS**
Dandruff see **HAIR**
DAPHNIA 5:481
 Crustacea 5:459
 illus. 5:459
Dark nebulae 3:226
DARWIN, CHARLES ROBERT 5:481-482
 Acquired characteristics 1:23-24
 Animal diseases 1:89
 Atoll 2:172

Evolution of man 7:654-659
 Huxley, Thomas Henry 9:860
 illus. 7:647
 Lamarck, Jean Baptiste 10:940
 survival of the fittest 5:482
 theory of evolution 5:482
DATA 5:482
DATES 5:482
 illus. 5:482
Da Vinci see **LEONARDO DA VINCI**
DAVISSON, CLINTON J. 5:482-483
Davy safety lamp 5:483
DAVY, SIR HUMPHRY 5:483
 Barium 3:225
 Calcium 4:323
 Chlorine 4:381
 Faraday, Michael 7:670-671
 illus. 5:483
 Potassium 14:1354
DAY AND NIGHT 5:483
 Astronomy 2:166-167
 Earth 6:543
 Equinox 7:634
 exp. 5:484
 illus. 5:483
 Measurement 11:1033-1036
 Seasons 16:1522-1523
Day lily see **LILY**
Daylight saving time see **TIME ZONES**
DC (direct current) see **ELECTRICITY**
DDT see **INSECTICIDES**
DEAD RECKONING 5:485
Deaf mute 5:485
DEAFNESS 5:485
 deaf mutes 5:485; 12:1128
 illus.: hand language 5:485
DEATH 5:485
Debierne, Andre 1:24
Decay see **DECOMPOSITION**
DECIBEL 5:486
 chart 5:486
 Noise 12:1155
 Weber-Fechner law of loudness 5:486
DECIDUOUS 5:486
 Forestry 8:716
 Leaves 10:949
 Poplar 14:1349
DECOMPOSER ORGANISM 5:486
DECOMPOSITION 5:486-487
 Compounds, stability of 6:432
 Hydrolysis 9:867
 illus. 5:487
 methods: electrolysis 5:486; heating 5:486; natural 5:486
DECOMPRESSION 5:487
 effect on body 5:487
 need for 5:487
 pounds per square inch 5:487
Deductive reasoning 8:770
DEEP-SEA DIVING 5:488-489
 illus. 5:488
 research submarine 5:488-489
 scuba 5:488
Deep well pump, illus. 14:1385
DEER FAMILY 5:489-490
 Antelope 2:113
 characteristics 5:489
 diet 5:489
 digestive system 5:489
 Gazelle 8:757
 geographic distribution 5:490
 Hoof 9:852
 illus.: 1:84; 14:1375; black tailed deer 5:489; bull moose 5:490; Virginia deer 5:489; Wapiti 5:490
 reproduction 5:490

DEER MOUSE 5:490
DEERE, JOHN 5:490
Deerhorn cactus, illus. 7:607
DEFOREST, LEE 5:491
  illus. 5:491
  Radio 15:1416-1418
DEGREE 5:491
  illus. 5:491
DEHYDRATION 5:491-492
  Food preservation 8:709-710
DELIQUESCENCE 5:492
DEPHINIUM 5:492
DELTA 5:492
  illus. 5:492
  Island 10:917
DEMOGRAPHY 5:492
  carrying capacity 5:492
  control 5:492
Dendrite see **NERVE CELL**
Deneb see **CYGNUS**
DENSITY 5:493
  Convection 5:445
  Gem 8:759
  Hydrometer 9:867
  illus. 5:493
  Specific gravity 17:1640
Dentine see **TEETH**
DEPTH SOUNDING 5:493-494
  Acoustic weapons 1:22
  illus. 5:494
  methods: echo 5:494; Kelvin-White
    machine 5:494; lead and line
    5:494
  Moho 11:1080-1081
  Oceanography 12:1190-1195
  Seismograph 16:1527
  Sonar 16:1584
  uses 5:493-494
DERMATITIS 5:495
DERMATOLOGY 5:495
Dermis see **SKIN**
Derringer, illus. 19:1839
DESERT 5:495
  animals 5:496
  Australia 2:177-181
  Cactus 4:321
  Camel 4:326-327
  characteristics 5:495-496
  Climate 4:397
  Dune 6:553
  famous deserts: Colorado 5:496;
    Great Basin 5:496; Mojave 5:496;
    Sonoran 5:496; Sahara 5:496
  illus. 5:496; 6:552; cactus 5:495;
    desert cottontail 5:495; oasis
    5:495; rattlesnake 5:495
  Irrigation 10:916
  Mesa 11:1046
  plants 5:496
  Yucca 19:1890
Destroyer see **SHIPS**
DETERGENT 5:496
  chemical composition 5:496
  Coal tar 5:414
  Liquid 10:968-970
  Soap 16:1570
  Surface tension 17:1695
  Wetting agent 19:1863
Detonator see **BOMB; EXPLOSIVES**
DEUTERIUM 5:497
  heavy water 5:497; 9:830
  Hydrogen 9:866
Devilfish, illus. 15:1432
DEW 5:497
  illus. 5:497
DEW POINT 5:497
  Frost 8:733
  Hygrometer 9:871
Dextrose see **SUGAR**

DIABETES 5:497
  acidosis 5:497
  Banting, Frederick Grant 3:224
  Cataract 4:353
  causes 5:497
  coma 5:497; 5:425
  Gangrene 8:750
  insipidius 5:497
  Islets of Langerhans 10:971
  juvenile 5:497
  Medicine 11:1038-1040
  mellitus 5:497
  Ophthalmoscope 13:1212
  Pituitary gland 14:1310
  Sweeteners, diet 18:1711
  treatment 5:497
DIAGNOSIS 5:497
DIAMOND 6:507
  Africa 1:36
  Carbon 4:337
  illus. 6:507; 9:819
  Mineral 11:1065-1067
  properties 6:507
  synthetic 6:507
  uses 6:507
DIAPHRAGM 6:508; 1:14
  Hiccough 9:844
  Lung 10:983-984
  Mammalia 11:1011-1012
DIARRHEA 6:508
  Astringent 2:154
  Paregoric 13:1249
DIASTOLE 6:508
  Blood pressure 3:270
  Heart 9:825
  Heartbeat 9:826
DIATOM 6:508; 1:58
  colonies 6:508
  Fossils 8:722
  illus. 18:1738
  uses 6:508
DICOTYLEDON 6:508
  Angiosperm 1:82
  illus. 6:508; 14:1324
  Leaves 10:948-949
  Monocotyledon 11:1090
Didymium see **NEODYMIUM**
DIEFFENBACHIA 6:509
Dielectric see **CONDENSOR**
DIES 6:509
Diesel see **ENGINE**
DIFFERENTIAL 6:509
DIFFRACTION 6:509
DIFFRACTION GRATING 6:509
  reflection 6:509
  transmission 6:509
DIFFUSION 6:509
  Absorption, physiological 1:15
  exp. 6:509
DIGESTIVE SYSTEM 6:510-513
  Ameba 1:70
  Amino acid 1:71
  Amylase 1:75
  Anatomy 1:76
  Animal 1:83
  Appendix 2:123
  Assimilation 2:151
  bile 6:512-513
  bladder, urinary 3:266
  carbohydrate 6:512; 4:337
  Crop 5:458
  Dysentery 6:537
  Echinodermata 6:550
  Enzymes 7:629-630
  exp.: effect of saliva 6:51C; peri-
    stalsis 6:512
  fat 6:512-513
  gallbladder 6:513; 8:747
  Gallstones 8:748

  Gizzard 8:778
  Herbivore 9:836-837
  Histology 9:848-849
  Hydrochloric acid 9:865
  illus.: earthworm 6:510; hydra
    6:510; man 6:511
  in man: anus 6:512; appendix 6:512;
    cardiac valve 6:511; cecum 6:512;
    chyme 6:511; colon 6:512; duo-
    denum 6:511; esophagus 6:511;
    ileum 6:511; jejunum 6:511; mu-
    cous glands 6:511; peristalsis
    6:511; pyloric sphincter 6:511;
    rectum 6:512; small intestine
    6:511; soft palate 6:511; villi
    6:511
  Jaundice 10:921
  Liver 10:972
  Metabolism 11:1048
  Nutrition 12:1184
  parts: anus 6:510; colon 6:510;
    liver 6:510; esophagus 6:510; in-
    testine 6:510; mouth 6:510; pan-
    creas 6:510; salivary glands
    6:510; stomach 6:510
  Peristalsis 13:1266
  Pharynx 13:1274
  Physiology 13:1289-1291
  Pisces (animal) 14:1308-1309
  Plants, medicinal 14:1328-
    1329
  protein 6:512
  Rectum 15:1438
  Ruminants 15:1483
  Salivary glands 15:1490
  Sphincter 17:1645
  Sugar 17:1683
  Tongue 18:1756-1757
Digital computer see **COMPUTER**
DIGITALIS 6:513
DILL 6:513
  illus. 6:513
DIMENSION 6:513
DINGO 6:513
DINOSAUR 6:514-516
  Anklosaurus 6:515
  Brontosaurus 6:514
  illus.: allosaurus 6:514, 516;
    brontosaurus 6:515; diplodocus
    6:515; enmontosaurus 6:516; pro-
    toceratops 6:515, 516; stego-
    saurus 6:514, 515; trachodon
    6:515; triceratops 6:515; tyran-
    nosaurus 6:514, 516
  Proceratops 6:515
  Pterodactyl 14:1382
  Reptilia 15:1449-1450
  Stegosaurus 6:514
  Trachodon 6:515
  Triceratops 6:515
  Tyrannosaurus 6:516
DIOECIOUS 6:516
  Monoecious 11:1090
DIPHTHERIA 6:517
  Black Death 3:265
  complications 6:517
  Medicine 11:1038-1040
  prevention 6:517
  symptoms 6:517
  treatment 6:517
Dipleurula 10:943
Dippers, Big and Little see **BIG AND
  LITTLE DIPPERS; URSA MAJOR
  AND MINOR**
DIRECT CURRENT 6:517
DIRECTION FINDER 6:517
  illus. 6:517
  loop antenna 6:517
  Navigation 12:1134-1135

DIRIGIBLE 6:518
  accidents 6:518
  Aircraft 1:48-50
  Airships 1:54
  buoyancy 6:518
  illus.: diagram 6:518; Zeppelin
    6:518
  nonrigid 6:518
  rigid 6:518
  uses 6:518
DISEASE 6:519; 3:210
  Carriers 4:345
  communicable 6:519
  Drugs 6:528-530
  Epidemic 7:630-631
  Germ theory 8:773
  Medicine 11:1038-1040
  non-communicable 6:519
  Pain 13:1235
  Symptom 18:1713
  treatment 6:519
  Typhoid fever 18:1784
Disinfectant see **ANTISEPTIC**
DISPERSION 6:519
  illus. 6:519
  Insoluble 9:884
  Light 10:959-963
  Solute 16:1582
  White light 19:1867
DISSECTION 6:520
DISSOCIATION 6:520
DISTILLATION 6:520
  Camphor 4:330
  Carbolic acid 4:337
  Carbon 4:338
  Carbonization 4:343
  Charcoal 4:370
  Coke 5:420
  Creosote 5:456
  Fossil fuels 8:719
  Gas 8:755
  illus. 6:520
  method 6:520
  Neon 12:1138
  Perfume 13:1264
  Tar 18:1717
Diver's palsy see **BENDS;
  DECOMPRESSION**
Diving see **OCEANOGRAPHY**
Diving bell see **BATHYSPHERE AND
  BATHYSCAPHE**
DIVISION OF LABOR 6:521
DIZZINESS 6:521
DNA see **NUCLEIC ACID**
DODO 6:521
  illus. 6:521
DOG 6:521-523
  body structure 6:521
  breeds: hound 6:523; non-sporting
    6:523; sporting 6:522-523;
    working 6:522
  Dingo 6:513
  habits 6:522
  illus.: ancestral dog 6:521; Boston
    terrier 6:523; chihuahua 6:523;
    collie 6:522; dachshund 6:523;
    feet 6:522; fox terrier 6:523;
    jackal 6:521; pointer 6:522;
    skeleton 6:522; teeth 6:522;
    wolf 6:521
  Jackal 10:920
  reproduction 6:521
DOGWOOD 6:524
  illus. 6:524
DOLDRUMS 6:524; 18:1764
DOLOMITE 6:524
DOLPHIN 6:524
  illus. 1:85; 11:1021
  Porpoise 14:1352

DOMAGK, GERHARD 6:524-525
  prontosil 6:525
Domain 1:60
DOMESTICATION 6:525
DOMINANCE 6:525
DONKEY 6:525
  Burro 4:316-317
Doppler, Christian 6:526
DOPPLER EFFECT 6:525-526
  illus. 6:525
  Sound interference 16:1591
  Star, double 17:1658-1659
  uses in astronomy 6:525
DORMOUSE 6:526
DORSAL FIN 6:526
Double star see **STAR, DOUBLE**
DOVE 6:526
  Bird nests 3:259
  illus. 6:526
DRACO 6:526-527
  illus. 6:526
  mythology 6:527
DRAGON 6:527
  illus. 6:527
  mythology 6:527
DRAGONFLY 6:527
  illus. 6:527
  Metamorphosis 11:1052
Drainage systems see **AFRICA;
  ASIA; AUSTRALIA; EUROPE;
  NORTH AMERICA; SOUTH
  AMERICA**
Dream see **SLEEP**
Drift see **CURRENTS, OCEAN**
DRIZZLE 6:527
Dromedary see **CAMEL**
Drone see **BEES**
DROUGHT 6:528
  Dust storm 6:534
  illus. 6:528
  Irrigation 10:916
DROWNING 6:528
  artificial respiration 6:528
Drug habit see **ADDICTION; DRUGS;
  NARCOTICS**
DRUGS 6:528-529
  Antibiotics 2:115-116
  as prevention 6:528
  as treatment 6:529
  aspirin 6:530; 2:151
  Chemotherapy 4:377
  Cocaine 5:415
  Disease 6:519
  hallucinogens 6:530
  heroin 6:530
  Hypodermic 9:872
  illus.: antibiotic fermentation
    tanks 6:529; laboratory 6:529;
    ointment mill 6:528; testing
    6:529
  morphine 6:530
  narcotics 6:530
  Ointment 13:1208
  opium 6:530
  Pharmacology 13:1272-1274
  Plants, medicinal 14:1328-1329
  prescription 6:530
  psychedelic 6:530
  Sedative 16:1523
  Sulfa drugs 17:1684
  Tincture 18:1753
  Tranquilizer 18:1766
  Vaccine 18:1793
DRUPE 6:530
  Blackberry 3:265
  Fruit 8:736
  illus. 6:530
Dry cell see **BATTERY**
DRY ICE 6:530-531

  exp.: effect on burning candle
    6:531; use in freezing 6:531
  sublimation 6:530-531
DUCK 6:532-533
  characteristics 6:532
  food 6:532
  Fowl 8:724
  habitat 6:532-533
  illus.: ducklings 6:532; Mallard
    drake 6:532; Mallard duck and
    ducklings 6:532; nest 6:532; wood
    duck 6:533
  protective coloration 6:532
  Swan 18:1709
DUCKBILL 6:531
  illus. 6:531
  Mammalia 11:1011-1012
  Monotreme 11:1091
  Spiny anteater 17:1649
DUCKWEED 6:533
DUCTILE 6:533
  Bessemer process 3:248
Ductless glands see **ENDOCRINE
  GLANDS**
DUNE 6:533
  composition 6:533
  illus. 6:533
  migration 6:533
  shapes 6:533
Duodenum see **DIGESTIVE SYSTEM**
Durian 14:1330
DUST 6:534
Dust bowls 6:534
DUST STORM 6:534
  illus. 6:534
Dutchman's breeches see **WILD
  FLOWERS**
Dwarf see **CRETIN; MIDGET**
DYE 6:534-535
  chemical composition 6:535
  exp. 6:534
  Forest products 8:712
  illus. 6:535
  indigo 6:535
  Madder 10:995
  methods 6:535
  Staining 17:1656
  synthetic 6:535
  vegetable 6:535
DYNAMICS 6:536
  Forces 8:710-711
  Mechanics 11:1037-1038
Dynamite see **EXPLOSIVES**
DYNAMO 6:536-537
  alternating-current generator 6:537
  Armature 2:138
  Direct current 6:517
  Electricity 6:570
  Electrolysis 6:576
  electromagnetic induction 6:536-
    537
  Faraday, Michael 7:670-671
  Fuel 8:740
  Generator 8:760
  Henry, Joseph 9:835
  illus. 6:536
  Induction 9:877
  Machinery 10:989-991
  Motor 12:1114-1116
DYNAMOMETER 6:537
  illus. 6:537
DYNE 6:537; 8:711
DYSENTERY 6:537
  amebic 6:537
  bacillary 6:537
  Infection 9:878
  symptoms 6:537
  treatment 6:537
DYSPROSIUM 6:537

EAGLE 6:538
  bald 6:538
  Bird nests 3:260; 6:538
  Birds of prey 3:262
  golden 6:538
  illus. 6:538
EAR 6:538-540
  anvil 6:539
  cochlea 6:540
  Deafness 5:485
  endolymph 6:540
  Equilibrium 7:633
  exp. 6:540
  Eustachian tube 6:539
  hammer 6:539
  illus.: animal 6:540; man 6:539
  labyrinth 6:540
  middle ear 6:539
  perilymph 6:540
  pinna 6:538
  Sense organs 16:1528-1529
  Sound 16:1585-1590
  stirrup 6:539
  tympanic membrane 6:538
  Vibration 19:1813
Eardrum see **EAR; FROG**
EARTH 6:541-545
  Antarctic Circle 6:543
  Arctic 2:133-134
  Arctic Circle 6:543
  Astronomy 2:167
  Atmosphere 2:168-171; 6:543
  Australia 2:177-181
  autumnal equinox 6:543
  Continent 5:444
  Cosmology 5:450
  Day and night 5:483
  Earth, early development of
    6:545-547
  eclipse 6:544-545
  Equator 7:632
  Equinox 7:634
  Europe 7:645
  frigid zone 6:543
  Geography 8:761-763
  Geologic time table 8:764-765
  Geology 8:768-769
  Geophysics 8:722
  Globe 8:783
  Horse latitudes 9:855
  illus.: Eratosthenes' measurement
    6:541; magnetic fields 6:545; mo-
    tion 6:543; parts 6:542; revolu-
    tion 19:1844; revolution around
    the sun 6:543; seasons 6:544
  interior: core 6:542; crust 6:542;
    mantle 6:542
  International Date Line 9:889
  International Geophysical Year:
    the Solid Earth 9:894
  Interstellar communication 10:907-
    909
  Island 10:917
  Jupiter 10:928-929
  Latitude 10:945
  layers 6:541
  Longitude 10:978
  Lunisolar precession 10:984-985
  magnetism 6:545
  Map-making 11:1016
  Mars 11:1023-1025
  Measurement 11:1033-1036
  meridians 6:544; 11:1046
  Midnight sun 11:1059
  Moho 11:1080-1081
  Moon 11:1092-1094
  Mountains 12:1116-1117
  Natural resources 12:1131-1133
  North America 12:1156-1160

  Paleontology 13:1237-1238
  parallels 6:544
  Planet 14:1312
  Plate tectonics 14:1334-1335
  Polar wandering 14:1344
  precession of the equinoxes 6:544
  revolution 6:543-545
  rotation 6:543-545; 15:1479
  satellite 6:544
  Seasons 16:1522-1523
  shape 6:541
  sidereal day 6:543
  Sky 16:1559
  solar day 6:543
  South America 16:1593-1597
  spatial relationships 6:543
  Stratigraphy 17:1676-1677
  Sundial 17:1692
  surface 6:541
  Surveying 18:1707
  Time zones 18:1751-1752
  torrid zone 6:543
  Tropic of Cancer 6:543
  Tropic of Capricorn 6:543
  vernal equinox 6:543
  Volcano 19:1822-1823
  Waterspout 19:1835
EARTH, EARLY DEVELOPMENT OF
  6:545-547
  Continent 6:444
  Continental Drift 5:444
  emergence 6:547
  Geologic time table 8:764-765
  illus.: billion years ago 6:546;
    half-billion years ago 6:546;
    stages in development 6:546
  Solar system, origin of 16:1579
  submergence 6:547
Earth's crust see **EARTH; GEOLOGY**
EARTHQUAKE 6:547
  Continental drift 5:444
  Faulting 7:673
  Focus 8:708
  illus. 6:547
  International Geophysical Year:
    the Solid Earth 9:894
  Moho 11:1080-1081
  Richter Scale 15:1459
  Seismograph 16:1527
  Tidal wave 18:1749
  Tsunami 18:1775
EARTHWORM 6:548
  characteristics 6:548
  Decomposer organism 5:486
  Digestive system 6:510
  food 1:83
  Hermaphrodite 9:841
  illus. 6:548; 15:1443; 15:1453;
    digestive system 6:510; reproduc-
    tive system 15:1447
  Leech 10:950
  reproduction 6:548
  usefulness 6:548
EBONY 6:548
  Hardwood 9:820
  illus. 6:548
ECCLES, SIR JOHN CAREW 6:549
Echidna see **SPINY ANTEATER**
ECHINODERMATA 6:549-550;
  17:1659-1660
  body structure 6:549-550
  digestive system 6:550
  illus.: brittle star 6:549; sea
    cucumber 6:549; sea urchin
    6:549; water vascular system
    6:550
  Marine biology 11:1019-1021
  nervous system 6:550
  reproduction 6:550

  Reproduction, asexual 15:1445
  respiratory system 6:550;
    15:1453-1455
  Sand dollar 15:1493
  Sea cucumber 16:1517
  Sea lily 16:1517-1518
  Sea urchin 16:1518
  Skeleton 16:1552-1555
  water vascular system 6:550;
    19:1834
ECHO 6:550
  Acoustics 1:22-23
  exp. 6:550
ECLIPSE 6:551
  annular 6:551
  corona 6:551
  Earth 6:544-545
  illus. 6:551
  moon 6:551; 11:1092-1094
  partial 6:551
  penumbra 6:551; 13:1262
  solar 6:551
  total 6:551
  umbra 6:551
ECOLOGY 6:552-553
  Biology 3:253
  biota 6:552
  Botany 3:285
  Ecosystem 6:555
  environment 6:552; 7:628
  factors 6:552
  Geography 8:763
  Gregarious 8:797
  Habitat 9:814
  illus.: barren environment 6:552;
    desert environment 6:552; marsh
    environment 6:552; mountain
    environment 6:552
  Nocturnal habits 12:1154-1155
  Pike 13:1294
  Strip mining 17:1678
  Succession 17:1682-1683
  Zoology 19:1895-1896
ECONOMIC BOTANY 6:553-554
  Balance of nature 3:214-221
  Biology 3:253
  Botany 3:285
  Fiber 7:678
  Forest products 8:712-715
  Fungus 8:741-742
  Hardwood 9:820
  Herb 9:836
  illus.: hybrid corn 6:553; soy
    bean 6:554; wheat 6:553
  Legume 10:951
  lower plants: bacteria 6:553;
    fungi 6:553; liverworts 6:553;
    mosses 6:553
  Rope 15:1477
  Tannin 18:1716
  Tea 18:1721-1722
  Seed 16:1524-1525
  seed plants: fibers 6:554; forest
    products 6:554; narcotics pro-
    duction 6:554; spices 6:554;
    vegetables 6:554
  Softwood 16:1571-1572
Economic zoology 3:254
ECOSYSTEM 6:555
  community 6:555
  Ecology 6:552-553
  Environment 7:628
  Geography 8:763
  Gregarious 8:797
  illus. 6:555
  International Control of Natural
    Resources 9:888-889
  Niche 12:1148
  Paleontology 13:1237-1238

Pond 14:1349
Predator-prey 14:1358-1359
Stratification 17:1676
Tundra 18:1778
Habitat 9:814
ECOTONE 6:556
ECTODERM 6:556
Embryology 6:595
ECZEMA 6:556
EDEMA 6:556
Edentata 11:1011
EDISON, THOMAS ALVA 6:556-557
Bulb, electric 4:312
illus.: laboratory 6:557; phono-
graph 6:556; vote recorder 6:557
Motion pictures 12:1112-1114
Radio 15:1416-1418
Sound recording 16:1592
EEL 6:558
illus. 6:558
EELWORM 6:558
Efferent fibers see **NERVOUS
SYSTEM**
EFFERVESCENCE 6:558
EFFLORESCENCE 6:558
EGGS 6:559
Albumin 1:56
Hatchery 9:822
Heredity 9:837-841
illus. 6:559
Menstruation 11:1044
Oviparous 13:1230
Ovum 13:1230
size: 6:559
structure 6:559
Yolk 19:1889-1890
EGGPLANT 6:558
illus. 6:558
EGRET 6:560
illus. 6:560
Heron 9:841-842
EHRICKE, KRAFFT A. 6:560
EHRLICH, PAUL 6:560
Eider duck see **DUCKS**
EINSTEIN, ALBERT 6:560-561;
2:167
Energy 7:613
illus. 6:561; 16:1514
Mach, Ernst 10:988-989
Mass 11:1027
Radiation 15:1408
Relativity 15:1443
Quantum mechanics 14:1390
EINSTEINIUM 6:562
Eland, illus. 1:34
Eland see **ANTELOPE**
ELASTICITY 6:562
Hooke, Robert 9:852
illus. 6:562
Modulus 11:1080
Momentum 11:1088
Rubber 15:1481-1482
Stress 17:1677-1678
ELDERBERRY 6:562
illus. 6:562
Electric arc welding see **ARC**
Electric eel see **EEL**
Electric eye see **ELECTRONICS**
Electric field see **ELECTRICITY;
MAGNET**
Electric motor, illus. 10:991
ELECTRICITY 6:563-572
alternating current 6:570
ammeter 6:566
Ampere 1:72
Ampere, Andre Marie 1:73
Antenna (electronic) 2:114
Armature 2:138
Battery 3:232-233

capacitators 6:570-571
capacitive reactance 6:571
charges 6:563-564
Chemical change 4:371-372
circuits: parallel 6:567-568;
series 6:567-568
Commutator 5:429
Conduction 5:439; 6:564-565
Converter 5:445
Copper 5:447
coulomb 6:566
current 6:585-586
Cycle 5:473
Direct current 6:517; 6:570
Dynamics 6:536
Dynamo 6:536-537
electric field 6:568
Electromagnet 6:577
Electromotive force 6:579
Electronics 6:581-585
Electroscope 6:585
Energy 7:614-615
exp. 6:565, 568, 570, 571
Faraday, Michael 7:670-671
fuel cell 6:572
Fuse 8:743
Galvanometer 8:748-749
generating 6:569
generator 6:566; 8:760-761
Geothermal energy 8:772
Heat barrier 9:828
Hydroelectric power 9:865-866
illus.: alternating current generator 6:572; cells 6:566; circuits
6:567; conductors and noncon-
ductors 6:564; generators 6:569;
how electricity is made 6:566; induction 9:876; magnetism 6:568;
negative charges 6:564; positive
and negative charges 6:563;
power line 6:563; wiring diagram
6:572; impedance 6:571
Inductance coil 9:876
Induction 9:876
inductive reactance 6:570
insulators 6:564-565
kilowatt 6:568
Kilowatt hour 10:933
Lightning 10:963-964
Magnet 10:995-997
magnetism 6:568-569
measurement 6:568
Millikan's electronic charge
11:1063
Motor 12:1114-1116
negative charge 6:563-564
ohm 6:566; 12:1196
Ohm, Georg Simon 12:1196
Ohmmeter 12:1197
Ohm's Law 6:566
Oscilloscope 13:1225
Peltier, Jean Charles Athanase
13:1260
Photoelectricity 13:1278-1280
photosensitive materials 6:572
Physics 13:1287-1288
Polar wandering 14:1344
positive charge 6:563-564
Radio 15:1416-1418
Radio tube 15:1420
radio waves 6:571
resistance 6:566
resonance 6:571; 15:1452-1453
Short circuit 16:1540
Sound recording 16:1592
Static electricity 17:1663
Switches, electric 18:1712
thermocouple 6:571
transformers 6:571; 18:1766

Transistor 18:1767-1768
Turbine 18:1778-1779
Vacuum tube 18:1793-1794
Volt 19:1823-1824
Volta, Alessandro 19:1824
voltage drop 6:566
voltmeter 6:566; 19:1824-1825
ELECTROCARDIOGRAPH 6:573
electrodes 6:573
illus. 6:573
P wave 6:573
QRS group 6:573
ELECTROCHEMISTRY 6:573
Electricity 6:563-572
Electrolysis 6:576
illus.: Volta's experiment 6:573
ELECTROENCEPHALOGRAPH
6:574
Brain 3:289
Epilepsy 7:631
illus.: 6:575; brain waves 6:574
ELECTRODE 6:574
Anode 2:109
Arc 2:128
Cathode 4:354
Electrolysis 6:575
electrolyte 6:574
Geiger counter 8:758
Hall-Heroult process 9:818
illus.: Voltaic cell 6:574; lead
alloy 1:63
Nickel 12:1148
Vacuum tube 18:1793-1794
ELECTROLYSIS 6:575-576
Aluminum 1:68
Anode 2:109
Bauxite 3:234
Cathode 4:354
Chemical change 4:371-372
Chlorine 4:381
Decomposition 5:486
Dissociation 6:520
Electrochemistry 6:573
Electrode 6:574
Electroplating 6:585
exp. 6:576
Faraday, Michael 7:670-671
Hydrolysis 9:867
importance 6:575
Ion 10:911-912
Lead 10:947
Metal 11:1049-1051
Oxide 13:1232
Serum 16:1530
Electrolyte see **BATTERY; ELEC-
TROLYSIS; ELECTROPLATING**
ELECTROMAGNET 6:577
advantages 6:577
Armature 2:138
Color 5:422-423
exp. 6:577
Galvanometer 8:748-749
Henry, Joseph 9:835
illus. 6:577
Magnet 10:995-997
Motor 12:1114-1116
Oersted, Hans Christian 12:1196
Solenoid 16:1581
Telegraph 18:1724
Telephone 18:1726-1727
Transformer 18:1766
uses 6:577
ELECTROMAGNETIC SPECTRUM
6:578
Diffraction 6:509
gamma rays 6:578
hysteresis 6:577
illus. 6:578
infrared light 6:578

Light 10:959-963
Optics 13:1215
Radiation 15:1408
Ray, infrared 15:1434-1435
Search for Extraterrestrial
  Intelligence (SETI) 16:1522
Short wave radio 16:1540-1541
ultraviolet light 6:578
ELECTROMOTIVE FORCE 6:579
ELECTRON 3:232; 6:579
  Ampere 1:72-73
  Cathode 4:354
  Cathode ray 4:354-355
  Electricity 6:563-573
  Electronics 6:581-585
  illus. 6:579
  International Geophysical Year:
    Atmosphere 9:891-892
  Magnet 10:995-997
  Moseley, Henry Gwyn-Jeffreys
    11:1097
  orbits 6:579
  Positron 6:579; 14:1353
  valence 6:579
ELECTRON BORROWING 6:580
  Electricity 6:572
  Electron 6:579
  Electron sharing 6:580-581
  electrovalent 6:580
  Molecular theory 11:1083
Electron microscope see **BIOPHYS-
ICS; MICROSCOPE, ELECTRON**
ELECTRON SHARING 6:580-581
  covalent 6:581
  Germanium 8:773
  illus. 6:580
Electron tube see **ELECTRONICS**
ELECTRONICS 6:581-585
  amplification 6:581-582
  Aviation 2:195
  Cathode 4:354
  Cathode-ray tube 4:355; 6:583
  DeForest, Lee 5:491
  Electricity 6:572
  Electron 6:579
  electronic eye 6:581, 584
  High fidelity 9:844
  illus.: simple electron tube 6:581
  Machinery 10:989-991
  modulation 6:581-582
  Musical instruments 12:1126
  Oscilloscope 13:1225
  Photoelectricity 13:1278-1280
  Printed circuit 14:1364
  Radio 15:1416-1418
  rectification 6:581-582
  semiconductor diode 6:581-583
  Short wave radio 15:1540-1541
  switching 6:581
  Television 18:1730-1732
  transistor 6:581-584; 18:1767-
    1768
  triode tube 6:582
  Vacuum tube 18:1793-1794;
    6:581-583
  X rays 19:1884-1886
ELECTROPLATING 6:585
  Electrode 6:574
  Electrolysis 6:576
  illus. 6:585
  Nickel 12:1148
ELECTROSCOPE 6:585
ELECTROSTATIC PRECIPITATOR
  6:585
  Garbage 8:750
ELECTROSTATICS 6:585
  Static electricity 17:1663
ELEMENTS 6:586-589
  Anhydride 1:82

Atom 2:172-174
atomic number 6:586
Berzelius, Jons Jakob 3:247
Carbon cycle 4:339
Carbon life 4:341
Chemistry 4:373-377
Curie, Pierre and Marie 5:465-466
Decomposition 5:486
Electron 6:579
Electron borrowing 6:580
Exclusion Principle 7:660
Half-life 9:817
Halogen 9:818
Heavy metals 9:830
  illus. 6:586
Ion 10:911-912
Isotope 10:918
Metal 11:1049-1051
Moseley, Henry 11:1097
Mixture 11:1079
names and symbols 6:587-589
Nonmetal 12:1155
Nuclear particles 12:1164-1165
Nuclear science 12:1170-1175
nucleus 6:586
Periodic Table 6:587-589
Radiation, uses of 15:1414-1415
Rare-earth elements 15:1429
structure 6:586
Substances, properties 17:1681-
  1682
Symbols, chemical 18:1713
Valence 18:1795; 6:587
ELEMENTS IN THE HUMAN BODY
  6:590
  Calcium 4:323
  Carbon 4:338
  illus. 6:590
  Nitrogen cycle 12:1150-1151
  Potassium 14:1354
ELEPHANT 6:591
  characteristics 6:591
  illus. 1:34; 6:591; 19:1894
  Mammalia 11:1011-1012
  Mammoth 11:1013
  Pachyderm 13:1235
  reproduction 6:591
Elephantiasis see **FILARIA**
Elimination see **EXCRETORY
SYSTEM**
Elk see **DEER FAMILY**
ELM 6:592
EMBALM 6:592
EMBOLISM 6:592
EMBRYO 6:592
EMBRYOLOGY 6:592-597
  Animals, classification of 1:94
  Baer, Karl Ernst von 3:212
  Biology 3:254
  Birth 3:264
  Cleavage 4:394
  Coelom 5:419
  Ectoderm 6:556
  Eggs 6:559
  embryonic membranes: allantois
    6:596-597; amnion 6:596; chorion
    6:597; placenta 6:597; yolk sac
    6:596
  Endoderm 7:610
  epigenesis 6:592
  Fertilization 7:678
  Fetus 7:678
  Gamete 8:749
  Gestation period 8:774
  illus.: chicken 6:597; cleavage
    in starfish 6:594; development of
    the chick 6:593; embryonic mem-
    brane 6:595; frog 6:594-595, 597;
    18:1753; man 6:597; shark 6:597

Larva 10:943
Multiple birth 12:1119
Nervous system 12:1141-1145
Notochord 12:1161
Ovum 13:1230
preformation theory 6:592
Reproduction, sexual 15:1446-
  1447
Reproductive systems 15:1447-
  1448
stages of development in vertebrates: blastula 6:595; cleavage
  6:594-595; fertilization 6:594;
  germ layers 6:595; neural tube
  6:595-596; mesoderm 6:596
stages of study 6:594
Teratology 18:1734
Weismann, August 19:1861
Yolk 19:1889-1890
Zoology 19:1895-1896, 1897
Zygote 19:1896
EMBRYOPHYTA 7:607-608
  cells 7:607
  characteristics 7:607
  illus.: black-eyed Susan 7:607;
    chart of plant classification
    7:608; club moss 7:607; deer-
    horn cactus 7:607; fern 7:607;
    fir tree 7:607; horsetail 7:607;
    liverwort 7:607; moss 7:607;
    silver maple 7:607
  Plants, classification of 14:1322-
    1327
  reproduction 7:608
EMERALD 7:609
  illus. 11:1065; 7:609
  Magnetite 10:997
Emery see **CORUNDUM**
Emmetropia 13:1216
EMPHYSEMA 7:609
  Aerosol 1:32
  Bronchitis 3:297
  causes 7:609
  symptoms 7:609
Emu see **BIRDS, FLIGHTLESS**
EMULSION 7:609
  exp. 7:609
  Film 7:681
  Soap 16:1570
Enamel see **PAINT; TEETH**
Encyst see **PARASITES**
ENDANGERED SPECIES 7:610;
  9:888-889
  Extinction 7:663-664
  Ivory 10:919
  Kite 10:935
  Kiwi 10:935
ENDOCRINE GLANDS 7:610
  Acne 1:22
  Adrenal glands 1:27-28; 7:610
  Anatomy 1:76
  Atrophy 2:174
  Gland 8:780
  Glandular tissue 8:781
  Gonad 8:787
  Histology 9:846-849
  Homeostasis 9:851
  Hormone 9:853
  illus. 7:611
  Insulin 9:887
  Islets of Langerhans 10:917
  pancreas 7:610; 13:1240
  Parathyroid 13:1249; 7:610
  Physiology 13:1289-1291
  Pituitary gland 7:610; 14:1310
  Progesterone 14:1371
  Secretion 16:1523
  Simmond's disease 16:1549
  Spleen 17:1650-1651

Thymus 18:1748
Thyroid 18:1749; 7:610
ENDODERM 7:610
Ectoderm 6:556
Embryology 6:595
Endolymph 6:540
ENDOSCOPE 7:610
ENDOSKELETON 7:610
Exoskeleton 7:661
ENDOTHERMIC 7:610
Exothermic 7:661
Heat of reaction 9:829
ENERGY 7:612-617
animal digestion 1:86
Atmosphere 2:169
Brake 3:290
Calorimetry 4:325-326
chemical 7:614-615
Chemical change 4:372
Color 5:422-423
conservation: law of 7:612
Dyne 6:537
electrical 7:614-615; 6:572
Electronics 6:581-585
Engineering 7:624
Engine 7:619
Explosives 7:663
Foot-pound 8:710
Fuel 8:738-740
Geothermal energy 8:772
Heat 9:826; 7:615
Heat of reaction 9:829
human body 7:613
illus.: atomic 7:616; conserva-
  tion 7:613; kinetic 7:612; mechan-
  ical 7:615; potential 7:613; power
  dam 7:614; principles of transfer
  7:617; windmill 7:614
Joule, James Prescott 10:925
kinetic 7:612, 614; 10:934
Machinery 10:989-991
Machines, simple 10:992-994
Matter 11:1031
Metabolism 11:1048
Motor 12:1114-1116
Neutrino 12:1145
nuclear 7:616
Physiology 13:1289-1291
potential 7:612, 614; 14:1354
Power 14:1355
Steam 17:1665
Thermodynamics 18:1741-1742
transfer 7:616-617
Wave 19:1836-1837
work 7:617; 19:1880
Energy conversion see **ENERGY;**
  MACHINERY
ENERGY CRISIS 7:618
Coal 5:413; 7:618
illus.: fossil fuels 7:618; solar
  energy 7:618
*International Control of Natural
  Resources* 9:888
nuclear energy 7:618
solar energy 7:618
ENGINE 7:619-623
Airplane: piston 1:52; rocket 1:52;
  turbojet 1:52; turboprop 1:52
Antifreeze 2:117
Automobile 2:184-186
Carburetor 4:323
Combustion 5:425
diesel 7:622-623
Dynamometer 6:537
Effect on agriculture 1:38
Ethyl 7:638
External-combustion 7:619-621
four stroke 7:622
Fuel 8:738-740

gas turbine 7:623
Helicopter 9:832
Horsepower 9:856
illus.: efficiency 7:619; internal
  combustion 7:622; piston 7:620;
  radial aircraft 7:623; recipro-
  cating-type steam 7:619; single-
  shaft gas turbine 7:623; triple-
  flow steam turbine 7:619; Wankel
  7:621; internal-combustion 7:621-
  623
Jet propulsion 10:922-923
Machinery 10:989-991
Motor 12:1114-1116
reciprocating 7:621-622
Thermodynamics 18:1741-1742
Train, railroad 18:1764-1765
Turbine 18:1778-1779
two-stroke 7:622
Wankel 7:623
ENGINEERING 7:624-628
Bridges 3:294-296
careers 7:628
education 7:625
fields: aeronautical 7:626; agricultural 7:626; architectural
  7:626; ceramic 7:626; chemical
  7:626-627; electrical 7:627;
  industrial 7:627; mechanical
  7:627; metallurgical 7:627; mining
  7:628; nuclear 7:628; sanitary
  7:628
history 7:624-625
illus.: aeronautical 7:625, 626;
  agricultural 7:626; architectural
  7:624, 626; ceramic 7:626; civil
  7:627; industrial 7:627;
  mechanical 7:627
Mechanics 11:1037-1038
Purification 14:1387
English Channel see **EUROPE**
English daisy, illus. 7:644
English sparrow, illus. 7:682
ENTOMOLOGY 7:628
ENVIRONMENT 7:628
Ecology 6:552
ENZYMES 7:629-630
aids in digestion 7:630
animal digestion 1:86
Biochemistry 3:251
Blood 3:269
Catalyst 4:352; 7:629
composition 7:629
Cori, Carl F. and Gerty T. 5:448
Digestive system 6:511
during embryology 7:630
exp. 7:629
Gene 8:760
in genetics 7:630
Plants, insectivorous 14:1328
Physiology 13:1289-1291
Eocene see **CENEZOIC ERA;**
  GEOLOGIC TIME TABLE
EPIDEMIC 7:630-631
Meningitis 11:1043
Typhoid fever 18:1784
Typhus fever 18:1784
Epidermis see **SKIN**
Epiglottis see **RESPIRATORY**
  SYSTEM
EPILEPSY 7:631
Barbiturates 3:225
Brain 3:289
Convulsion 5:446
Electroencephalograph 6:574-575
grand mal 7:631
petit mal 7:631
seizure 7:631
symptoms 7:631

Epinephrine see **ADRENALIN**
EPIPHYTE 7:631
illus. 7:631
EPITHELIAL TISSUE 7:632
Cancer (disease) 4:331
Cuticle 5:471
Glandular tissue 8:781
Histology 9:846
illus. 7:632; 9:847
Integumentary system 9:887
Mucous membrane 12:1117
Thyroid gland 18:1749
EPOCH 7:632
EQUATION 7:632
EQUATOR 7:632
Great circle 8:796
illus. 7:632
Latitude 10:945
Equatorial calms 6:524
EQUILIBRIUM 7:633
Ear 6:540
exp. 7:633
Homeostasis 9:850-851
Mechanics 11:1037-1038
Equilibrium of forces see **FORCES**
EQUINOX 7:634
autumnal 7:634
Earth 6:543
illus. 7:634
Lunisolar precession 10:984-985
Measurement 11:1033-1036
Midnight sun 11:1059
parallelism 7:634
Saturn 16:1509-1510
Solstice 16:1581
vernal 7:634
Virgo 19:1816
ERG 7:634
ERA 7:634
ERBIUM 7:634
Ergot on rye, illus. 13:1247
Ermine see **WEASEL**
EROSION 7:635-636
Agriculture 1:40
Bay 3:234
Bridge 3:294
Escarpment 7:636
Gardening 8:751-753
Glacial ages 8:779
illus. 7:635; 7:636
Island 10:917
Mesa 11:1046
Mulch 12:1118
Natural bridge 12:1131
Peneplain 13:1261
Plateau 14:1335
River 15:1459-1460
Sand 15:1493
soil conservation 7:635-636
Soil types 16:1573
Waterfall 19:1834-1835
Weathering 19:1858
Erythrocite see **BLOOD**
Erythromycin 2:116
ESCARPMENT 7:636
cuesta 7:636
illus. 7:636
ESKER 7:636
Esophagus see **DIGESTIVE SYSTEM**
ESSENTIAL OILS 7:637
ESTER 7:637
Aspirin 2:151
Fat 7:672
ESTIVATION 7:637
Hibernation 9:843
ESTROGEN 7:637
Giant 8:775
Gonad 8:787
Steroid 17:1671

ESTROUS CYCLE 7:637
Estrogen 7:637
Menstruation 11:1044
ESTUARY 7:637
ETHER 7:637
Alcohol 1:56
Anesthetic 1:81
Hygrometer 9:871
Surgery 17:1696
Ethologist 1:88
ETHOLOGY 7:637-638
Lorenz, Konrad 10:978
ETHYL 7:638
illus.: effect on piston 7:638
Ethyl alcohol see **ALCOHOL**
ETHYLENE 7:638
Ethylene glycol see **ORGANIC COMPOUNDS**
EUCALYPTUS 7:638-639
Australia 2:177
illus. 7:639
Plants, tropical 14:1331
Eugenics see **BIOLOGY; GALTON, SIR FRANCIS**
EUGLENA 7:639
digestion 7:639
habitat 7:639
illus.: 7:639; 7:688; 14:1379
locomotion 1:86
Protozoa 14:1378-1379
Euglenophyta 18:1738
Eumycophyta 18:1739
EUONYMUS 7:639
illus. 7:639
EUROPE 7:640-645
animals: carnivores 7:644; deer 7:644; domestic 7:644; muskrats 7:644; rabbits 7:644
Climate 4:394-397; 7:642
Continent 5:444
Geography 8:761-763
Geology 8:768-769
illus.: 7:643; animals 7:643; bad-ger 7:643; brown bear 7:643; chamois 7:643; chestnut tree 7:644; crested porcupine 7:643; English daisy 7:644; European bison 7:643; European hare 7:643; European wild boar 7:643; fox 7:643; ibex 7:643; jackal 7:643; lemming 7:643; meadow mouse 7:643; mouflon 7:643; olive tree 7:644; otter 7:643; plants 7:644; rat 7:643; red deer 7:643; reindeer 7:643; Scotch broom 7:644; shrew 7:643; squirrel 7:643; stock 7:644; stork 7:643; sweet peas 7:644; tulip 7:644; weasel 7:643; white birch 7:644; wolf 7:643
map 7:640, 641
mountains: Alps 7:640; Apennines 7:640; Balkans 7:640; Caledonian 7:640; Carpathians 7:640; Cauca-sus 7:640; Dolomites 7:640; Her-cynian 7:640; Huronian 7:640
Natural resources 12:1131-1133; bauxite 7:645; coal 7:645; iron 7:645; natural gas 7:645; petroleum 7:645
plains 7:642
plants: Central plains 7:645; cold forests 7:645; Mediterranean 7:644-645; Oceanic zone 7:645
rivers and drainage: Black Sea 7:642; Caspian Sea 7:642; Dnei-per 7:642; Dniester 7:642; Don 7:642; Elbe 7:642; English Channel 7:642; Oder 7:642; Po

7:644; Rhine 7:642; Rhone 7:644; Seine 7:642; sea and land 7:642; Ural 7:642; Vistula 7:642; Volga 7:642
European ash, illus. 9:820
European hare, illus. 7:643
EUROPIUM 7:646
Eustachian tube see **EAR**
EUTROPHICATION 7:646
Bog 3:277
EVAPORATION 7:646
Boiling point 3:278
Combustion 5:425
Distillation 6:520
exp. 7:646
Homeostasis 9:851
Humidity 9:858-859
Liquid 10:970
Physical states and changes 13:1286-1287
Steam 17:1665
Sublimation 17:1680
Water cycle 19:1832-1833
Water vapor 19:1834
EVERGREEN 7:646
Juniper 10:927
Leaves 10:949
EVOLUTION 7:647-654; 10:943
Acquired characteristics 1:23-24
Adaptation 1:24-25
Amphibians 1:74
Animal 1:82-87
Animals, classification of 1:92
Australia: duckbill 2:180
Biology 3:253
Burbank, Luther 4:316
common ancestor 7:650-651
Darwin, Charles Robert 5:481
Division of labor 6:521
early theories 7:647-648
Ecology 6:552-553
Ectoderm 6:556
environmental effects 7:649
first plants and animals 7:651
fossil records 7:650; 8:791-723
Galapagos Islands 8:745
Geologic time table 8:764-765
geological periods 7:652-654
Heredity 9:837-841
Horse 9:854-855
illus.: animal 7:651; embryonic parallelism in vertebrates 7:653; horse 7:648, 649; Irish elk 7:650; plant 7:652; scientists 7:647
Lamarck, Jean Baptiste Pierre 10:940
Mendel, Gregor Johann 11:1042
Mesozoic Era 11:1047
Mimicry 11:1064
natural selection 7:648
Paleozoic Era 13:1239
pattern 7:650
Peripatus 13:1265
Plants, classification of 14:1322-1327
Prehistoric mammals 14:1359-1360
Primates 14:1362-1363
Protective coloration 14:1375-1376
Protozoa 14:1378-1379
Specialization 17:1640
Trilobite 18:1772
EVOLUTION OF MAN 7:654-659
anthropoid ape 7:654
Australopithecus 7:656-657
Cenezoic Era 4:361-362
classification of man 7:654
Chellean man 7:657

Cro-Magnon man 7:659
Evolution 7:647-654
Geologic time table 8:764-765
Heidelberg man 7:658
Homo sapiens 9:851
Human being 9:858
illus.: 7:655; Chellean man 7:658; Java man 7:657; Neanderthal 7:659; Zinjanthropus 7:656
Java man 7:657
modern man 7:659
Neanderthal man 6:658-659
Paleontology 13:1237-1238
Peking man 7:657
Phylogeny 13:1286
physical changes 7:656
Pleistocene Era 7:656
Prezinjanthropus 7:656
Primates 14:1362-1363
Race 14:1396
Rhodesian man 7:658
Solo man 7:658
Stone age 17:1674
Tools 18:1757-1759
Zinjanthropus 7:656
Ewe see **SHEEP**
EXCLUSION PRINCIPLE 7:660
EXCRETORY SYSTEM 7:660-661
Anatomy 1:76
bladder 7:661
Bladder, urinary 3:266
Digestive system 6:510-513
human 7:660
illus. 7:660
Kidney 10:932-933; 7:660
Nephridia 12:1138
Physiology 13:1289-1291
renal tubule 7:661
ureter 7:660-661
urethra 7:660-661
Urine 18:1791
Exocrine glands see **ENDOCRINE GLANDS**
EXOSKELETON 7:661
EXOTHERMIC 7:661
Heat of reaction 9:829
Fuel 8:738
EXPANSION 7:661-662
exp. 7:661, 662
Freezing point 8:729
Gas 8:754-756
Heat 9:827
Ice 9:873
EXPERIMENT 7:662
Experimental Aircraft Association 1:49
EXPIRATION 7:663
EXPLOSIVES 7:663
Bomb 3:279-282
Combustion 5:425
composition 7:663
detonation 7:663
Forest products 8:713
Gun 9:810
Gunpowder 9:811
high 7:663
Nitroglycerine 12:1150-1151
primary 7:663
propellants 7:663
Weapons 19:1838-1841
Exponents 1:60
Extension see **MUSCLE SYSTEM**
External combustion engine 7:619-621
EXTINCTION 7:663-664
causes 7:663-664
prevention 7:664
EXTRASENSORY PERCEPTION 7:664

EXTREMITIES 7:664
EYE 7:664-667
  Accommodation 1:19
  aqueous humor 7:667
  Astigmatism 2:153-154
  blind spot 7:667
  blindness 3:267
  Cataract 4:353
  Color 5:423
  conjunctiva 7:664
  Conjunctivitis 5:439
  cornea 7:664
  Corpuscular theory 5:449
  Cross-eyes 5:458
  exp. 7:666
  Farsightedness 7:671
  Glaucoma 8:782-783
  illus. 7:665
  iris 7:664
  Lens, man-made 10:953
  movements 7:668
  Nearsightedness 12:1136
  optic nerve 7:667
  Ophthalmoscope 13:1212
  Optometry 13:1215-1217
  Perspective 13:1269
  pupil 7:664
  retina 7:667
  rods and cones 7:667
  Sense organs 16:1528-1529
  sight 7:667
  structure 7:664-667
  Tears 18:1722
  vitreous humor 7:664, 667
EYE, BINOCULAR 7:668
  Eye 7:664-667
  illus. 7:668
  Perspective 13:1269
EYE, COMPOUND 7:668
  Eye 7:667
  Eye, simple 7:668
  illus. 7:668
  ommatidia 7:668
EYE, SIMPLE 7:668
  Eye 7:664-667
  illus.: spider 7:668
FABRE, JEAN 7:669
Factor see **ALGEBRA;**
  MATHEMATICS
FAHRENHEIT 7:669
  Degree 5:491
FAINT 7:669
Fairy ring see **MUSHROOM**
FALCON 7:669
  Birds of prey 3:262
  illus. 7:669
  Petrel 13:1270
Fall see **SEASONS**
FALLING BODIES 7:670
  Galileo 8:746
  Gravity 8:794-795
  Motion 12:1111-1112
Falling star see **METEOR**
Fallopian tubes see **ESTROUS CY-**
  CLE; MENSTRUATION;
  REPRODUCTIVE SYSTEMS
FALLOUT 7:670
FALLOW 7:670
False nettle, Illus. 12:1145
Family see **ANIMALS, CLASSI-**
  FICATION OF; PLANTS,
  CLASSIFICATION OF
Family tree 13:1258
Fang see **SNAKES**
Fanworms, illus. 11:1020
FARAD 7:670
FARADAY, MICHAEL 7:670-671
  Armature 2:138
  Condenser 5:438

Dynamo 6:536
Generator 8:760
Henry, Joseph 9:835
  illus. 7:670
Induction 9:877
Radio 15:1416-1418
Farm see **AGRICULTURE**
Farm implements
  illus.: combine 1:39; 1:41; corn
  picker 1:38, 1:41; grain drill
  1:39, 1:41; plow 1:41
FARSIGHTEDNESS 7:671
  Astigmatism 2:153-154
  Eye 7:664-667
  illus. 7:671
  Nearsightedness 12:1136
FAT 7:672
  animal digestion 1:86
  Cholesterol 4:383
  Connective tissue 5:439
  Digestive system 6:512
  Elements in the human body 6:590
  Ester 7:637
  exp. 7:672
  Fat, adipose tissue 7:672
  Fatty acids 7:673
  Lanolin 10:942
  Oil 12:1197
  Tallow 18:1715
FAT, ADIPOSE TISSUE 7:672
FATIGUE 7:673
  Muscle system 12:1122
Fathometer see **DEPTH SOUNDING**
FATTY ACIDS 7:673
  animal digestion 1:86
  Assimilation 2:151
  Lanolin 10:942
  Metabolism 11:1048
FAULTING 7:673
  Earthquake 6:547
  Escarpment 7:636
  illus. 7:673
FAUNA 7:673
Fawn see **DEER FAMILY**
FEATHER 7:673-674
  Bird 3:256
  illus. 7:673, 674
  parts 7:674
  Skin modification 16:1558
FELDSPAR 7:674
  Clay 4:392
  illus. 7:674; 9:819
  Kaolin 10:930
  Pegmatite 13:1259
  Porcelain 14:1350
Felis domesticus 1:91
Felis leo 1:91, 92
Female see **HEREDITY**
Femur see **SKELETON**
Fen see **MARSH**
FENNEL 7:675
  illus. 7:675
Fer de lance see **SNAKES**
FERMENTATION 7:675; 3:210
  Acids and bases 1:20
  Carbon cycle 4:339
  Glycolysis 8:783
  Yeast 19:1888-1889
FERMI, ENRICO 7:675
  illus. 7:675
FERMIUM 7:676
FERNS 7:676
  exp. 7:677
  illus. 1:65; 7:607; 7:676;
    14:1325, 1327; 14:1331; 18:1763
  Plants, classification of 14:1322-
    1327
  reproduction 7:676
  rhizomes 7:676

Ferret see **WEASEL**
Fertile see **NUCLEAR SCIENCE**
  GLOSSARY
FERTILIZATION 7:678
  Menstruation 11:1044
  Ovum 13:1230
  Pistil 14:1308-1309
  Plant 14:1314-1317
  Spallanzani, Lazzaro 17:1638
  Sperm 17:1644
  Zygote 19:1896
FERTILIZER 7:678
  chemical elements 7:678
  illus. 7:678
  Nitrogen cycle 12:1150-1151
  Shrub 16:1543-1544
FETUS 7:678
FEVER 7:678
FIBER 7:678
  illus. 7:678
FIBIGER, JOHANNES ANDREAS
  7:679
Fibrin and fibrinogen see **BLOOD;**
  CIRCULATORY SYSTEM
FIBROUS TISSUE 7:679
  Histology 9:846-849
  Joints, skeletal 10:924-925
  Sprain 17:1653
Fibula see **SKELETON**
FIELD, CYRUS WEST 7:679
  Cables 4:320
FIG 7:680
  illus. 7:680
FILARIA 7:680
  elephantiasis 7:680
  illus. 7:680
  life cycle 7:680
  Nemathelminthes 12:1137-1138
  Parasites 13:1247-1249
Filbert see **NUTS**
FILM 7:681
  Bromide 3:297
  color 7:681
  composition 7:681
  developing 7:681
  Forest products 8:713
  illus. 7:681
  Motion pictures 12:1112-1114
  Photochemistry 13:1277-1278
FILTER 7:681
FIN 7:682
  illus. 7:682
FINCH 7:682
  Crossbill 5:458
  Goldfinch 8:786
  Grosbeak 9:807
  illus.: English sparrow 7:682;
    grosbeak 7:682; purple finch
    7:682
  Junco 10:926
  Linnet 10:967
FIORD 7:682
  illus. 7:682
FIR 7:683
  Evergreen 7:646
  illus. 7:683
Fir tree, illus. 7:607
FIRE 7:683
  Combustible 5:425
  Combustion 5:425
  Kindling temperature 10:933
FIRE EXTINGUISHER 7:683-684
  automatic sprinklers 7:684
  Carbon dioxide 4:340
  exp. 7:684
  Fire 7:683
  foam 7:683
  illus. 7:683
  soda-acid 7:683

Firearms see **WEAPONS**
Firebrat, illus. 9:881
Firefly see **BEETLE**
FIRST AID 7:684-686
  animal bites 7:686
  Artificial respiration 2:143
  bleeding 7:685
  Burns 4:316; 7:685
  cuts and lacerations 7:685
  foreign bodies in the eye 7:686
  Fracture 8:727
  frostbite 7:686; 8:734
  general directions 7:684
  Heimlich's Choke Maneuver 9:831
  illus.: cardiopulmonary resuscita-
    tion 7:685
  Poison 14:1342; 7:685
  Resuscitation 15:1455
  Shock 16:1539; 7:684
  snake bites 7:686
  strains 7:686
  suffocation 7:685
  sunstroke 7:686
FISCHER, EMIL 7:686
FISCHER, HANS 7:686
FISH 7:686
  Chordata 4:384
  Haddock 9:815
  illus. 7:687; 15:1454
  Marine biology 11:1019-1021
  perch 13:1263
  Pisces (animal) 14:1307-1308
  Shark 16:1533
  Swordfish 18:1712
Fish hawk see **OSPREY**
FISSION 3:209; 7:620; 7:688
  illus. 7:688
  Reproduction, asexual 15:1445
Fissionable see **NUCLEAR SCIENCE**
  GLOSSARY
FITTONIA 7:688
  illus. 7:688
Fjord see **FIORD**
FLAGELLA 7:688
  Euglena 7:639
  illus. 18:1738
  Sperm 17:1644
Flame thrower 19:1841
FLAMINGO 7:688-689
  illus. 7:688
FLATFISH 7:689
Flatworm see **PLANARIA;**
  PLATYHELMINTHES
Flax see **LINEN**
FLEA 7:689
  illus. 7:689
FLEMING, ALEXANDER 2:115;
  7:689; 13:1261
Fleming, Sir John A. 15:1417
FLEMING, SIR SANFORD 7:689
FLESH 7:689
FLICKER 7:690
  Bird houses 3:258
  illus. 7:690
FLIGHT, PRINCIPLES OF 7:690-691
  Aerodynamics 1:28-29
  Aeronautics 1:30-31
  Air pressure 1:47
  Aircraft 1:48-50
  Airplane 1:52-53
  Aviation 2:191-197
  Bernoulli, Daniel 3:245-246
  birds 7:690
  controls 7:691
  drag 7:690-691
  gravity 7:690; 8:794-795
  illus. 7:690-691
  Jet propulsion 10:922-923
  ornithopters 7:690

  Supersonic 17:1695
  thrust 7:690-691
Flightless birds see **BIRDS,**
  FLIGHTLESS
Flint see **ROCKS**
Floe see **ICEBERG**
FLOOD 7:692
  flash flood 7:692
  flood plain 7:692
  Levee 10:956
  prevention 7:692
  River 15:1459-1460
FLORA 7:692
FLORY, PAUL J. 7:692
FLOTATION 7:692
FLOUNDER 7:692
  Flatfish 7:689
  illus. 7:692; 14:1375
  Sole 16:1580
FLOUR 7:693
FLOWER 7:693-694
  Calyx 4:326
  complete 7:693
  composite 7:693
  Fruit 8:734-736
  hormones 7:694
  Horticulture 9:856
  illus.: blue-eyed grass 7:694;
    butter-and-eggs 7:694; dandelion
    7:694; Joshua 7:694; parts 7:693
    trees 7:693; trumpet creeper
    7:694
  parts 7:693
  photoperiodism 7:694
  Pollination 14:1347
  purpose 7:694
  Stigma 17:1672
FLUID 7:694
Fluke see **LIVER FLUKE;**
  PLATYHELMINTHES
Fluorescent light see **BULB,**
  ELECTRIC
FLUORINE 7:694
  Fluorite 7:695
  Fluorocarbons 7:695
FLUORITE 7:695
  Fluorine 7:694-695
  illus. 9:819
FLUOROCARBONS 7:695
  freon 7:695
FLUOROSCOPE 7:695-696
  illus. 7:695
  parts 7:695
  uses 7:696
  X rays 19:1884-1886
FLY 7:696-697
  characteristics 7:696-697
  Gnat 8:783-784
  harmfulness 7:696
  illus. 7:696-697
  Metamorphosis 11:1052
  reproduction 7:697
  usefulness 7:696
FLYCATCHER 7:697
  illus. 7:697
  Peewee 13:1259
FLYING FISH 8:707
  characteristics 8:707
  illus. 8:707
  reproduction 8:707
Flying machine of Leonardo Da Vinci,
  illus. 1:28
Flying saucer see **UNIDENTIFIED**
  FLYING OBJECT
FM (frequency modulation) see
  RADIO
Focal length 11:1007
FOCUS 8:708
  illus. 8:708

Foetus see **FETUS**
FOG 8:708
  advection 8:708
  exp. 8:708
  radiation 8:708
FOLDING 8:708
  illus. 8:708
Foliage see **LEAVES**
FOLLICLE (BOTANICAL) 8:709
  Fruit 8:735
FOLLICLE (REPRODUCTIVE) 8:709
Food see **MALNUTRITION;**
  NUTRITION
FOOD CHAIN 8:709
  food pyramid 8:709
  food web 8:709
  Plankton 14:1313
FOOD PRESERVATION 8:709-710
  Agriculture 1:39
  Bacteriology 3:210-211
  causes of spoilage 8:709
  Dehydration 5:491-492
  methods 8:710
Food pyramid see **FOOD CHAIN**
Food vacuole see **PROTOZOA**
Foot see **MEASUREMENT;**
  SKELETON
Foot and mouth disease see **ANIMAL**
  DISEASES
Food-candle see **CANDELA**
FOOT-POUND 8:710
  Horsepower 9:856
  Joule 10:925
  Torque 18:1761
  Work 19:1880
FORCES 8:710-711
  Dynamics 6:536
  Dyne 6:537; 8:711
  Erg 7:634
  Foot-pound 8:710
  Gravity 8:794-795
  illus. 8:710, 711
  Inertia 9:877
  Machinery 10:989-991
  Mass 11:1027
  Mechanics 11:1037-1038
  methods of measuring 8:711
  Modulus 11:1080
  Momentum 11:1088
  Newton's Laws of Motion 8:710-711
  resultant force 8:711
Force arm see **MACHINES, SIMPLE**
Forces in level flight, illus. 1:29
Forcing houses 8:797
Ford, Henry, automation 2:182
Forecast see **WEATHER**
  FORECASTING
Forest, Lee de see **DEFOREST, LEE**
Forest preserve see **PRESERVES**
FOREST PRODUCTS 8:712-715
  bark 8:713
  Economic botany 6:554
  exp. 8:712
  Forestry 8:716-717
  Hardwood 9:820
  illus. 8:715
  Lumber 10:979
  map 8:714
  Paper 13:1242
  Pine 13:1295-1296
  wood 8:712-713
  illus. 8:713
  wood secretions 8:713
FORESTRY 8:716-717
  care and management of timber
    8:716-717
  current research 8:717
  fire protection 8:717
  Forest products 8:712-715

illus. 8:716, 717
kinds of forests: coniferous 8:716;
  deciduous 8:716
Lumber 10:979
Natural resources 12:1131-1133
plant disease 8:717
planting 8:716
reforestation 8:717
FORGET-ME-NOT 8:718
illus. 8:718
FORGING 8:718
FORMALDEHYDE 8:718
Fumigant 8:741
properties 8:718
uses 8:718
FORMULA 8:718-719
Compound 5:431
illus. 8:718
structural 8:719
Symbol, chemical 18:1713
FORSYTHIA 8:719
illus. 1:81; 8:719
FOSSIL FUELS 8:719
FOSSILS 8:719-723
Animals, classification of 1:92
Cave 4:357
Cenozoic Era 4:361-362
Coelacanth 5:417
Cuvier, Georges 5:472
Cycad 5:473
Evolution of man 7:654-659
exp. 8:722
fossil animals 8:723
fossil plant 8:722
Geologic time table 8:764-765
illus.: history 8:721; molds 8:720,
  722; petrified wood 8:720; three-
  toed horses 8:723; zebra 8:723
impressions 8:720
index fossils 8:721
Mammoth 11:1013
Mastodon 11:1028
molds and casts 8:720
original remains 8:720
Paleontology 13:1237-1238
Petrification 13:1270
replaced remains 8:720
Reptilia 15:1449-1450
Stratigraphy 17:1677
FOUNDING 8:723
Iron 10:913-915
FOUR-O'CLOCK 8:723
illus. 8:723
Night-blooming plants 12:1148-
  1149
FOWL 8:724-726
Animal husbandry 1:89-90
chicken 8:724; 4:378
duck 8:724
egg production 8:726
goose 8:724; 8:788
Hatchery 9:822
illus.: adult silver Cornish hen
  8:724; Beltsville white turkeys
  8:725; chicks 8:725; Cochin hen
  8:724; guinea hen 8:726; New
  Hampshire rooster 8:725; partridge 8:726; pheasant 8:726;
  Wyandotte cock 8:725; Wyandotte
  hen 8:725; young experimental
  breed turkeys 8:725
Peacock 13:1256
Pigeon 13:1293
poultry industry 8:726
special breeding 8:726
turkey 8:724; 18:1780
FOX 8:726-727
characteristics 8:726
illus. 7:643; 8:726; 19:1894

reproduction 8:727
Fox terrier, illus. 6:523
FOXGLOVE 8:727
Digitalis 6:513
illus.: false foxglove 8:727
Plants, medicinal 14:1328-1329
FRACTURE 8:727
compound 8:727
greenstick 8:727
simple 8:727
FRANCIUM 8:727
FRANCK, JAMES 8:727
Frankincense see **FOREST
PRODUCTS**
FRANKLIN, BENJAMIN 8:728
contributions to science 8:728
Gulf Stream 9:810
inventions 8:728
FREEZING POINT 8:728-729
Centigrade or Celsius 4:363
exp. 8:729
Ice 9:873
illus. 8:729
Liquid 10:968-970
Raoult's Law 15:1428-1429
Freon 7:695
FREQUENCY 8:730
FREUD, SIGMUND 8:730
FRICTION 8:729-731
Abrasives 1:14
Bearing 3:237
Brake 3:290
effect of velocity 8:731
exp. 8:730; 8:731
Falling bodies 7:670
laws of friction 8:731
Lubrication 10:979
Resistance 15:1452
rolling 8:731
sliding 8:731
Frigid zone 6:543
FRISCH, KARL VON 8:732
Lorenz, Konrad 10:978
FROG 8:732-733
characteristics 8:733
circulatory system 8:733
exp. 8:732
illus.: bullfrog 8:732; embryo
  6:597; 18:1753; embryonic devel-
  opment 6:594-595; metamorpho-
  sis 11:1052; tree 8:733
Metamorphosis 11:1052
protection 1:87
respiratory system 8:733
Tadpole 18:1715
Frond see **FERN**
Front see **AIR MASSES; CYCLONE;
WEATHER; WEATHER FORE-
CASTING**
Frontal lobe see **BRAIN**
FROST 8:733
exp. 8:733
FROSTBITE 8:734
FRUIT 8:734-736
Apple 2:123
Berry 3:246
Blackberry 3:256
Capsule 4:336
dry: achene 8:734; anthocarp
  8:735; capsule 8:735; caryopsis
  8:735; follicle 8:735; legume
  8:735; nut 8:735; samara 8:734;
  schizocarp 8:735
fleshy: berry 8:736; drupe 8:736;
  multiple 8:736; pome 8:736
Flower 7:693-694
Horticulture 9:856
illus.: almond 8:735; apple 8:735;
  banana 8:735; bean 8:735; bitter-

sweet 8:735; blackberry 8:734;
  blueberry 8:734; cherry 8:734;
  strawberry 8:735
Melon 11:1041
Nuts 12:1184
Parthenocarpy 13:1251
Peach 13:1255-1256
Seed 16:1524-1525
Shrub 16:1543-1544
Strawberry 17:1677
FRUIT FLY 8:736-737
exp. 8:737
Fly 7:696-697
gentic studies 8:736
Heredity 9:838
illus. 8:736
FSH (follicle stimulating hormone)
  see **ESTROUS CYCLE;
MENSTRUATION**
FUCHSIA 8:738
illus. 8:738
FUCUS 8:738
illus. 8:738
FUEL 8:738-740
Atomic (nuclear) fuel 8:739
Battery 3:233
Coal 5:413
Combustion 5:425
Forest products 8:712
fuel cell 8:740
heat energy 8:738
illus.: chemical reaction (burning)
  8:739; fuel cell 8:749; nuclear
  engine 8:739; solar energy 8:740
radiant energy 8:738
requirements 8:738
Rocket engine 15:1463-1467
Rocket propellant 15:1468-1469
solar energy 8:740
supply 8:739
Fuel cell see **BATTERY; ELECTRO-
CHEMISTRY; ELECTROLYSIS;
FUEL**
Fulcrum see **MACHINES, SIMPLE;
TORQUE**
FULLER'S EARTH 8:740
Clay 4:392
FULTON, ROBERT 8:740-741
FUMAROLE 8:741
FUMIGANT 8:741
Cyanide 5:472
Insecticides 9:883
Greenhouse 8:796-797
FUNGICIDES 8:741
FUNGUS 8:741-742
algae-like 8:742
Antibiotics 2:115-116
Bacteria 3:209
Bacteriology 3:210-211
Blight 3:267
characteristics 8:741
classification 8:741
club 8:742
Germ theory 8:773
illus. 8:742; 14:1322, 1325;
  18:1739
imperfect 8:742
Meningitis 11:1043
Microbe 11:1054
Mold 11:1081-1082
Morel 11:1096
Mushrooms 12:1124
Parasites 13:1247-1249
Plant diseases 14:1318-1319
Plants, classification of 14:1322-
  1327
reproduction 8:742
Ringworm 15:1459
Rot 15:1479

Rust 15:1484
sac 8:472
slime 8:742
varieties 8:741
Yeast 19:1888-1889
FUR 8:742
guard hair 8:742
illus. 8:742
Seal 16:1521
FURNACE 8:743
FUSE 8:743
exp. 8:743
Short circuit 16:1540
Fusion see **NUCLEAR SCIENCE GLOSSARY**
G 8:744
Gabbro see **ROCKS**
GABOR, DENNIS 8:744
GADOLINIUM 8:744
Gagarin, Yuri 5:450
GAILLARDIA 8:744
GAJDUSEK, DANIEL CARLETON 8:744
GALACTIC 8:744
GALAPAGOS ISLANDS 8:745
GALAXY 8:745
illus. 8:745
Interstellar communication 10:907-909
Milky Way 11:1062
Nebula 12:1136
GALE 8:745
GALEN 8:745
galenicals 8:745
Medicine 11:1038-1040
GALENA 8:746
illus. 8:746
Lead 10:947
Mineralogy 11:1067-1069
GALILEO 2:166; 8:746-747
Acceleration 1:17
Astronomy 2:166
Barometer 3:227-228
Copernicus, Nicolaus 5:447
illus. 8:746
Jupiter 10:928-929
Mechanics 11:1037-1038
Pendulum 13:1260-1261
pulselogia 8:746
GALL 8:747
GALLBLADDER 8:747; 6:513
Gallstones 8:748
Liver 10:972
GALLIUM 8:747
Gallon see **MEASUREMENT**
GALLSTONES 8:748
GALTON, SIR FRANCIS 8:748
GALVANI, LUIGI 8:748
illus. 8:748
Galvanic cell see **BATTERY**
GALVANOMETER 8:748-749
Ammeter 1:72
exp. 8:749
fixed coil 8:749
moving coil 8:749
Game preserve see **PRESERVES**
GAMETE 8:749
Ovum 13:1230
GAMETOPHYTE 8:749; 1:65
Liverworts 10:973-974
Moss 12:1108-1109
Spore formation 17:1653
Gametophyte generation, illus. 1:65
GAMMA GLOBULIN 8:750
Immunity 9:874
Gamma ray see **NUCLEAR SCIENCE GLOSSARY; RAY, GAMMA**
Gander see **FOWL; GOOSE**
GANGLION 8:750

GANGRENE 8:750
GANNET 8:750
GAR 8:750
GARBAGE 8:750
Leaching 10:947
Pollution 14:1347-1348
GARDENIA 8:750
GARDENING 8:751-753
Greenhouse 8:796-797
history 8:751
illus.: design 8:752; informal 8:751
indoor gardens 8:751
planning for flowers 8:752
planning vegetable gardens 8:753
rock gardens 8:751
Shrub 16:1543-1544
Sweet pea 18:1710
Vegetable 19:1807
vegetable gardens 8:752
Garibaldi, illus. 11:1019
GARLIC 8:753
illus. 8:753
GARNET 8:753
illus. 8:753; 11:1065
Garter snake see **SNAKES**
GAS 8:754-756
Air 1:42
Argon 2:134
Bernoulli, Daniel 3:245-246
Charles' Law 4:370-371
Condensation 5:437
density 8:754
Diffusion 6:509; 8:755
Dirigible 6:518
Elements 6:586-589
Expansion 7:661-662
exp. 8:754
explosions 8:755
Fluid 7:694
Fluorine 7:694
gas laws 8:756
Gay-Lussac's Gas Law 8:757
Heat of vaporization 9:830
illus. 8:754, 755; 11:1031
Ionization 10:912
kinetic theory 8:755; 10:934
Molecular theory 11:1083
Physical states and changes 13:1286-1287
Pressure 14:1361
properties 8:754
Raoult's Law 15:1428-1429
Rarefaction 15:1430
uses 8:756
White damp 19:1867
Gas laws 8:756
Gasoline engine, illus. 10:989, 991
Gasoline see **ENGINE; ETHYL; FUEL**
Gastric juice see **DIGESTIVE SYSTEM**
GASTROVASCULAR CAVITY 8:756
Gastrula see **EMBRYOLOGY**
Gatling gun, Illus. 19:1840
GAUGE 8:756
GAY-LUSSAC'S GAS LAW 3:287; 8:757
Gas 8:754-756
illus. 8:757
GAZELLE 8:757
illus. 8:757
GEAR 8:758
Gecko see **LIZARDS**
GEIGER COUNTER 8:758
Cloud chamber 5:408
illus. 8:758; 15:1409, 1411
Isotope 10:918
operation 8:758
Particle detector 13:1252

Pharmacology 13:1272-1274
Radiation detector 15:1411
Radiation, protection from 15:1413
GELATIN 8:758
GEM 8:759
Amethyst 1:71
Carat 4:336
Crystal 5:460
Diamond 6:507
Garnet 8:753
illus.: aquamarine 8:759; black opals 8:759; facet cut stone 8:759; golden beryl 8:759; malachite 8:759; tourmaline 8:759; rhodolite garnet 8:759
Mineral 11:1065-1067
Olivine 13:1209
Onyx 13:1209
Opal 13:1209-1210
Pearl 13:1256-1257
Quartz 14:1391-1392
Ruby 15:1483
Sapphire 15:1496
synthetic 8:759
Topaz 18:1760
Tourmaline 18:1762
GEMINI 8:760
illus. 8:760
mythology 8:760
Gemini spacecraft 17:1633
GENE 8:760
Chromosomes 4:385
Clubfoot 5:412
Dominance 6:525
Heredity 9:838
illus. 8:760
Locus 10:977
Mutation 12:1128
Nucleic acid 12:1178
GENERATOR 8:760-761
armature 8:761
Automobile 2:184-186
Commutator 5:429
Direct current 6:517
Dynamo 6:536
Electricity 6:566
Electromagnet 6:577
energy sources 8:761
Hydroelectric power 9:865-866
illus. 6:569, 572; 8:761
Turbine 18:1778-1779
Genetics see **FRUIT FLY; HER-EDITY; MENDEL, GREGOR JOHANN**
Genitals see **REPRODUCTIVE SYSTEMS**
Gentian see **WILD FLOWERS**
Genus see **ANIMALS, CLASSI-FICATION OF; PLANTS, CLASSIFICATION OF**
Geographic grid 8:762
GEOGRAPHY 8:761-763
Australia 2:177-181
cultural environment 8:761
Fauna 7:673
Flora 7:692
human geography 8:763
illus.: system of coordinates 8:763
Map-making 11:1016
mathematical 8:762
natural environment: mineral resources 8:762; climate 8:762; fauna 8:762; flora 8:762; ground water 8:762; relief 8:762; topography 8:762; type of soil 8:762
Natural resources 12:1131-1133
South America 16:1593-1597
Time zones 18:1751-1752
Topography 18:1760

GEOLOGIC TIME TABLE 8:764-765
Archaeopteryx 2:129
Archeozoic era 2:132
Cenezoic era 4:361-362; 8:765
Coal 5:412-413
Continent 5:444
Earth, early development of 6:545-547
Epoch 7:632
Era 7:634
Evolution 7:647-654
Evolution of man 7:654-659
Fauna 7:673
Flora 7:692
Geology 8:768-769
Glacial ages 8:779
illus.: chart 8:766-767; Cretaceous sea life 8:765; Middle Cambrian 8:764; Mississippian 8:764; Oligocene deposits 8:765; Permian sea 8:764; Pleistocene 8:765
Mesozoic Era 8:765; 11:1047
North America 12:1156-1160
Paleontology 13:1237-1238
Paleozoic era 8:764; 13:1239
Plants, classification of 14:1322-1327
Plants, tropical 14:1329-1331
Precambrian era 8:764
Proterozoic era 14:1377
GEOLOGY 8:768-769
age of earth 8:769
areas of study 8:768
Canyons 4:334
Cave 4:357
Continental drift 5:444
Earth, early development of 6:545-547
Earthquake 6:547
Erosion 7:635-636
Escarpment 7:636
Estuary 7:637
Faulting 7:673
Fiord 7:682
Folding 8:708
Geologic time table 8:764-765
Geophysics 8:772
illus. 8:769
importance of 8:768
Intrusion 10:910
Joints 10:924
Limnology 10:965-966
Mesa 11:1046
Moho 11:1080-1081
Moraine 11:1095
Mountains 12:1116-1117
Natural gas 12:1131
Plate tectonics 14:1334-1335
Plateau 14:1335
Quicksand 14:1392-1393
Rocks 15:1471-1474
Sinkhole 16:1550
Soil types 16:1573
Speleology 17:1644
Stratigraphy 17:1676-1677
Weathering 19:1858
GEOMETRY 8:770-772
basic terms and assumptions: axioms 8:770; basic definitions 8:770; postulates 8:770; primitives 8:770
deductive reasoning 8:770
geometric figures 8:771
Mathematics 11:1029-1030
Plane 14:1312
Pythagoras 14:1389
Solid 16:1581
Surveying 18:1707

GEOPHYSICS 8:772
GEOTHERMAL ENERGY 8:772
Geotropism see **TROPISM**
GERANIUM 8:772
Gardening 8:752
Geriatrics see **AGING**
GERM 8:773
Antibiotics 2:115-116
Antibody 2:116
Bacteria 3:209
Immunity 9:874
Microorganism 11:1054
Germ layer theory see **EMBRYOLOGY; HEREDITY; WEISMANN, AUGUST**
GERM THEORY 8:773
GERMANIUM 8:773
illus.: shared electrons 8:773
GERMINATION 8:774
exp. 8:774
Radicle 15:1416
GESTATION PERIOD 8:774
Animals, life span 1:97
chart 8:774
Elephant 6:591
Embryology 6:592-597
Horse 9:854
Pregnancy 14:1359
GEYSER 8:775
Geothermal energy 8:772
Hot springs 9:857
illus. 8:775
GIANT 8:775
Pituitary gland 14:1310
somatotropin 8:775
Giant star see **STARS**
GIAQUE, WILLIAM F. 8:775
GIBBON 8:776
Ape 2:121
communication 8:776
Gorilla 8:789
illus. 8:776
locomotion 8:776
Primates 14:1362-1363
reproduction 8:776
GIBBS, JOSIAH WILLARD 8:776
GILA MONSTER 8:776-777
illus. 8:776
Poison gland 14:1343
GILBERT, GROVE KARL 8:777
GILL 8:777
illus. 8:777
Lung 10:983-984
Metamorphosis 11:1052
GINGER 8:777
illus. 8:777
GINKGO 8:778
Gymnosperm 9:813
illus. 8:778; 9:812
GINSENG 8:778
illus. 8:778
GIRAFFE 8:778
illus. 1:34; 8:778
GIZZARD 8:778
Glacial acetic acid 1:19
GLACIAL AGES 8:779
Cenozoic Era 4:361-362
Earth, early development of 6:547
erosion 8:779
Evolution of man 7:654-659
Geologic time table 8:764-765
International Geophysical Year: Glaciers 9:892-893
maps 8:779
Moraine 11:1095
Pleistocene Epoch: Illinoisian 8:779; Kansan 8:779; Nebraskan 8:779; Wisconsin 8:779
Stone Age 17:1675

GLACIER 8:780
alpine 8:780
Cave 4:357
Cliff 4:394
continental 8:780
Esker 7:636
Evolution of man 7:654-659
Geology 8:768-769
Iceberg 9:874
illus. 8:768, 780
International Geophysical Year: Glaciers 9:892-893
Kaleidoscope 10:930
Kettle 10:932
Moraine 11:1095
Piedmont 8:780
Sea level 16:1517
Valley 18:1795
GLADIOLUS 8:780
illus. 8:780
GLAND 8:780
Glanders see **ANIMAL DISEASES**
Glandular fever see **MONONUCLEOSIS**
GLANDULAR TISSUE 8:780-781
Epithelial tissue 7:632
Gland 8:780
Thymus 18:1748
GLASER, DONALD 8:781
GLASS 8:781-782
history 8:781
illus.: handblowing 8:782
Magnifying power 11:1007
making 8:782
obsidian 8:781
Optical instruments 13:1214-1215
properties 8:781-782
Sand 15:1493
Silicon 16:1545
Staining 17:1656
Glass snake, illus. 10:975
Glasses see **LENS, MAN-MADE**
GLAUCOMA 8:782-783
Blindness 3:267
causes 8:782
treatment 8:782-783
Glenn, John H. see **SPACE TRAVEL**
Gliding joint see **JOINTS, SKELETAL**
GLOBE 8:783
GLOBULIN 8:783
GLOMAR CHALLENGER 8:783
illus. 9:895
International Oceanographic Decade 9:896
Oceanography 12:1190-1195
GLOXINIA 8:783
illus. 8:783
Violet 19:1815
Glucose see **SUGAR**
GLUTELIN 8:783
GLUTEN 8:783
Glycerol see **FATTY ACIDS**
GLYCOLYSIS 8:783; 10:938
GNAT 8:783-784
Gneiss see **ROCKS**
Gnetales 9:813
GNU 8:784
illus. 8:784
GOAT 8:784-785
Angora 8:784
Cashmere 4:347
illus.: Alpine buck 8:784; Angora 8:784; Black Nubian 8:784; Saanen 8:784; Toggenburg 8:784
Kashmir 8:784
nubian 8:784
reproduction 8:785
Sheep
Toggenburg 8:784

Goat, the see **CAPRICORNUS**
GODDARD, ROBERT HUTCHINGS
  8:785
GOITER 8:785
  exophthalmic 8:785
  nodular 8:785
  simple 8:785
GOLD 8:785-786
  Africa 1:36
  Carat 4:336
  illus.: in quartz vein 8:786; panned
    8:785; uses 8:786
  Mineral 11:1065-1067
  properties 8:786
  where found 8:786
Goldenrod see **WILD FLOWERS**
GOLDFINCH 8:786
GOLDFISH 8:786-787
  care of 8:786-787
  characteristics 8:786
  illus.: blue-finned veiltail 8:787;
    comet 8:787; fantail 8:787; lion-
    head 8:787; moor 8:787
  Tropical fish 18:1772-1773
  varieties 8:787
GOLDSCHMIDT, VICTOR MORITZ
  8:787
Golgi bodies see **CELLS**
GONAD 8:787; 15:1447
  Androgen 1:79
  Pituitary gland 14:1310
GONORRHEA 8:787; 19:1809
GOOGOL 8:787
GOOSE 8:788
  Fowl 8:724
  habitat 8:788
  illus. 1:25; 8:788
  varieties 8:788
GOOSEBERRY 8:788
  illus. 8:788
Gooseneck barnacle 5:459
GOPHER 8:788
  characteristics 8:788
  diet 8:788
  illus. 8:788
  reproduction 8:788
GORILLA 8:789
  Ape 2:121
  captivity 8:789
  communication 8:789
  habitat 8:789
  illus. 8:789; 19:1894
  Primates 14:1362-1363
GOURD 8:789
  illus. 8:789
GOUT 8:789
  Arthritis 2:140
  symptoms 8:789
  treatment 8:789
GRACKLE 8:790
  illus. 8:790
GRAFTING 8:790
  illus. 8:790
  methods 8:790
  purposes 8:790
Grain see **BARLEY; CEREAL
  GRAINS; CORN; GRASSES; RICE;
  RYE; WHEAT**
Gramicidin see **BACTERIOLOGY**
GRAND BANKS 8:791
  Gulf Sream 9:810
  North Atlantic Drift 12:1160
  Ocean 12:1188-1190
  Pelagic 13:1259
Grand Canyon see **NORTH
  AMERICA**
Granite see **ROCKS**
GRANULATION 8:791
  Inflammation 9:878-879

GRAPE 8:791
  illus: Concord 8:791; Niagara
    8:791; red Caco 8:791; vine
    8:791
Grapefruit see **CITRUS FRUITS**
GRAPHITE 8:792
  Carbon 4:338
GRASSES 8:792-793
  Bamboo 3:223
  Barley 3:226
  Citronella 4:390
  classification 8:792
  flowers 8:793
  illus.: buffalo grass 8:792; Indian
    8:792; Bermuda 8:792
  importance 8:792
  leaves 8:792
  Lupine 10:985
  Reed 15:1440
  roots 8:792
  Sorghum 16:1584
  stems 8:792
  Timothy 18:1752
GRASSHOPPER 8:793
  Animals, classification of 1:94
  Animals, life span 1:97
  characteristics 8:793
  Circulatory system 4:387
  classification 8:793
  illus. 1:96; 15:1454; katydid
    8:793; laying eggs 8:793; short-
    horned lubber 8:793
  Metamorphosis 11:1052
  reproduction 8:793
Grasshopper mouse 12:1117
GRAVEL 8:793
GRAVITY 8:794-795
  Air pressure 1:43
  Balance 3:213
  Earth 6:544-545
  Equilibrium 7:633
  exp.: center of gravity in human
    body 8:794; pull of gravity
    8:795
  Falling bodies 7:670
  Forces 8:710-711
  illus.: chart 8:795; earth compared
    with moon 8:795
  Inertia 9:877
  *International Geophysical Year: the
    Solid Earth* 9:894
  Inverse-square law 10:910-911
  Jupiter 10:928-929
  Mass 11:1027
  Moon 11:1092-1094
  Newton, Sir Isaac 12:1147
  Newton's Law of Universal
    Gravitation 8:794
  Pendulum 13:1260-1261
  Resistance 15:1452
  Siphon 16:1551
  Solar system 16:1575-1578
  weight 8:795; 19:1860
Great auk see **AUK; BIRDS,
  FLIGHTLESS**
Great Barrier Reef see **AUSTRALIA**
Great Basin Desert 5:496
GREAT CIRCLE 8:796
  illus. 8:796
  Map-making 11:1016
Great Lakes see **NORTH AMERICA**
Great swallower, illus. 11:1021
Greater dog see **CANIS MAJOR AND
  CANIS MINOR**
GREBE 8:796
  illus. 8:796
GREENHOUSE 8:796-797
  coldframes 8:797
  conservatory 8:797; 5:441
  construction 8:797

  forcing houses 8:797
  Gardening 8:751-753
  heating 8:796
  hotbeds 8:797
  illus. 8:797
  Jade (Plant) 10:920
  shading 8:796
  types 8:796
  uses 8:796
  ventilation 8:796
  warmhouse 8:797
  water 8:796
Greenockite 4:322
Greenwich see **TIME ZONES**
GREGARIOUS 8:797
Grenade see **BOMB; EXPLOSIVES**
Gristle see **CARTILAGE TISSUE**
GROSBEAK 9:807
  illus. 7:682; 9:807
Ground effect machines see **AIR-
  CUSHION VEHICLES**
GROUND (ELECTRIC) 9:807
GROUNDHOG 9:807
  characteristics 9:807
  habitat 9:807
  hibernation 9:807
  illus. 9:807
GROUNDWATER 9:807-808
  Leaching 10:946-947
GROUPER 9:808
GROUSE 9:808
  illus. 9:808
Grub 3:242
Guanaco 10:975
  illus. 16:1596
Guard hair 8:742
GUAVA 9:808
  illus. 9:808
Guided missile see **BOMB; MISSILE**
Guinea hen see **FOWL**
GUINEA PIG 9:808-809
  feeding of young 9:809
  habitat 9:808
  illus. 9:809
  laboratory uses 9:809
  reproduction 9:808-809
GULF 9:809
  map 9:809
GULF STREAM 9:809-810
  climatic control 9:810
  diagram 9:809
  Grand Banks 8:791
  Labrador Current 9:810
  North Atlantic Drift 9:810; 12:1160
  North Equatorial Current 9:809
  prevailing westerlies 9:810
  Sargassum 15:1497
  Sea level 16:1517
Gulf Stream Countercurrent
  5:470
GULL 9:810
  illus. 9:810
  Tern 18:1734-1735
Gulper, illus. 11:1021
Gum (anatomical) see **TEETH**
GUM ARABIC 9:810
GUM (BOTANICAL) 9:810
GUN 9:810
  Gunpowder 9:811
GUNPOWDER 9:811
  composition 9:811
  hazards of making 9:811
  Weapons 19:1838
GUPPY 9:811
  characteristics 9:811
  classification 9:811
  exp.: raising guppies 9:811
  Oviviparous 13:1230
  reproduction 9:811
  Tropical fish 18:1772-1773

GYMNOSPERM 9:812-813
  Cone 5:439
  conifers 9:812
  cycad 9:812
  Embryophyta 7:607-608
  evolution 9:812
  Ginkgo 8:778; 9:813
  Gnetales 9:813
  illus.: 14:1327; cycad 9:812; gink-
    go 9:812; hemlock 9:812; ponder-
    osa pine 9:812
  Mesozoic Era 11:1047
  Pine 13:1295-1296
  Plants, classification of 14:1322-
    1327
  Polycotyledon 14:1347-1348
  Seed 15:1524-1525
  Softwood 16:1571-1572
GYPSUM 9:813
  Calcium 4:323
  Cement 4:361
  illus. 9:819
  Plaster 14:1332
  Plaster of Paris 14:1332
Gyroplane see **AUTOGIRO**
GYROSCOPE 9:813
  aid in navigation 9:813
  Autogiro 2:181
  Compass 5:430
  gimbals 9:813
  illus.: 9:813
  missiles 9:813
  Navigation 12:1134-1135
  rotor 9:813
  satellites 9:813
  Sperry, Elmer Ambrose 17:1645
HABER PROCESS 9:814
  Ammonia 1:72
  illus. 9:814
  Nitrogen 12:1150
HABITAT 9:814
HABITUATION 9:815
HADDOCK 9:815
  illus. 9:815
HAFNIUM 9:815
HAHN, OTTO 9:815
HAHNIUM 9:815-816
HAIL 9:816
HAIR 9:816
  color 9:816
  curly 9:816
  purposes 9:816
  Skin 16:1556-1557
  Skin modification 16:1558
  straight 9:816
Hair follicle see **SKIN**
HALE, GEORGE ELLERY 9:816-817
HALF-LIFE 9:817
  Atom 2:173
  diagram 9:817
  Radioactive elements 15:1420-
    1421
  Rubidium-strontium dating method
    15:1483
Halibut see **FLOUNDER**
Hall, Charles Martin 9:818
  Aluminum 1:68
HALL-HEROULT PROCESS 9:818
  illus. 9:818
HALLEY, EDMUND 9:817
Halley's comet 5:426
HALOGEN 9:818
  Chlorine 4:381
  Iodine 10:911
HAMSTER 9:818-819
  habitat 9:818
  illus. 9:818
  laboratory uses 9:819
  reproduction 9:818

Hangar see **AVIATION**
Hansen's disease see **LEPROSY**
Hard water see **WATER**
Hardening of the arteries see
  ARTERIOSCLEROSIS
HARDNESS SCALE 9:819
  exp. 9:819
  illus.: apatite 9:819; calcite
    9:819; corundum 9:819; diamond
    9:819; feldspar 9:819; fluorite
    9:819; gypsum 9:819; quartz
    9:819; talc 9:819; topaz 9:819
  Mineral 11:1065-1067
  Mineralogy 11:1067-1069
  Rocks 15:1471-1474
  Tourmaline 18:1762
HARDWOOD 9:820
  beech 9:820
  deciduous 9:820
  ebony 9:820
  Forest products 8:712
  illus.: black walnut 9:820; Euro-
    pean ash 9:820; white oak 9:820
  Ironwood 10:916
  mahogany 9:820
  maple 9:820
  oak 9:820
  teak 9:820
  uses 9:820
  wood 9:820
Hare see **RABBIT**
HARELIP 9:821
  Cleft palate 4:394; 9:821
HARVEST 9:821
Harvestman see **DADDY LONGLEGS**
HARVEY, WILLIAM 9:821
  Animal diseases 1:89
  Galen 9:745
  illus. 9:821
  Medicine 11:1038-1040
HATCHERY 9:822
HAWK 9:822
  Birds of prey 3:263
  characteristics 9:822
  Falcon 7:669
  illus. 9:822
HAWORTH, WALTER 9:822
HAWTHORNE 9:822
  illus. 9:822
Hay see **GRASSES**
HAY FEVER 9:823
HAZE 9:823
Hazelnut see **NUTS**
HEADACHE 9:823
Health see **MALNUTRITION; NUTRI-
  TION; PURIFICATION; SANITA-
  TION; SEWAGE DISPOSAL;
  VITAMIN; VITAMIN DEFICIENCY**
HEART 9:823-825
  Artery 2:139
  Blue baby 3:272
  Bundle of His 9:825
  Circulatory system 4:387-389
  Diastole 6:508
  Digitalis 6:513
  Electrocardiograph 6:573
  exp. 9:823
  fish 9:823-824
  frog 9:824
  Heart murmur 9:826
  Heartbeat 9:826
  human 9:824
  illus.: 14:1385; 18:1795; fish
    9:824; frog 9:824; human 9:825;
    lizard 9:824
  mitral valve 9:824
  Muscle tissue 12:1123
  nodal tissue 9:825
  pacemaker 9:825

  pericardium 9:824; 13:1265
  Rheumatic fever 15:1457
  Richard, Dickenson Woodruff
    15:1459
  Stethoscope 17:1672
  Thrombosis 18:1747
  Vein 19:1808-1809
  vena cava 9:824
HEART MURMUR 9:826
  functional 9:826
  Heart 9:823-825
  pathological 9:826
HEARTBEAT 9:826
HEARTWOOD 9:826
  illus. 9:826
  Rosewood 15:1478
  Sapwood 15:1496
HEAT 9:826-827
  Absolute zero 1:15
  Calorie 4:325
  Conduction 5:438
  Conductor 5:439
  Convection 5:445
  Dynamics 6:536
  Endothermic 7:610
  Energy 8:612-617; 9:827
  Exothermic 7:661
  exp.: conductors 9:827
  Fuel 8:738-740
  Furnace 8:743
  Heat barrier 9:828
  Heat of fusion 9:828
  Heat of reaction 9:829
  illus.: British Thermal Unit 9:827;
    calorie 9:827
  Insulator 9:887
  kinetic theory 9:827
  Physical states and changes
    13:1286-1287
  Physics 13:1287-1288
  temperature 9:826
  Thermometer 18:1743-1744
  Thermostat 18:1744-1745
  Trade winds 18:1764
HEAT BARRIER 9:828
  illus.: thermos bottle 9:828
  Insulator 9:887
  Refrigeration 15:1441-1442
HEAT OF FUSION 9:828
  Calorimetry 4:326
  Freezing point 8:728
  illus. 9:828
  Thermochemistry 18:1740
HEAT OF REACTION 9:829
  Chemical change 4:371-372
  illus.: body states 9:829; calori-
    meter 9:829
  Thermochemistry 18:1740
HEAT OF VAPORIZATION
  9:830
  Calorimetry 4:326
  Heat 9:826-827
  illus. 9:830
  Thermochemistry 18:1740
HEATHER 9:830
  illus. 16:1545
  Laurel 10:945
Heavy hydrogen see **DEUTERIUM;
  ELEMENTS; HEAVY WATER;
  HYDROGEN**
HEAVY METALS 9:830
  pollutants 9:830
HEAVY WATER 9:830-831; 5:497
  Hectares 9:716
Hedgehog see **INSECTIVORE**
HEIMLICH'S CHOKE MANEUVER
  9:831
  Artificial respiration 2:143
  cafe coronary 9:831

HELICOPTER 9:831-832
Aeronautics 1:131
Autogiro 2:181
control 9:831
Convertiplane 5:445
engine 9:832
illus. 9:832
uses 9:831
Heliochronometer, illus. 5:407
HELIOGRAPH 9:832
HELIOTROPE 9:833
illus. 9:833
Heliotropism see **TROPISM**
HELIUM 9:833
discovery 9:833
Hydrogen 9:866
properties 9:833
sources 9:833
Helldiver see **GREBE**
HEMATITE 9:833
illus. 9:833
Magnetite 10:995-997
Hemisphere see **EARTH**
HEMLOCK 9:834
illus. 9:812; 9:834
Hemoglobin see **BLOOD**
HEMOPHILIA 9:834
Heredity 9:840
HEMP 9:834
Hen see **CHICKEN; FOWL**
HENCH, PHILIP 9:834-835
HENRY, JOSEPH 9:835
Electromagnet 6:577
illus. 9:835
Morse, Samuel Finley Breese
11:1097
Radio 15:1416-1418
Hepatica see **WILD FLOWERS**
HEPATITIS 9:835
infectious 9:835
Jaundice 10:921
Mononucleosis 11:1090
serum 9:835
toxic 9:835
HERB 9:836
Caraway 4:336
Catnip 4:356
Celery 4:358
Clematis 4:394
Composite flower 5:431
Dill 6:513
Garlic 8:753
Ginger 8:777
Ginseng 8:778
herbal 9:836
herbalist 9:836
herbicide 9:836
illus. 9:836
Mustard 12:1127-1128
Oregano 13:1222
Parsley 13:1251
Parsnip 13:1251
Peppermint 13:1263
Petunia 13:1272
Philodendron 13:1275
Potentilla 14:1355
structure 9:836
Sunflower 17:1673
Tarragon 18:1718
uses 9:836
Watercress 19:1832
Weed control 19:1858-1859
HERBACEOUS 9:836
Dahlia 5:475
HERBARIUM 9:836
HERBICIDE 9:836
HERBIVORE 9:836-837; 3:216
gnawing animals 9:837
hoofed animals 9:837

HERCULES 9:837
illus. 9:837
mythology 9:837
HEREDITY 9:837-841
Acquired characteristics 1:23-24
Albino 1:55
alleles 9:839
Alternation of generations 1:65
Blood types 3:271
Botany 3:285
Breeding 3:293
cross breeding 9:841
Dominance 6:525; 9:838, 840
Fowl 8:724-726
Fruit fly 8:737
Galton, Sir Francis 8:748
Gene 8:760
gene flow 9:841
genes and evolution 9:841
genetic drift 9:841
Hemophilia 9:834
Hybridization 9:862
illus.: chromosome (banded) 9:838;
inheritance of dominant character-
istics 9:840; Mendelian inheri-
tance 9:839; inheritance 9:837-
838; of sex 9:840
Locus 10:977
Mendel, Gregor Johann 11:1042
Mendel's experiments 9:838-839
Mitosis and meiosis 11:1076-1078
Multiple birth 12:1119
mutation 9:841; 12:1128
natural selection 9:841
Nucleic acid 12:1178
Nucleoprotein 12:1178-1179
physical traits 9:837
Plant 14:1314-1317
recessive 9:838; 15:1438
Rh factor 15:1456
sex linkage: color blindness 9:840;
hemophilia 9:840; 16:1530-1531
symbols and diagrams 9:839
Zoology 19:1895-1896, 1897
Zygote 19:1896
HERMAPHRODITE 9:841
animal reproduction 1:87
Monoecious 11:1090
Hermit crab, illus. 5:459
HERNIA 9:841
Heroin see **MORPHINE**
HERON 9:841-842
Egret 6:560
habitat 9:841
illus. 9:842
reproduction 9:841-842
Heroult, Paul Louis Touissant 9:818
Aluminum 1:68
HERRING 9:842
Alewife 1:57
Anchovy 1:79
illus. 9:842
Sardine 15:1497
HERSCHEL, WILLIAM 9:842
HERTZ 9:842
HERZBERG, GERHARD 9:842
HESS, VICTOR 9:842
Heterosis 9:862
HIBERNATION 9:843
Bat 3:230
Bear 3:236
Estivation 7:637
exp.: frog 9:843
Fat, adipose tissue 7:672
Groundhog 9:807
physiological effects 9:843
Sleep 16:1560
HIBISCUS 9:843-844
illus. 14:1331; 16:1543

HICCOUGH 9:844
HICKORY 9:844
illus. 9:844
Hide see **LEATHER**
HIGH FIDELITY 9:844
HIGH PRESSURE CENTER 9:844
Air masses 1:46
Indian summer 9:876
map 9:844
HILL, ARCHIBALD VIVIAN 9:844
Himalaya Mountains see **ASIA**
Hindenburg 1:54
Hinge joint see **JOINTS, SKELETAL**
HIPPOCRATES 9:845
Galen 8:745
Medicine 11:1038-1040
HIPPOPOTAMUS 9:845
characteristics 9:845
habitat 9:845
reproduction 9:845
Histamine see **ALLERGY**
HISTOGRAM 9:845
illus. 9:845
HISTOLOGY 9:846-849
Anatomy 1:76
Bone 3:282-283
Botany 3:284-285
Cartilage tissue 4:346
Cytology 5:474
Epithelial tissue 7:632
exp.: making tissue slides 9:848
Fibrous tissue 7:679
Glandular tissue 8:781
illus.: main tissues of the body
9:847
Microtome 11:1058
Muscle tissue 12:1122-1123
Organ 13:1222
organ systems: circulatory 9:849;
digestive 9:848-849; gland 9:849;
respiratory 9:849; skin 9:849
Ovary 13:1229
Physiology 13:1289-1291
Secretion 16:1523
Skeleton 16:1552-1555
Skin modification 16:1558
specialization 9:846
Staining 17:1656
Testis 18:1736-1737
Tissue culture 18:1753-1754
tissue in body: blood 9:848; epi-
thelial 9:846; muscle 9:846; ner-
vous 9:846; sustentative 9:846
Vitamin 19:1817-1818
Histones 4:385
Hive see **BEE**
HIVES 9:849
Eczema 6:556
Hog see **PIG**
Hoist, illus. 10:989
HOLLY 9:850
illus. 9:850
HOLLYHOCK 9:850
illus. 9:850
HOLMIUM 9:850
HOLOGRAM 9:850
Gabor, Dennis 8:744
HOMEOSTASIS 9:850-851
advanced plants 9:851
Equilibrium 7:633
human body 9:851
Obesity 12:1187
one-called plants and animals
9:851
Physiology 13:1289-1291
Stress 17:1677-1678
HOMO SAPIENS 1:91; 9:851
HOMOGENEOUS 9:851
HOMOGENIZATION 9:851

Honeydew melon see **MELON**
Honey see **BEE**
HONEYSUCKLE 9:851
Elderberry 6:562
illus. 9:851
Snowberry 16:1570
HOOF 9:852
even-toed 9:852
illus. 18:1785; cattle 9:852; deer
  9:852; horse 9:852; rhinoceros
  9:852
odd-toed 9:852
Pig 13:1293
Hoof and mouth disease see **ANIMAL
DISEASES**
HOOKE, ROBERT 9:852
Hooke's Law 9:852
HOOKWORM 9:852
Parasites 13:1247-1249
HOP 9:852
HOREHOUND 9:853
illus. 9:853
HORMONE 9:853
Adrenalin 1:28
Atrophy 2:174
Biochemistry 3:251
Endocrine glands 7:610
Estrogen 7:637
Giant 8:775
Glandular tissue 8:781
Islets of Langerhans 10:917
Multiple birth 12:1119
Progesterone 14:1371
Puberty 14:1383
HORMONES, PLANT 9:853
auxins 9:853
cytokinins 9:853
ethylene 9:853
florigen 9:853
gibberellins 9:853
Gland 8:780
Horticulture 9:856-857
illus.: plants treated 9:853
HORN 9:853-854
illus.: cow 9:853; goat 9:853;
  horned toad 9:853; rhinoceros
  9:853; sheep 9:853; triceratops
  9:853
Skin modification 16:1558
Hornblende see **ROCKS**
Horned toad see **LIZARD**
Hornet see **WASP**
Hornworts, illus. 4:308
Horoscope see **ASTROLOGY**
HORSE 9:854-855
breeding 9:854
diet 9:855
Donkey 6:525
evolution 9:854-855
filly 9:854
foal 9:854
gelding 9:854
illus.: evolution 7:648; Hackney
  9:854; Palomino 9:854; prehistoric
  7:649; Shire 9:854; Standard-bred
  racing 9:855
locomotion 9:855
mare 9:854
Mustang 12:1127
stallion 9:854
yearling 9:854
HORSE CHESTNUT 9:855
illus. 9:855
HORSE LATITUDES 9:855; 18:1764
HORSEPOWER 9:856
Dynamometer 6:537
illus. 9:856
Motor 12:1114-1116
Work 19:1880

HORSETAILS 9:856
illus. 7:607; 9:856; 18:1763
HORTICULTURE 9:856-857
Agriculture 1:38-41
Arboretum 2:127-128
Breeding 3:293
Burbank, Luther 4:316
Economic botany 6:554
Fruit 8:736
illus.: new wheat strains 9:857
research 9:857
Hotbed 8:797
HOT SPRINGS 9:857
illus. 9:857
Hothouse see **GREENHOUSE**
Housefly see **FLY**
HUCKLEBERRY 9:858
illus. 9:858
HUMAN BEING 9:858
Caucasoid 9:858
Evolution of man 7:654-659
Homo sapiens 9:851
Mongoloid 9:858
Negroid 9:858
Race 14:1396
Humerus see **SKELETON**
HUMIDITY 9:858-859
absolute 9:858
diagram 9:858; capacity of air
  9:859
Hygrometer 9:870-871
relative 9:858
Vapor 18:1796
Weather 19:1843-1846
HUMMINGBIRD 9:859
Bird nests 3:259
illus. 9:859
Pollination 14:1346-1347
Humor, aqueous and vitreous see
EYE
HUMUS 9:859
Loam 10:975
HURRICANE 9:859-860
Cyclone 5:473
eye 9:860
forecasting 9:859-860
illus.: eye 9:860; 19:1849;
  tracking by radar 9:860
typhoon 9:860; 18:1784
Husbandry see **ANIMAL
HUSBANDRY**
HUXLEY, JULIAN SORREL 9:860
HUXLEY, THOMAS HENRY 9:860
Huxley, Julian Sorrell 9:860
HUYGENS, CHRISTIAN 9:861
HYACINTH 9:861
illus. 9:861
Stem, underground 17:1668-1669
HYBRIDIZATION 9:861-862; 1:40
allele 9:861
Burbank, Luther 4:316
Chicken 4:378
Economic botany 6:554
Fruit 8:736
Heredity 9:837-841
Horticulture 9:856-857
hybrid vigor 9:862
illus.: corn 9:861; mule 9:862
Mendel, Gregor Johann 9:861
Mule 12:1118
Pedigree 13:1258
Peony 13:1262
HYDRA 9:862
Animals, classification of 1:95
Coelenterata 5:417-419
diet 9:862
exp.: attacking food 9:863
Gastrovascular cavity 8:756
habitat 9:862

illus. 9:862; 15:1446; digestive
  system 6:510; reproduction
  15:1445
Nematocyst 12:1138
reproduction 9:862; 15:1445
HYDRANGEA 9:863
illus. 9:863
HYDRATES 9:863
HYDRAULIC ACTION 9:864
illus. 9:864
Machinery 10:989-991
Pascal's Law 9:864
Pressure 14:1361
Hydraulic press, illus. 10:989
HYDROCARBON 9:864; 13:1222-
1223
Biochemistry 3:251
Carbon 4:337-338
ethane 9:864
Ethyl 7:638
Fossil fuels 8:719
methane 9:864; 11:1053
Methane series 11:1053
Natural gas 12:1131
Oil wells 13:1207-1208
Paraffin 13:1244; 9:864
Silicone 16:1547
HYDROCHLORIC ACID 9:865
aid in digestion 1:20
Chloride 4:380
Chlorine 4:381
Digestive system 6:512
Hydrocyanic acid 1:64
Hydrocyanic gas 8:741
HYDROELECTRIC POWER 9:865-
866
Dam 5:480; 9:866
illus.: dam 9:865; installation
  9:866; turbine 9:865
Turbine 18:1778-1779
waterfall 9:866; 19:1835
HYDROGEN 9:866-867
Aeronautics 1:30
Airships 1:54
Deuterium 5:497
Hydrocarbon 9:864
illus.: forms 6:586
Nitrogen cycle 12:1150-1151
production 9:866
Protein 14:1376-1377
Rocket engine 15:1463
HYDROGEN BOND 9:867
Hydrogen chloride 9:865
Hydrogen peroxide see **HYDROGEN;
OXIDE**
HYDROID COLONY 9:867
polymorphism 9:867
HYDROLYSIS 9:867
Hydrogen 9:866-867
Ionization 10:912
HYDROMETER 9:867-868
Hydrophobia see **RABIES**
HYDROPONICS 9:868; 1:39
exp. 9:868
HYDROXIDE 9:869
HYDROXYL 9:869
HYENA 9:869; 1:13
illus. 9:869
HYGIENE 9:869
care of teeth 9:869
drinking water 9:869
exercise 9:869
nutrition 9:869
HYGROMETER 9:870-871
chemical 9:871
dew-point 9:871
direct-reading 9:871
exp. 9:870
hygrographs 9:871

Hyperopia see **FARSIGHTEDNESS**
Hyperplasia 9:871
HYPERTENSION 3:270; 9:871
  Ophthalmoscope 13:1212
HYPERTONIC SOLUTION 9:871
HYPERTROPHY 9:871
  Muscular dystrophy 12:1123
  Skin modification 16:1558
Hypocotyl see **SEED**
HYPODERMIC 9:872
  illus. 9:872
  needle 9:872
  syringe 9:872
HYPOTENSION 9:872; 3:271
HYPOTHALAMUS 9:872
  illus. 9:872
  oxytocin 9:872
  vaso presin 9:872
Hypothesis see **SCIENTIFIC METHOD**
HYPOTONIC SOLUTION 9:872
IBIS 9:873
  illus. 9:873
IBEX 9:873
  Goat 8:785
  illus.: 7:643; 9:873
ICE 9:873
  exp. effect of salt 9:873
  Refrigeration 15:1441-1442
Ice ages see **GLACIAL AGES; GEOLOGIC TIME TABLE**
ICEBERG 9:874
  illus. 9:874
  International Geophysical Year: Glaciers 9:893
Ichneuman fly 14:1375
Igneous rock see **ROCKS**
Ignition see **AUTOMOBILE; ENGINE**
Iguana 4:369
Ileum 6:511
Ilex, illus. 16:1545
Ilium see **SKELETON**
Illumination see **BULB, ELECTRIC; LIGHT**
IMMUNITY 9:874
  Diphtheria 6:517
  Inflammation 9:878
  Nephritis 12:1138-1139
  Serum 16:1530
  Transplant 18:1770
Impala see **ANTELOPE**
Impatiens see **TOUCH-ME-NOT**
IMPETIGO 9:874
  causes 9:874
  symptoms 9:874
  treatment 9:874
Impetus see **INERTIA; MOTION**
IMPRINTING 9:874
IMPULSE 9:875
Inbreeding see **HYBRIDIZATION**
Incandescent lamp see **BULB, ELECTRIC**
Inchworm see **WORMS**
Incisor see **TEETH**
Inclined plane see **MACHINES, SIMPLE**
INCUBATOR 9:875-876
  exp. hatching baby chicks 9:875
  Hatchery 9:822
  human 9:875-876
  poultry 9:875
Incus 6:539
Index fossil see **FOSSILS; PALEONTOLOGY**
Indian cucumber-root, illus. 11:1090
Indian paintbrush see **WILD FLOWERS**
INDIGESTION 9:876

Indigo see **DYE**
INDIUM 9:876
INDUCTANCE COIL 9:876
INDUCTION 9:876-877
  Armature 2:138
  illus.: electric 9:876
  Inductance coil 9:876
  Magnet 10:995-997
  Radio 15:1416-1418
  Telegraph 18:1724
Inelastic collision see **MOMENTUM**
Inert gas see **ELEMENTS; GAS**
INERTIA 9:877
  Gas 8:754
  Momentum 11:1088
  Newton's Law of Motion 9:877
  Resistance 15:1452
  Rocket sled 15:1470
Infantile paralysis see **POLIOMYELITIS**
INFECTION 9:877-878
  Antiseptic 2:118
  Blood count 3:270
  blood poisoning 9:878
  Inflammation 9:879
  Influenza 9:879
  Impetigo 9:874
  Lymphatic system 10:986-987
  Mange 11:1013
  Mastoid 11:1028
  Pain 13:1235
  symptoms 9:877
  Tooth decay 18:1759-1760
  Wound 19:1882
INFINITY 9:878
  illus. 9:878
INFLAMMATION 9:878-879
  Acne 1:22
  Appendix 2:123
  Astringent 2:154
  Blood 3:268-269
  body defenses 9:878
  Infection 9:877-878
INFLUENZA 9:879
  strains 9:879
  symptoms 9:879
  vaccines 9:879
INFRARED ASTRONOMICAL SATELLITE (IRAS) 9:879
  extragalactic research 9:879
  galactic astronomy 9:879
Infrared ray see **ELECTROMAGNETIC SPECTRUM; RAY, INFRARED**
Inheritance of characteristics see **HEREDITY**
Injection see **DRUGS; HYPODERMIC**
INK 9:879-880
  electrostatic 9:880
  exp. homemade 9:880
  newspaper black 9:880
  printing 9:880
  writing and drawing 9:880
Inoculation see **IMMUNITY; VACCINE**
INORGANIC 9:880
INSECTA 9:880-882
  Ants 2:120
  Aphid 2:122
  Arthropoda 2:140-142
  Autotomy 2:190
  Bees 3:239-240
  Beetles 3:242-243
  body structure 9:880-882
  Bugs 4:311-312
  Butterflies 3:317-318
  Caddis fly 4:321
  Chitin 4:380
  complete metamorphosis 9:882

  Cricket 5:457
  Dragonfly 6:527
  Entomology 7:628
  exp. collecting 9:882
  Flea 7:689
  Fly 7:696-697
  Gnat 8:783-784
  Grasshopper 8:793
  illus.: ant 9:881; caterpillar 9:881; cockroach 9:881; firebrat 9:881; Japanese beetle 9:881; milkweed bug 9:881; reproductive systems 15:1446
  incomplete metemorphosis 9:882
  life cycles 9:882
  Louse 10:978
  Mandible 11:1013
  Molting 11:1087
  Mosquito 12:1107
  nervous system 9:882
  Protective coloration 14:1375-1376
  Silverfish 16:1549
  Spiracle 17:1649
  Thorax 18:1745
  Walking stick 19:1827
  Wasp 19:1829
INSECTICIDES 9:883
  Acetic acid 1:19
  contact poisons 9:883
  Fumigant 8:741; 9:883
  Greenhouse 8:796-797
  illus. 9:883
  Moths 12:1110
  Nicotine 12:1148
  Poison 14:1342
  spray insecticides 9:883
  stomach poisons 9:883
INSECTIVORE 9:884
  aardwolf 9:884
  habitat 9:884
  hedgehog 9:884
  illus.: hedgehog 9:884; shrew 9:884
  Mammalia 11:1011-1012
  odor 9:884
  shrew 9:884; 16:1542
Insectivorous plants see **PLANTS, INSECTIVOROUS**
INSIGHT 9:884
INSOLUBLE 9:884
INSPIRATION 9:884
INSTINCT 9:884
INSTRUMENT LANDING SYSTEM 9:885
  Aeronautics 1:30-31
  Airplane 1:52-53
  Aviation 2:191-197
  illus.: pigeon 9:884
  Direction finder 6:517
  Flight, principles of 7:690-691
  illus. 9:885
  Instrument panel 9:886
  Navigation 12:1134-1135
  Radar 14:1396-1397
INSTRUMENT PANEL 9:885-886
  Aeronautics 1:30-31
  Airplane 1:52-53
  Aviation 2:191-197
  engine and system instruments 9:886
  flight instruments 9:885-886
  Flight, principles of 7:690-691
  illus.: 9:885, 886
  Navigation 12:1134-1135
  navigation instruments 9:885-886
INSULATOR 9:887
INSULIN 9:887
  Animal husbandry 1:89
  Banting, Frederick Grant 3:224
  Diabetes 5:497

Hormone 9:853
Islets of Langerhans 10:917
Pancreas 13:1240
Vigneaud, Vincent du 19:1813-1814
Intake valve see **ENGINE**
Integer see **ARITHMETIC; INFINITY; NUMBER SYSTEMS**
INTEGUMENTARY SYSTEM 9:887
Intercontinental Ballistic Missile 11:1074
Interdependence see **BALANCE OF NATURE; ECOSYSTEM**
Internal combustion engine 7:621-623
Internal combustion engine see **AUTOMOBILE; ENGINE**
INTERNAL MEDICINE 9:887
internists 9:887
responsibilities
INTERNATIONAL BUREAU OF WEIGHTS AND MEASURES 9:887-888
International System of Units 9:896
INTERNATIONAL CONTROL OF NATURAL RESOURCES 9:888-889
endangered species 9:888-889
international agreements: fur seals 9:889; International Whaling Commission 9:889; monitoring 9:889
Whale 19:1865
Wilderness 19:1871, 1874
INTERNATIONAL DATE LINE 9:889
illus. 9:889
Measurement 11:1033-1036
Time zones 18:1751-1752
International Geophysical Cooperation 9:891
INTERNATIONAL GEOPHYSICAL YEAR 9:890-892
areas of study 9:890
Geology 8:768
illus.: Soviet scientist 9:890
organization 9:890
Poles, North and South 14:1345
Sun 17:1686-1891
INTERNATIONAL GEOPHYSICAL YEAR: ANTARTICA 9:890-891
illus. 9:891
International Geophysical Cooperation 9:891
INTERNATIONAL GEOPHYSICAL YEAR: ATMOSPHERE 9:891-892
illus. 9:893
satellite program 9:892
sun 9:891
Van Allen belt 9:892
INTERNATIONAL GEOPHYSICAL YEAR: GLACIERS 9:892-893
Iceberg 9:874
INTERNATIONAL GEOPHYSICAL YEAR: THE SOLID EARTH 9:894
crust 9:894
gravity 9:894
illus. 9:894
mantle 9:894
Moho 11:1080-1081
INTERNATIONAL HYDROLOGICAL DECADE 9:894-895
areas for study 9:894-895
INTERNATIONAL OCEANOGRAPH-IC DECADE 9:895-896
Law of the Sea Conference 9:896
pollution 9:895

INTERNATIONAL SYSTEM OF UNITS 9:896-897; 10:985
basis of units: amount of substance 9:896; electric current 9:896; force 9:896; length 9:896; light intensity 9:896; mass 9:896; temperature 9:896; time 9:896
illus.: 9:896, 897
International Bureau of Weights and Measures 9:888
Mole 11:1082
prefixes 9:897
temperature scales 18:1733
Internode 4:309
INTERSTELLAR COMMUNICATION 10:907-909
illus.: Cygnus A galaxy 10:909; radio telescope 10:907; size of outer space 10:909; optical telescope 10:909; stars and distance away 10:908
international cooperation 10:909
life on other planets 10:907
Milky Way 11:1062
problems 10:908
Radio telescope 10:908; 15:1419
Sound interference 16:1591
Stars 17:1660-1662
Intestine see **DIGESTIVE SYSTEM**
INTRAVENOUS 10:909
INTRUSION 10:910
illus. 10:910
Lava 10:945
Volcano 19:1822-1823
INVENTION 10:910
INVERSE SQUARE LAW 10:910-911
astronomy 10:911
Candela 4:332
gravity 10:910
illus. 10:910
Light 10:962
INVERTEBRATE 10:911
Chordata 4:383
Involuntary muscle see **MUSCLE SYSTEM; MUSCLE TISSUE**
Io moth, illus. 14:1375
IODINE 10:911
ION 10:911-912
Chemistry 4:373-377
Electrolysis 6:575-576
Electron borrowing 6:580
illus. 10:911
in solution 10:912
Ionization 10:912
Molecular theory 11:1083
illus. 14:1375
properties 10:911, 912
solubility 10:912
Water 19:1830-1831
IONIZATION 10:912
anode 2:109
International Geophysical Year: Atmosphere 9:891-892
Ion 10:911-912
Millikan's electronic charge 11:1063
Ionosphere see **ATMOSPHERE**
IRIDESCENCE 10:912
IRIDIUM 10:913
IRIS (PLANT) 10:913
Gardening 8:752
illus. 10:913
Iris (visual) see **EYE**
Irish moss see **THALLOPHYTES**
IRON 10:913-915
beneficiation 10:914
cast iron 10:915

deposits: MesabisRange 10:913; St. Johns, Newfoundland 10:913; Steep Rock Lake, Ontario 10:913
Hematite 9:833
illus.: loading ore 10:914; open pit mine 10:914; pig iron ladle 10:915; varieties of ore 10:914
Magnetite 10:997
Open pit mine 13:1212
Ore 13:1221
pig iron 10:914
properties 10:913
slag 10:915
Steel 17:1666-1668
wrought iron 10:915
IRON LUNG 10:915
illus. 10:915
Poliomyelitis 14:1346
IRONWOOD 10:916
illus. 10:916
IRRADIATION 10:916
IRRIGATION 10:916
illus. 10:916
ISLAND 10:917
Archipelago 2:133
Atoll 2:172
continental 10:917
high-water mark 10:917
illus.: volcano 10:917
Mid-Atlantic Ridge 11:1058
volcanic origin 10:917
oceanic 10:917
ISLETS OF LANGERHANS 10:917
Insulin 9:887
Pancreas 13:1240
ISOBAR 10:918
ISOTHERMAL LINES 10:918
ISOTONIC SOLUTION 10:918
ISOTOPE 10:918
Atom 2:174
Chemistry 4:374
deuterium 10:918; 5:497
Geiger counter 10:918
Half-life 9:817
Heavy water 9:830
illus. 10:918
Nuclear particles 12:1164-1165
radioisotope 10:918
Thulium 18:1747
ISTHMUS 10:919
illus.: Panama 10:919
Itch mite see **MITE**
IVORY 10:919
Tusks 18:1783
IVY 10:919
illus. 10:919
JACKAL 10:920
Dog 6:521
illus.: 6:521; 7:643; 10:920
Jackass see **DONKEY**
Jackfruit 14:1330
Jack-in-the-pulpit see **WILD FLOWERS**
Jackrabbit, illus. 1:84
Jacob's Ladder see **WILD FLOWERS**
JADE 10:920
JADE (PLANT) 10:920
illus. 10:920
Jaguar see **CAT FAMILY**
illus. 16:1596
Japanese beetle, illus. 9:881
Japanese beetle see **INSECTA**
Japanese (Kurashio) Current 5:470
Japonica see **CAMELLIA**
JASMINE 10:920
illus.: 10:920; 12:1149; 13:1264
Night-blooming 12:1148-1149
Jasper see **QUARTZ**
illus. 14:1392

JAUNDICE 10:921
  Hepatitis 9:835
Java man see **EVOLUTION OF MAN**
Jaw see **DIGESTIVE SYSTEM;**
  MANDIBLE; SKELETON; TEETH
Jay see **BLUE JAY; CROW**
Jejunum see **DIGESTIVE SYSTEM**
JELLYFISH 10:921
  Animals, classification of 1:95
  characteristics 10:921
  Ctenophora 5:463
  habitat 10:921
  illus.: 1:85; Atlantic jellyfish
    10:921; Hawaiian jellyfish 10:921
JENNER, EDWARD 10:921-922
  Medicine 11:1038-1040
  Smallpox 16:1562
  Vaccine 18:1792
JERBOA 10:922
  illus.: 1:84; 10:922
Jessamine see **JASMINE**
Jet see **GEM; MINERAL**
Jet engine, illus. 10:991
Jet lag 3:254
JET PROPULSION 10:922-923
  Aircraft 1:48-50
  Airplane 1:52-53
  Aviation 2:191-197
  exp. 10:923
  Engine 7:619-623
  Hero's Aeolopile 10:922
  illus.: 10:922; ramjet 10:923
  Missile 11:1071-1075
  ram jet 10:922
  thrust 10:923
  Turbine 18:1778-1779
  turbofan engine 10:923
  turbojet 10:922
  turboprop 10:923
JET STREAM 10:924
  Calm, regions of 4:325
  Horse latitudes 9:855
  illus. 10:924
  Squall line 17:1654
Jewelweed see **TOUCH-ME-NOT**
Jimson weed see **WILD FLOWERS**
JOINTS 10:924
  Arthritis 2:140
  Skeleton 16:1552-1555
JOINTS, SKELETAL 10:924-925
  ball-and-socket 10:925
  hinge 10:925
  illus.: ball-and-socket 10:925;
    hinge 10:925; pivot 10:925
  immovable 10:924
  pivot 10:924
  Skeleton 16:1552-1555
Jonquil see **NARCISSUS**
JOSHUA 10:925
  illus.: 7:694; 10:925
  Plants, succulent 14:1329
JOULE 10:925
  Energy 7:612:617
  Kilowatt hour 10:933
JOULE, JAMES PRESCOTT 10:925
Judas tree see **REDBUD**
Jugular vein see **CIRCULATORY**
  SYSTEM
JUMPING BEAN 10:926
Jumping mouse see **JERBOA;**
  MOUSE
JUNCO 10:926
  illus. 10:926
JUNGLE 10:926-927
  agriculture 10:926-927
  illus.: plant and animal life
    10:927; tropical rain forest
    10:927
  plants and animals 10:926

June bug see **INSECTA**
JUNIPER 10:927
  illus. 10:927
JUPITER 10:928-929
  Giant red spot 10:928
  gravity 10:928
  illus.: Jupiter Orbiter Probe
    10:929; seen through telescope
    10:928; with moons 10:928
  Jupiter Orbiter Probe 10:929
  Planet 14:1312
  rotation 10:928
JUPITER ORBITER PROBE 10:929
  illus. 10:929
JUTE 10:929
  illus. 10:929
KALEIDOSCOPE 10:930
  illus. 10:930
Kallima, illus. 11:1064
KAME 10:930
KANGAROO 10:930
  Australia 2:177
  characteristics 10:930
  habitat 10:930
  illus. 10:930
  Marsupial 11:1026
  reproduction 10:930
  Wallaby 19:1827
Kangaroo rat see **RAT; RODENTIA**
  (RODENT)
KAOLIN 10:930
  Clay 4:392
  Feldspar 7:674
  Porcelain 14:1350
KAPOK 10:930
  illus. 16:1593
KARST TOPOGRAPHY 10:930-931
Katydid see **ARTHROPODA;**
  GRASSHOPPER
Kelly, William 3:247
KELP 1:58; 10:931
  illus. 10:931
  Seaweed 16:1523
KELVIN, WILLIAM THOMPSON,
  LORD 10:931
  Cryogenics 5:460
KEPLER, JOHANNES 2:166; 10:931
  Copernicus, Nicolaus 5:447
  laws of planetary motion 10:931
  Orbit 13:1217-1218
KEROSENE 10:932
KESTREL 10:932
KETTLE 10:932
Kid see **GOAT**
KIDNEY 10:932-933
  Excretory system 7:660-661
  functions 10:932
  illus. 10:932
  Nephritis 12:1138-1139
  structure 10:932
  Urine 18:1791
KILLDEER 10:933
  Bird nests 3:260
  illus. 10:933
Killer whale see **WHALE**
KILN 10:933
Kilo see **MEASUREMENT**
Kilocycle see **RADIO**
KILOWATT HOUR 10:933
  Electricity 6:568
  Watt-hour meter 19:1836
Kilowatt-hour meter see **WATT-**
  HOUR METER
KINDLING TEMPERATURE 10:933
Kinematics 11:1037
KINESTHETIC SENSE 10:934
  Sense organs 16:1528-1529
Kinetic energy see **ENERGY**
Kinetic Molecular Theory 4:307

KINETIC THEORY 10:934
  Charles' Law 4:370-371
  Expansion 7:661-662
  Heat 9:827
  Molecule 11:1083-1084
King crab see **CRAB**
King snake see **SNAKES**
KINGFISH 10:934
  illus.: king whiting 10:934
KINGFISHER 10:934-935
  Bird nests 3:260
  illus. 10:935
  Kookaburra 10:936-937
  Tern 18:1735
KINGLET 10:935
  illus. 10:935
KIWI 10:935; 3:261
  illus. 10:935
Knee see **SKELETON**
KNOT 10:935
KOALA 10:936
  Australia 2:181
  characteristics 10:936
  diet 10:936
  illus. 10:936
  Marsupial 11:1026
  reproduction 10:936
KOCH, ROBERT 10:936
  Bacteriology 3:210
  illus. 10:936
KOHLRABI 10:936
  Cabbage 4:320
KOOKABURRA 10:936-937
  illus. 10:937
Koppen system 4:397
KREBS, SIR HANS 10:937
KRYPTON 10:937
Kumquat see **CITRUS FRUITS**
KURCHATOVIUM 10:937
KUSCH, POLYKARP 10:937
KYMOGRAPH 10:937
LABORATORY 10:938
  Chemistry 4:376-377
  illus.: 6:557; 10:938
Labrador Current 9:810
Labrador duck, illus. 12:1159
LABURNUM 10:938
  illus. 10:938
Labyrinth 6:540
Labyrinth see **EAR**
Lacrimal gland see **EYES; TEARS**
Lactase 6:512
Lactation see **MAMMALIA**
LACTIC ACID 10:938
  Cancer (disease) 4:331
  Fatigue 7:673
LACTOGEN 10:938
Lactose see **ENZYME; SUGAR**
Ladybug see **BEETLE**
Lady's slipper see **ORCHID**
LAENNEC, RENE 10:939
Lagomorpha 11:1011
LAGOON 10:939
  illus. 10:939
LAKE 10:939-940
  barrier 10:939
  glacial 10:939
  illus.: Crater Lake 10:940
  Lagoon 10:939
  Limnology 10:965-966
  sinkhole 10:940
Lake trout see **TROUT**
LAMARCK, JEAN BAPTISTE
  PIERRE 10:940
  Acquired characteristics 1:23-24
  Evolution of man 7:654-659
  illus.: 7:647; 10:940
Lamb see **SHEEP**
Lamination see **PLYWOOD**

LAMP 10:941
LAMPBLACK 10:941
  Carbon 4:338
LAMPREY 10:941
  alewife 1:57
  Eel 6:558
  illus. 10:941
  Pisces (animal) 14:1307-1308
LAND, EDWIN HERBERT 10:941
  Color 5:423
Landslide see **AVALANCHE**
Langerhans, islets of see **ISLETS OF LANGERHANS**
Langley, Samuel see **AVIATION**
LANOLIN 10:942
Lantana 14:1330
LANTHANUM 10:942
  Lutetium 10:985
LAPLACE, PIERRE SIMON, MARQUIS DE 10:942
Lapwing see **PLOVER**
Lard see **FAT; PIG**
LARK 10:942
  illus. 10:942
Larkspur see **DELPHINIUM**
LARVA 3:242; 10:943
  Animals, classification of 1:94
  Balance of nature 3:218-219
  Bee 3:240
  Butterflies 4:317
  Caddis fly 4:321
  Canker worms 4:333
  Caterpillar; :354
  characteristics 10:943
  Chordata 4:384
  dipleurula 10:943
  Filaria 7:680
  Fly 7:697
  habitat 10:943
  illus.: lo moth 10:943; mosquito 10:943
  Jumping bean 10:926
  Liver fluke 10:973
  Mealworm 11:1032
  Metamorphosis 11:1052
  Moths 12:1108-1109
  naiads 10:943
  nauplius 10:943
  Platyhelminthes 14:1336-1337
  Tadpole 18:1715
  trochophore 10:943
LARYNGITIS 10:944
LARYNX 10:944
  Adam's apple 10:944
  epiglottis 10:944
  illus. 10:944
  Laryngitis 10:944
  Mutism 12:1128
  Transplant 18:1770
LASER 10:944
  Maser 11:1026
LATENT HEAT 10:944
LATERAL 10:944
LATEX 10:944
LATHE 10:945
LATITUDE 10:945
  Earth 6:544
  Geography 8:762
  International Geophysical Year: the Solid Earth 9:894
Laudanum see **OPIUM**
Laurel 10:945
  illus. 10:945
LAVA 10:945
  basalt 10:945
  granite 10:945
  illus. 10:945
  magma 10:945
  Mid-Atlantic Ridge 11:1058

  obsidian 10:945
  pumice 10:945
LAVENDER 10:946
  illus. 10:946; 13:1264
LAVOISER, ANTOINE LAURENT 10:946
  illus. 10:946
  Oxidation 13:1231-1232
  Oxygen 13:1232-1233
Law of the Conservation of Energy 4:326
Law of the Sea Conference 9:896
LAWRENCIUM 10:946
LEACHING 10:946-947
LEAD 10:947
  Metal 11:1049-1051
  Mineral 11:1065
  poisoning 10:947
LEAFLET 10:947
Leaning Tower of Pisa, illus. 1:17
Leap year 4:324
LEATHER 10:947
  Lye 10:985
  Tannin 18:1716
LEAVES 10:948-949
  Angiosperm 1:81-82
  Bud 4:309
  Cactus 4:321
  classification 10:948
  compound 10:948
  Cotyledon 5:452
  dicotyledon 10:948
  exp.: making lead guide 10:949
  Herbaceous 9:836
  Homeostasis 9:851
  illus.: alternate 10:948; com-
    plete 10:948; compound 10:948;
    cross-section 10:948; opposite
    10:948; palmate 10:948; parallel
    10:948; pinnate 10:948; simple
    10:948
  internal structure 10:949
  Leaflet 10:947
  monocotyledon 10:948; 11:1090
  Maple 11:1015
  Plant 14:1314-1317
  Photosynthesis 13:1285
  Pine 13:1295-1296
  simple 10:948
LEECH 10:950
  illus. 10:950
LEEK 10:950
  illus. 10:950
LEEUWENHOEK, ANTON VAN 10:950
  Bacteriology 3:210
  Medicine 11:1038-1040
Leghorn see **CHICKEN**
LEGUME 10:951
  Clover 5:411
  Follicle (botanical) 8:709
  Fruit 8:735
  illus. 10:951
  Lentil 10:954
  Locust (tree) 10:977
  Mesquite 11:1047
  Mimosa 11:1064
  Nitrogen cycle 12:1150-1151
  Soil testing 16:1572
  Soybean 16:1597
  Sweet pea 18:1710
LEMMING 7:643; 10:951
  illus.: 10:951; 12:1117
Lemon see **CITRUS FRUIT**
LEMUR 10:952
  Gorilla 9:789
  habitat 10:952
  illus. 10:952
  Primates 14:1362-1363

Lens, animal see **EYE**
LENS, MAN-MADE 10:952-953
  achromatic 10:953
  Camera 4:328-329; 10:952
  chromatic 10:953
  concave 10:953
  convex 10:953; 5:445
  Eye 7:664-667
  eyeglasses 10:952
  Focus 8:708
  illus.: 10:952, 953
  Magnifying power 11:1007
  Mirror 11:1070
  optical instruments 10:952-953;
    13:1214-1215
  Optics 13:1215
  Periscope 13:1266
  Perspective 13:1269
  Prism 14:1370
  Projector 14:1372-1373
  Telescope 18:1728-1730
LENTIL 10:954
  illus. 10:954
LEO 10:954
  illus. 10:954
  mythology 10:954
  Virgo 19:1816
LEONARDO DA VINCI 10:954-955
  artistic pursuits 10:955
  Aviation 2:191
  Helicopter 9:832
  history of anatomy 1:76
  illus.: 10:954; double crane
    10:955; printing press 10:955
  investigations 10:955
  Mechanics 11:1037-1038
  Renaissance 10:954
Leopard, illus. 14:1375
Leopard see **CAT FAMILY**
LEPROSY 10:955
  cause 10:955
  treatment 10:955
LETTUCE 10:956
  illus. 10:956
Leucocytes 3:269
LEUKEMIA 10:956
  Blood 3:268-269
  cause 10:956
  Chemotherapy 4:377
  chronic 10:956
  treatment 10:956
LEVEE 10:956
Lever see **MACHINES, SIMPLE**
LIBRA 10:956
  illus. 10:956-957
  mythology 10:957
LICHEN 10:957
  characteristics 10:957
  classification 10:957
  habitat 10:957
  illus.: 14:1324, 1326; 18:1738;
    reindeer moss 10:957
  litmus paper 10:957
  Plants, classification of
    14:1322-1327
  uses 10:957
LICORICE 10:957
  illus. 10:957
LIE DETECTOR 10:957
LIFE, CHARACTERISTICS OF 10:958
  Death 5:485
  illus. 10:958
  Plant 14:1314-1317
Life cycle see **AGING; BIRTH; DEATH**
LIFE, ORIGIN OF 10:958, 17:1652
  heterotroph theory 10:958
  photosynthetic plants 10:958

Lift, illus. 1:29
Lift pump, illus. 14:1385
Life see **AERODYNAMICS**
Lifting bodies 1:50
Ligament see **FIBROUS TISSUE**
Ligature 10:958
LIGHT 1:16; 10:959-963
  Absorption of light 1:16
  Atom 2:172-174
  Bulb, electric 4:312
  Candela 4:322
  chemiluminescence 10:959
  color 10:960
  Colorimeter 5:424
  composition 10:959
  Corpuscular theory 5:449
  Diffraction 6:509; 10:962
  Doppler effect 6:525
  electroluminescence 10:959
  Electromagnetic spectrum 6:578
  exp.: direction light travels
    10:960; preventing total reflection
    of light 10:960; reflections—how
    others see you 10:959
  Focus 8:708
  Huygens, Christian 9:861
  illus.: diffraction 10:962; inter-
    ference 10:962; inverse square
    law 10:963; measurement of
    speed of light 10:961; refraction
    10:962
  importance to life 10:963
  Inverse square law 10:910-911
  Iridescence 10:912
  Light year 10:963
  Luminescence 10:980
  measurement 10:962
  Mirage 11:1070
  Mirror 11:1070
  Newton, Sir Isaac 12:1147
  Opaque 13:1210
  Optical instruments 13:1214-1215
  particle model 10:962
  Pigment 13:1294
  Photoelectricity 13:1278-1280
  Photometer 13:1284
  Physics 13:1287-1288
  Prism 14:1370
  Quantum mechanics 14:1390-1391
  Rainbow 15:1427
  Ray, alpha 15:1433
  Ray, beta 15:1433
  Ray, ultraviolet 15:1435
  Reflection 15:1440
  Relativity 15:1443
  speed 10:962
  sources 10:959
  Spectograph 17:1642
  Spectrum 17:1643
  Sun 17:1686-1691
  Telescpoe 18:1728-1730
  Translucent 18:1769
  Transparent 18:1769
  Tyndall effect 18:1783
  Wave 19:1836-1837
  wave model 10:962
  White light 19:1867
LIGHT YEAR 10:963
  Light 10:959-963
LIGHTNING 10:963-964
  exp.: measuring distance of
    thunderstorm 10:964
Ligustrum, illus. 16:1545
LILAC 10:964
  illus. 10:964
Lilienthal, Otto 1:29
LILY 10:964-965
  care of 10:965
  illus.: Calla 10:965

Tulip 18:1776
  varieties 10:965
LILY-OF-THE-VALLEY 10:965
  illus. 10:965
Lima bean see **LEGUME**
LIME (CHEMICAL) 10:965; 4:391
Lime (fruit) see **CITRUS FRUIT**
Limestone 4:369
  Pyrite 14:1389
LIMNOLOGY 10:965-966
LIMPET 10:966
  illus.: 10:966; 11:1085
LINDEN 10:966
  illus. 10:966
Linear accelerator see
  ACCELERATORS (PARTICLE)
Linear venation see **LEAVES**
LINEN 10:966
  processing 10:966
  uses 10:966
LINNAEUS, CAROLUS 10:967
  illus. 10:967
  Plants, classification of 14:1322-
    1327
LINNET 10:967
LINSEED OIL 10:967
Lion, illus. 1:34
Lion see **CAT FAMILY**
Lipase 6:513
Lipase see **DIGESTIVE SYSTEM;**
  LIVER
LIPSCOMB, WILLIAM N. 10:967
LIQUID 10:968-970
  evaporation 10:970
  Fluid 7:694
  illus. 11:1031; compression of gas
    10:968; effect of pressure on
    boiling point 10:969; equaliza-
    tion 10:968; movement of
    molecules 10:970
  Mercury (element) 11:1044
  Molecular theory 11:1083
  molecules 10:968
  nonviscous 10:968
  Physical states and changes
    13:1286-1287
  Siphon 16:1551
  surface tension 10:969
  vapor 10:970
  Viscosity 19:1817; 10:968
  Water 19:1830-1831
LIQUID AIR 10:970
LISTER, JOSEPH 2:118; 10:971
  Medicine 11:1038-1040
  Sterilization 17:1671
  Surgery 17:1696-1697
Liter see **MEASUREMENT**
Literal numbers 1:60
LITHIUM 10:971
Lithography see **PRINTING**
Lithophyte see **LICHEN; MARINE**
  BIOLOGY
LITMUS TEST 10:971
Little America see **ANTARCTICA**
Little Dipper see **BIG AND LITTLE**
  DIPPERS; URSA MAJOR AND
  URSA MINOR
Little dory, illus. 11:1021
Live oak see **OAK**
LIVER 10:972
  bile 10:972
  detoxification of waste 10:972
  Digestive system 6:510, 512
  functions 10:972
  Gallbladder 8:747
  Glandular tissue 8:780
  Hepatitis 9:835
  illus.: back view 10:972; relation
    to other organs 10:972

Jaundice 10:921
Liver fluke 10:973
  metabolism of fatty acids and
    amino acids 10:972
  Migratory cells 11:1061
  Mononucleosis 11:1090
  plasma proteins 10:972
  Protein 14:1376-1377
LIVER FLUKE 10:973
  characteristics 10:973
  illus.: life cycle 10:973
  Liver 10:972
  Parasites 13:1249
  Platyhelminthes 14:1336-1337
  reproduction 10:973
LIVERWORTS 10:973-974
  characteristics 10:974
  classification 10:973
  illus.: 4:308; 7:607; 10:974;
    14:1326
  Plants, classification of
    14:1322-1327
  reproduction 10:974
  uses 10:974
Living fossils 18:1717
LIZARD 10:974-975
  Chameleon 4:369
  classification 10:974
  defenses 10:974
  diet 10:974
  illus.: 1:84; collared lizard
    10:975; glass snake 10:975;
    horned toad 10:975
  locomotion 10:974
  reproduction 10:974
  Reptilia 15:1449-1450
LLAMA 10:975
  Alpaca 1:64
  illus. 10:975
LOAM 10:975
LOBELIA 10:976
  illus. 10:976
LOBSTER 10:976
  Animals, classification of 1:95
  characteristics 10:976
  classification 10:976
  Crustacea 5:459
  diet 10:976
  habitat 10:976
  illus.: 5:459; 10:976
  reproduction 10:976
Lobworm see **SANDWORM**
Lock see **CANAL**
Lockjaw see **TETANUS**
LOCOMOTION 10:976
  Kinesthetic sense 10:934
Locomotive see **TRAIN; RAILROAD**
LOCOWEED 10:976
  illus. 10:977
LOCUS 10:977
Locust (insect) see **ARTHROPODA;**
  GRASSHOPPER; INSECTA
LOCUST (TREE) 10:977
LODE 10:977
Lodestone see **MAGNETITE**
Lodgepole pine see **FORESTRY**
LOESS 10:977
LOGANBERRY 10:977
Long, Crawford 17:1696
Long ton see **MEASUREMENT**
LONGEVITY 10:977
LONGITUDE 10:978
  Earth 6:544
  Geography 8:762
  illus. 10:978
  International Geophysical Year:
    the Solid Earth 9:894
  Latitude 10:945
  Meridian 11:1046

LOON 10:978
Loop antenna 6:517
LORENZ, KONRAD 10:978
Imprinting 9:874
Lotus 14:1330
Lotus see **WATER LILY**
LOUSE 10:978
chewing 10:978
nits 10:978
reproduction 10:978
sucking 10:978
LOVEBIRD 10:978
illus. 10:978
LOW-PRESSURE CENTER 10:979
Air masses 1:46
LUBRICATION 10:979
Lumbago see **ARTHRITIS**
LUMBER 10:979
board foot 10:979
hardwood 10:979
illus.: loading logs 10:979
Maple 11:1015
Pine 13:1295-1296
softwood 10:979
uses 10:979
Lumen see **CANDLE POWER**
LUMINESCENCE 10:980
Cathode-ray tube 4:355
chemiluminescence 10:980
electroluminescence 10:980
illus. 10:980
Light 10:959-963
photoluminescence 10:980
Luminous flux 4:332
Luminous intensity 4:332
LUNAR BASE 10:980-983
building 10:982
components: control system 10:981;
   ecological system 10:981; laboratory system 10:981; maintenance
   system 10:981; power generation
   system 10:981
illus.: 10:981, 982
importance 10:983
location 10:982
Moon 11:1092-1094
Lunar eclipse see **ECLIPSE**
LUNG 10:983-984
alveoli 10:984
bronchi 10:984
Expiration 7:663
Gill 8:777
illus.: 10:983; 14:1341
lung damage 10:984
Mammalia 11:1011-1012
Metamorphosis 11:1052
pleura 10:983
Pleurisy 14:1337
Pneumonia 14:1341
trachea 10:984
LUNGFISH 10:984
illus. 10:984
LUNISOLAR PRECESSION 10:984-
985
illus. 10:984
LUPINE 10:985
LUTETIUM 10:985
LUX 4:332; 10:985
Lycophyta 18:1763
LYE 10:985
LYMPHATIC DUCT
Capillary 4:335
LYMPHATIC SYSTEM 10:986-987
Adenoids 1:26
Anatomy 1:76
Blood 3:268
Capillary 4:335
circulation 10:986-987
contents of lymph 10:987

Histology 9:846-849
illus. 10:986
importance of 10:987
Migratory cells 11:1061
Mononeucleosis 11:1090
Spleen 17:1651
Tonsils 18:1757
Lynx see **CAT FAMILY**
LYREBIRD 10:987
illus. 10:987
MACADAM 10:988
illus. 10:988
MACAW 10:988
Parrot 13:1250
McCormick, Cyrus see
   AUTOMATION
MACE 10:988
illus. 10:988
Nutmeg 12:1183
MACH, ERNST 10:988-989
MACHINERY 10:989-991
Bearing 3:237
Cogwheel 5:419
Conveyor belt 5:446
Gear 8:758; 10:989
historical development 10:990
illus.: electric motor 10:991;
   gasoline engine 10:991; hoist
   10:989; hydraulic press 10:989;
   jet engine 10:991; solar battery
   10:991; stationary gasoline en-
   gine 10:989; waterwheel 10:991;
   windmill 10:991
Lathe 10:945
Lubrication 10:979
Machines, simple 10:994
Mechanical advantage 11:1037
Monorail 11:1091
Printing 14:1364-1367
purposes of complex machines
   10:990
Tools 18:1757-1759
MACHINES, SIMPLE 10:992-994
Bicycle 3:249
block and tackle 10:993
Energy 7:612-617
exp.: inclined plane 10:992; wheel
   and axle 10:994; pulley
   10:994
illus.: inclined plane 10:993;
   lever 10:993; pulley 10:993;
   screw 10:993; wedge 10:993;
   wheel 10:993
inclined plane 10:993
lever 10:992
Mechanical advantage 11:1037
Machinery 10:989-991
Power 14:1355
pulley 10:993
screw 10:944
Tools 18:1757-1759
Torque 18:1761
wedge 10:994
wheel 10:993
Windlass 19:1876
Work 19:1880; 10:992
MACKEREL 10:995
illus. 10:995
MADDER 10:995
Madonna Lily see **LILY**
Maelstrom see **WHIRLPOOL**
Maggot see **FLY; LARVA**
MAGMA 10:995
Crystal 5:461
Intrusion 10:910
Island 10:917
Lava 10:945
Volcano 19:1822-1823
MAGNESIA 10:995

MAGNESIUM 10:995
Metal 11:1049; 1051
Talc 18:1715
Water 19:1830-1831
MAGNET 10:995-996
Ammeter 1:72
Ampere, Andre Marie 1:73
cause of magnetic properties
   10:997
Compass 5:430
distribution 10:996
Earth 6:545
Electricity 6:572
Electromagnet 6:577
Generator 8:760-761
illus. compass 10:996; electro-
   magnet 10:977; patterns of mag-
   netic fields 10:996; poles
   10:996; produced by electricity
   6:568
Induction 9:876
line of force 10:996
Machinery 10:989-991
Magnesia 10:995
magnetic field 10:996
molecular theory of magnetism
   10:997
Polar wandering 13:1344
Pole (general) 14:1345
poles 10:996
Permeability 13:1267-1268
Magnetic pole see **COMPASS;
   POLES, NORTH AND SOUTH**
MAGNETITE 10:997
MAGNIFYING POWER 11:1007
focal length 11:1007
Lens, man-made 10:953
telescope 11:1007
MAGNITUDE 11:1008
illus. 11:1008
Stars 17:1660-1662
MAGNOLIA 11:1008
illus. 11:1008
MAGPIE 11:1008-1009
illus. 11:1008
MAHOGANY 11:1009
illus. 11:1009
Hardwood 9:820
Maidenhair tree see **GINKGO**
Maize see **CORN**
Major phylum of animal life, illus. 1:93
Malachite see **COPPER**
MALARIA 11:1009
Infection 9:878
Koch, Robert 10:936
mosquito 11:1009; 12:1107
Pharmacology 13:1272-1274
Protozoa 14:1378-1379
quinine 11:1009; 14:1393
symptoms 11:1009
treatment 11:1009
Male see **HEREDITY;
   REPRODUCTION, SEXUAL**
MALIGNANT 11:1009
Mallard see **DUCKS**
MALLEABLE 11:1010
Malleus see **EAR**
MALLOW 11:1010
Hibiscus 9:843-844
illus. 11:1010
MALNUTRITION 1:39; 11:1010
causes 11:1010
Nutrition 12:1184
six required elements 11:1010
MALPIGHI, MARCELLO 11:1010
Malpighian tube 11:1010
Medicine 11:1038-1040
Malpighian tube 11:1010
Maltase 6:512

MAMMALIA 11:1011-1012
Animal cages 1:88-89
Artiodactyla 11:1012
Bat 3:229-230
breast 3:292
Carnivora 11:1012
Cetacea 11:1012
Chiroptera 11:1012
Chordata 4:383-385
Cow 5:453
Edentata 11:1011
Eggs 6:559
Embryology 6:592-597
Estrous cycle 7:637
Fetus 7:678
Fox 8:726-727
Gestation period 8:774
Gnu 8:784
Hair 9:816
illus.: Buffalo 11:1011;
chart 11:1012
Insectivora 11:1011
Lactogen 10:938
Lagomorpha 11:1011
Marsupial 11:1026, 1011
Mastodon 11:1028
Milk 11:1061
Molting 11:1087
monotremes 11:1011, 1091
Mouse 12:1117
Monkey 11:1089
Opossum 13:1213
Pinnipedia 11:1012
placental 11:1011
Porpoise 14:1352
Primate 11:1012; 14:1362-
1363
Proboscidea 11:1012
respiratory system 11:1012
Reproductive systems
15:1447-1448
Rodent 11:1011; 15:1474-
1475
Sea lion 16:1518
Seal 16:1521
Shrew 16:1542
skeleton 11:1012
Spiny anteater 17:1649
Sweat glands 18:1710
Viviparous 19:1818
Walrus 19:1828
Whale 19:1865
Wombat 19:1879
MAMMOTH 11:1013
Behemoth 11:1013
Cenozoic Era 4:362
illus. 11:1013
Prehistoric mammals
14:1359-1360
Man see **ANTHROPOLOGY;
EVOLUTION: EVOLUTION OF
MAN; HUMAN BEING; MAMMALIA;
PRIMATES**
Manatee, illus. 12:1159
MANDIBLE 11:1013
illus.: bird 11:1013; human
11:1013; insect 11:1013
MANGANESE 11:1013
MANGE 11:1013
Scab 16:1510
MANGO 11:1014
illus. 11:1014
Plants, tropical 14:1329-
1330
MANGROVE 11:1014
illus. 11:1014
MAN-OF-WAR, PORTUGUESE
10:921; 11:1014
illus. 11:1014

MANOMETER 11:1014
Pressure gauge 14:1361
Manta ray see **RAY**
Mantis, illus. 11:1064
MANURE 11:1014-1015
Greenhouse 8:797
MANZANITA 11:1015
MAP-MAKING 11:1015-1017
Cartography 4:346
Globe 8:783
great circle routes 11:1016
illus.: aerial map 11:1017;
ground map 11:1017; Mer-
cator projection 11:1016;
terrestrial globes 11:1017
Interrupted Homolosine 11:1016
Lambert's conformal 11:1016
Mercator 11:1015
Navigation 12:1135
polar 11:1016
problems 11:1015
Projection 14:1371
projections: geometric 11:1015-
1016; globe-skin 11:1015-1016;
perspective 11:1015-1016
Surveying 18:1707
Topography 18:1760
MAPLE 11:1015
Hardwood 9:820
illus.: silver 11:1015; sugar
11:1015
Marble see **ROCKS**
MARCONI, GUGLIELMO 11:1018
illus. 11:1018
Mare see **BABY ANIMALS; HORSE**
MARIGOLD 11:1018-1019
Calendula 4:324
illus. 11:1019
MARIJUANA 11:1019
research 11:1019
source 11:1019
MARINE 11:1019
MARINE BIOLOGY 11:1019-1020
benthic zone 11:1020
Coelenterata 5:417-419
Fucus 8:738
illus.: blue marlin 11:1021; dol-
phin 11:1021; garibaldi 11:1019;
great swallower 11:1021;
gulper 11:1021; little dory
11:1021; ocean perch 11:1021;
Pacific albacore 11:1021; pilot
fish 11:1021; red dory 11:1021;
shark 11:1021; sperm whale
11:1021; starfish 11:1019; viper
fish 11:1021
Lobster 10:976
lower pelagic zone 11:1021
Ocean 12:1188-1190
Ocean environments 11:1019-1021
Pelagic 13:1259
Plankton 14:1313
Salamander 15:1489-1490
Swordfish 18:1712
Marine nematode, illus. 19:1881
Mariner 17:1634
Mariposa see **LILY**
MARJORAM 11:1022
illus. 11:1022
Mint 11:1070
MARLIN 11:1022
illus.: 11:1021, 1022
Swordfish 18:1712
MARMOSET 11:1022
illus.: 11:1022; 16:1597
Primates 14:1362
MARMOT 11:1022
illus. 11:1022
Marrow see **BLOOD; BONE**

MARS 11:1023-1025
atmosphere 11:1024
exploration 11:1025
illus.: 11:1023, 1024
life 11:1025
Planet 14:1312
seasons 11:1024-1025
spatial relationships 11:1023
Viking Project 19:1814
MARSH 11:1025
illus. 6:552
importance 11:1025
Marsh deer, illus. 16:1596
Marsh gas see **METHANE**
MARSUPIAL 11:1026
Australia 2:180
care of young 11:1026
illus.: opossum 11:1026; pelvic
structure 11:1026
Kangaroo 10:930
Koala 10:936
Mammalia 11:1011-1012
Mouse 12:1117
Opossum 13:1213
Wallaby 19:1827
Wombat 19:1879
Marten see **WEASEL**
MARTIN 11:1026
Bird houses 3:258
illus.: purple 11:1026
Petrel 13:1270
MASER 11:1026
Laser 10:944
Mason wasp 14:1375
MASS 11:1027
conservation 11:1027
exp.: charged oil drop 11:1027
Forces 8:710-711
illus. 11:1027
mass of the earth 11:1027
Momentum 11:1088
weight 11:1027; 19:1860
Mass defect see **NUCLEAR
SCIENCE GLOSSARY**
Mass number see **NUCLEAR
SCIENCE GLOSSARY**
Mass production 19:1869
Master gland see **ENDOCRINE
GLAND; PITUITARY**
MASTODON 11:1028
Cenozoic Era 4:362
illus. 11:1028
Prehistoric mammals 14:1359-
1360
MASTOID 11:1028
MATCHES 11:1028
illus. 11:1028
Phosphorus 13:1276-1277
safety 11:1028
MATHEMATICS 11:1028-1030
applied 11:1030
Arithmetic 2:136-137
Biometry 3:254
Chemistry 4:373-377
history 11:1029
illus.: puzzle 11:1029, 1030
importance 11:1030
Infinity 9:878
Locus 10:977
Measurement 11:1033-1036
Nuclear science 12:1170-1175
Numeral systems 12:1179-1183
Parallax 13:1245
Physics 13:1287-1288
postulates 11:1029
primitives 11:1029
Probability 14:1370
Statistics 17:1664-1665
symbolic language 11:1030

MATTER 11:1031
Antimatter 2:117
Atom 2:172-174
Chemistry 4:373-377
illus.: gas 11:1031; liquid
11:1031; solid 11:1031
inorganic 11:1031
law of conservation of energy
11:1031
measurement 11:1031
Molecule 11:1083-1084
organic 11:1031
Physical states and changes
13:1286
properties 11:1031
stages 11:1031
May apple see **WILD FLOWERS**
MAY FLY 11:1032
MAYER, MARIA 11:1032
Meadow mouse illus. 7:643
MEADOWLARK 11:1032
flight 11:1032
illus. 11:1032
nests 11:1032
MEALWORM 11:1032
MEASLES 11:1032
cause 11:1032
symptoms 11:1032
MEASUREMENT 11:1033-
1036
Ampere 1:73
basic quantities 11:1036
Caliper 4:325
Carat 4:336
charts 11:1034-1035
Chemistry 4:373-377
Density 5:493
Dyne 6:537
Erg 7:634
Foot-pound 8:710
history 11:1033, 1036
illus.: 11:1036; parts of the body
11:1033
instruments 11:1036
*International Bureau of Weights
and Measures* 9:888
Mass 11:1027
Metric system 11:1054
Ohm 12:1196
Power 14:1355
standards: comparator 11:1036;
international prototypes
11:1036; kilogram 11:1036
Sundial 17:1692
Surveying 18:1707
Volume 19:1825
Weight 19:1860
MECHANICAL ADVANTAGE
11:1037
illus. 11:1037
Machines, simple 10:992-994
MECHANICS 11:1037-1038
aerodynamics 11:1038
dynamics 11:1037
Forces 8:710-711
history 11:1037
kinematics 11:1037
MEDAWAR, PETER B. 11:1038
MEDIAN 11:1038
Medicinal plants see **ECONOMIC
BOTANY; HERB; PLANTS,
MEDICINAL**
MEDICINE 11:1038-1040
Biophysics 3:255
Diagnosis 5:497
Disease 6:519; 11:1039
Drugs 6:528-530
Fever 7:678
Fluoroscope 7:695-696

Freud, Sigmund 8:730
Galen 8:745; 11:1039-1040
Germ theory 8:773
Gravel 8:793
Harvey, William 9:821
Hippocrates 9:845; 11:1039
history 11:1038-1039
illus.: antiseptic 11:1040;
early Egyptian 11:1039
Infection 9:878
Malpighi, Marcello 11:1010
modern 11:1040
Paracelsus, Philippus Aureolus
13:1243
Pasteur, Louis 13:1252-1253
Pathology 13:1254-1255
Pharmacology 13:1272-1274
public health 11:1040
Surgery 17:1696-1697
Vesalius, Andreas 19:1812-1813
Vitamin deficiency 19:1818
MEDULLA 11:1040
MEDULLA OBLONGATA 11:1041
Brain 3:289
cranial nerves 11:1041
fourth ventricle 11:1041
illus. 11:1041
Poliomyelitis 14:1346
reflexes 11:1041
Medusa see **COELENTERATA**
Meiosis see **MITOSIS AND MEIOSIS**
Meitner, Lise see **HAHN, OTTO**
Melanin 1:55
MELON 11:1041
illus.: muskmelon 11:1041;
watermelon 11:1041
muskmelon 11:1041
watermelon 11:1041
Melt see **PHYSICAL STATES AND
CHANGES**
Membrane see **MENINGES;
MUCOUS MEMBRANE;
PERICARDIUM; PERITONEUM**
MEMORY 11:1042
MENDEL, GREGOR JOHANN
11:1042
Breeding 3:293
Heredity 9:837-841; 11:1042
illus. 7:647; 11:1042
Pedigree 13:1258
unit-characteristics 11:1042
MENDELEEV'S PERIODIC TABLE
11:1042-1043
Actinide elements 1:24
Californium 4:324-325
Cerium 4:368
Chemistry 4:374
Curium 5:466
Deuterium 5:497
Elements 6:586-589
periodic law 11:1042
Plutonium 14:1340
Praseodymium 14:1356
Radium 15:1424-1425
Symbol, chemical 18:1713
MENDELEVIUM 11:1043
Mendelian laws see **HEREDITY;
MENDEL, GREGOR JOHANN**
MENINGES 11:1043
MENINGITIS 11:1043
Paralysis 13:1245
MENSTRUATION 11:1044
Estrogen 7:637
Estrous cycle 7:637
Follicle (reproductive) 8:709
Ovary 13:1229
Pituitary gland 14:1310
Pregnancy 14:1359
Progesterone 14:1371

Puberty 14:1383
Reproductive systems 15:1447-
1448
Mercator 11:1015
Mercury barometer see **BAROMETER**
MERCURY (ELEMENT) 11:1044
cinnabar 11:1044
Mineral 11:1065-1067
pollution 11:1044
poisonous nature 11:1044
Thermometer 18:1743-1744;
11:1044
MERCURY (PLANET) 11:1044-1046
atmosphere 11:1045
distance from earth 11:1046
illus. 11:1045
Jupiter 10:928-929
orbit 11:1045
phases 11:1045
Planet 14:1312
speed 11:1045
temperature 11:1045
Mercury spacecraft 17:1633, 1635
Merganser see **DUCKS**
MERIDIAN 11:1046
Earth 6:544
MERISTEM 11:1046
MESA 11:1046
arroyo 11:1046
butte 11:1046
illus. 7:635; 11:1046
Plateau 14:1335
Mesoderm see **CLEAVAGE;
EMBRYOLOGY**
MESON 11:1046
Proton (elementary particle)
14:1377
Mesophyll see **LEAVES**
Mesothorium see **THORIUM**
MESOZOIC ERA 11:1047
Cretaceous Period 11:1047
Dinosaur 6:516
illus., tyrannosaurus 11:1047
Jurrassic Period 11:1047
Pterodactyl 14:1382
Prehistoric mammals 14:1359-
1360
Triassic Period 11:1047
MESQUITE 11:1047
illus. 11:1047
METABOLIMETER 11:1048
METABOLISM 11:1048
Absorption, physiological 1:16
amino acid 1:71
anabolic 11:1048
animals 11:1048
Arteriosclerosis 2:139
Assimilation 2:151
basal metabolic rate 11:1048
Biochemistry 3:251
Botany 3:284
catabolic 11:1048
Cleavage 4:393
Cretin 5:456
Diabetes 5:497
Endocrine glands 7:610
Estivation 7:637
Fatty acids 7:673
Histology 9:846-849
illus. 11:1048
Metaboliter 11:1048
Mitosis and meiosis 11:1076-1078
Nutrition 12:1284
Physiology 13:1289-1291
plants 11:1048
Schwann, Theodor 16:1513
Sleep 16:1560
Thyroid 18:1748
Vitamin 18:1818

Metacarpal bone see **SKELETON**
METAL 11:1049-1051
  Assaying 2:151
  Conduction 5:439
  Copper 5:447
  Dies 6:509
  Electrochemistry 6:573
  extraction 11:1049
  Founding 8:723
  Gold 8:785
  Halogen 9:818
  history 11:1049
  Holmium 9:850
  Hydroxide 9:869
  illus.: cassiterite (tin ore)
    11:1049; world map 11:1050
  importance of 11:1049
  Ionization 10:912
  Lead 10:947
  Metallurgy 11:1049-1051
  Mineral 11:1065-1067
  Mineralogy 11:1067-1069
  Nonmetal 12:1155
  Pickling 13:1292
  Pewter 13:1272
  Silver 16:1549
  Steel 17:1666-1668
  Tin 18:1752-1753
  Tungsten 19:1778
  working: casting 11:1050; deep-
    drawing 11:1051; extrusion
    11:1051; molding 11:1050; sin-
    tering 11:1051
Metalloid see **METAL**
METALLURGY 11:1051
Metamorphic rock see **ROCKS**
METAMORPHOSIS 9:880-882;
  11:1052
  adult 11:1052
  Amphibians 1:74-75
  Animals, classification of 1:91-96
  Arthropoda 2:140-142
  Beetles 3:242-243
  Butterflies 4:317
  Caterpillar 4:354
  Cocoon 5:417
  complete 11:1052
  Dragonfly 6:527
  Filaria 7:680
  Flea 7:689
  Fly 7:697
  Frogs 8:732-733
  Fruit fly 8:737
  Gnat 8:784
  illus: frog 11:1052
  incomplete 11:1052
  Larva 10:943; 11:1052
  Lobster 10:976
  Louse 10:978
  Molting 11:1087
  Mosquito 12:1107
  Moths 12:1108-1109
  nymphs 11:1052
  pupa 11:1052
  Silkworm 16:1548
  Tadpole 18:1715; 11:1052
  Tick 18:1749
  Toad 18:1755
Metaphase see **MITOSIS AND**
  MEIOSIS
Metatarsal see **SKELETON**
Metazoan see **ZOOLOGY**
METCHINIKOFF, ELIE 11:1052
METEOR 11:1052-1053
  chemical composition 11:1053
  illus. 11:1053
  irons 11:1053
  meteorite 11:1053
  Moon 11:1092-1094

origins 11:1053
stones 11:1053
stony-irons 11:1053
Tektites 18:1724
METHANE 11:1053
  Butane 4:317
  Compounds, stability of 5:432
  illus., molecule 11:1053
  Natural gas 12:1131
METHANE SERIES 11:1053
Methanol see **ALCOHOL**
Metric measurement: conversion
  factors 1:98
METRIC SYSTEM 11:1054
  illus. 11:1054
  International Bureau of Weights
    and Measures 9:887-888
  Lavoisier, Antoine Laurent 10:946
  Measurement 11:1033-1036
MICA 11:1054
  biotite 11:1054
  illus. 11:1054
  muscovite 11:1054
  Pegmatite 13:1259
MICROBE 11:1054
  Bacteria 3:209
MICROFILM 11:1054
Microgram see **MEASUREMENT**
Micrometer see **CALIPER**
MICROORGANISM 11:1054
Microphone see **RADIO**
Micropyle see **SEED**
MICROSCOPE 11:1055-1056
  Ameba 1:70
  compound 11:1055
  exp. 11:1056
  Germ theory 8:773
  illus.: 11:1007, 1055; 13:1214
  Lens, man-made 10:952-953
  Magnifying power 11:1007
  Malpighi, Marcello 11:1010
  Medicine 11:1038-1040
  Microtome 11:1058
  Optical instruments 13:1214-1215
  resolving power 11:1057
MICROSCOPE, ELECTRON 11:1057
  angstroms 11:1057
  Biophysics 3:225
  Compound 5:432
  illus. 11:1057; 13:1214
  Microscope 11:1055-1056
  Optical instruments 13:1214-1215
  usefulness 11:1057
Microscopic measurements see
  MEASUREMENT
MICROTOME 11:1058
  parts 11:1058
  specimen preparation 11:1058
Microwave see **ELECTRONICS**
MID-ATLANTIC RIDGE 11:1058
  illus. 11:1058
  Seamount 16:1521
MIDBRAIN 11:1058
Middle ear 6:539
MIDGET 11:1059
  causes 11:1059
  Giant 8:775
MIDNIGHT SUN 11:1059
MIGRAINE 11:1059
  Headache 9:823
MIGRATION 11:1059-1061
  accidental 11:1059
  Bird 3:257
  Bobolink 3:277
  flyways 11:1060
  illus: accidental 11:1060; normal
    11:1060; periodic 11:1060; spor-
    adic 11:1060; through man
    11:1060

normal 11:1059
periodic 11:1060
sporadic 11:1060
through man 11:1060
Warbler 19:1829
MIGRATORY CELLS 11:1061
MILDEW 11:1061
  Cineraria 4:386
MILK 11:1061
  Homogenization 9:851
Milk sugar see **SUGAR**
Milkweed see **SEED DISPERSAL;**
  WILD FLOWERS
Milkweed bug, illus. 9:881
MILKY WAY 11:1062
  Crux 5:460
  Galaxy 8:745
  illus. 11:1062
  Solar system 16:1575-1578
  Stars 17:1660
  Sun 17:1686-1691
MILLET 11:1062
  illus. 11:1062
MILLIBAR 11:1062
Milligram see **MEASUREMENT**
MILLIKAN'S ELECTRIC CHARGE
  11:1063
  Electron 6:579
  exp.: oil drop 11:1063
  illus. 11:1063
  Mass 11:1027
Millimeter see **MEASUREMENT**
MILLIPEDE 11:1063
  Arthropoda 2:140-142
  Centipede 4:363
  illus. 11:1063
MIMICRY 11:1064
  illus.: Kallima 11:1064; mantis
    11:1064; Monarch 11:1064;
    spider mite 11:1064; syrphus
    11:1064; Viceroy 11:1064;
    walking stick 11:1064
  Protective coloration 14:1375-
    1376; 11:1064
  selective evolution 11:1064
MIMOSA 11:1064
  illus. 11:1064
Mine, illus. 19:1841
Mine, military see **WEAPONS**
MINERAL 11:1065-1067
  Amethyst 1:71
  Asbestos 2:144
  Assaying 2:151
  Calcium carbonate 4:323
  crystal shape 11:1065
  Dolomite 6:524
  exp. 11:1066
  Fertilizer 7:678
  Fluorite 7:695
  Garnet 8:753
  Geology 8:786
  illus: emerald 11:1065; quartz
    11:1065; tourmaline 11:1067
  Lode 10:977
  mineral compound 11:1065
  Mineralogy 11:1067-1069
  Natural resources 12:1131-1133
  Olivine 13:1209
  Open pit mining 13:1212
  Ore 13:1221; 11:1065
  simple mineral element 11:1065
  sources 11:1066
  Tourmaline 18:1762
MINERAL WATER 11:1067
MINERALOGY 11:1067-1069
  chemical 11:1067-1069
  Crystallography 5:462-463;
    11:1067-1068
  descriptive 11:1069

determinative 11:1069
illus: space lattices in struc-
  ture of crystal 11:1068; tools
  for testing hardness 11:1069
Jade 10:920
Metal 11:1049-1051
Mineral 11:1065-1067
optical 11:1069
physical 11:1068
Mining see **COAL; METAL;
  MINERAL; OPEN PIT MINE**
Mink see **WEASEL**
MINNOW 11:1069
illus. 11:1069
MINT 11:1070
illus. 11:1070
Lavender 10:946
Oregano 13:1222
Peppermint 13:1263
Minuteman missile see
  MISSILE
Miocene see **CENOZOIC ERA;
  GEOLOGIC TIME TABLE**
MIRAGE 11:1070
illus. 11:1070
MIRROR 11:1070
concave 11:1070
illus. 11:1070
Kaleidoscope 10:930
Light 10:959-963
opaque 11:1070
Optical instruments 13:1214-
  1215
plane 11:1070
Reflection 15:1440
Telescope 18:1728-1730
Miscarriage 1:14
MISSILE 11:1071-1075
Anti-Ballistic Missile Defense
  System 11:1074-1075
Ballistics 3:221
Bomb 3:279-282
components: engine 11:1072; guid-
  ance and control system 11:1071-
  1072; on-board instruments
  11:1072; warhead 11:1071
cruise missile 11:1075
Gyroscope 9:813
illus: 19:1841; cruise 11:1073;
  guidance and control system
  11:1074; guided 11:1073; Hawk
  surface-to-air missile 11:1072;
  Saturn V 11:1071; typical U.S.
  missiles 11:1073
Intercontinental Ballistic
  Missile 11:1074
launching base 11:1072-1075
mobility in depth 11:1075
range 11:1071
Rocket 15:1461-1463
Rocket engine 15:1463-1467
Weapons 19:1838-1841
MISTLETOE 11:1075
illus. 11:1075
MISTRAL 11:1075
MITE 11:1075
illus. 11:1075
Mitochondria see **CELLS**
MITOSIS AND MEIOSIS 11:1076-
  1078
Cells 4:359-360
Heredity 9:837-841
Histology 9:846-849
Hybridization 9:862
illus: 11:1077; simple cell
  division 11:1076
Moss 12:1108-1109
Ovary 13:1229
Paramecium 13:1245-1246

process of meiosis: diakinesis
  11:1078; diplotene 11:1078;
  leptotene 11:1078; pachytene
  11:1078; zygotene 11:1078
process of mitosis: anaphase
  11:1078; interphase 11:1076;
  metaphase 11:1076; prometa-
  phase 11:1076; prophase
  11:1076; telophase 11:1078
Reproduction, asexual 15:1445
Testis 18:1736-1737
Zygote 19:1896
MIXTURE 11:1079
illus. 11:1079
Solution 16:1582
Mobile cannon, illus. 19:1840
MOCKINGBIRD 11:1079
illus. 11:1079
Moderator see **NUCLEAR SCIENCE
  GLOSSARY**
Modified Pioneer 17:1634
MODULUS 11:1080
Elasticity 6:562
illus. 11:1080
Mohair see **GOAT**
Mohave desert see **DESERT**
MOHO 11:1080-1081
illus. 11:1080
Mohs Hardness Scale 9:819
MOISSAN, HENRI 11:1081
Mojave Desert 5:496
Molar see **TEETH**
MOLASSES 11:1081
MOLD 11:1081-1082
exp. 11:1082
Fermentation 7:675
illus. 11:1081
Parasites 13:1249
Penicillin 13:1261
Plants, classification of
  14:1322-1327
MOLE 11:1082
Birthmark 3:264
Wart 19:1829
MOLE (MAMMAL) 11:1082
illus. 11:1082
Molecular compound 4:375
Molecular crystal compound 4:375
MOLECULAR THEORY 11:1083
Absolute zero 1:15
Brownian movement 4:307
changes 13:1286-1287
Kinetic theory 10:934
Modulus 11:1080
Molecule 11:1084
Molecular weight 11:1083
motion 11:1083
Physical states and changes
  13:1286-1287
Surface tension 17:1695
Temperature 18:1733
Thermodynamics 18:1741-1742
MOLECULAR WEIGHT 11:1083
Molecule 11:1083-1084
MOLECULE 11:1083-1084
Charles' Law 4:370-371
Chemistry 4:375
Compound 5:431; 11:1083
Detergent 5:496
Diffusion 6:509
Evaporation 7:646
Gay-Lussac's Gas Law 8:757
illus: water 11:1083
Kinetic theory 10:934
minimum potential energy 11:1084
Modulus 11:1080
Molecular theory 11:1083
monatomic 11:1083
Osmosis 13:1226-1227

Surface tension 17:1695
Vibration 19:1813
MOLLUSCA 11:1084-1086
Abalone 1:13
Aquaculture 2:124
Argonaut 2:134
body structure 11:1084
Chiton 4:380
Clam 4:392
Cockle 5:415
Cuttlefish 5:471
exp. 11:1086
illus: bay scallop 11:1085; blue
  mussels 11:1085; body structure
  11:1085; chiton 11:1085; limpet
  11:1085; nudibranch 11:1085;
  scallop 11:1085; snail 11:1085;
  whelk 11:1085
Limpet 10:966
Marine biology 11:1019-1021
Mussel 12:1127
Nautilus 12:1133
Octopus 12:1196
Oyster 13:1234
Pearl 13:1256-1257
Respiratory system 15:1453-1455
Scallop 16:1511
Shell 16:1534
Skeleton 16:1552-1555
Slug 16:1561
Snail 16:1564
Squid 17:1655
Whelk 19:1866
MOLTING 11:1087
amphibians 11:1087
birds 11:1087
illus: cicada 11:1087; snake
  11:1087
Insecta 9:880-882
mammals 11:1087
Metamorphosis 11:1052
Regeneration 15:1442-1443
reptiles 11:1087
Silkworm 16:1548
MOLYBDENUM 11:1087
MOMENT 11:1087
MOMENTUM 11:1088
exp. 11:1088
Forces 8:710-711
formula 11:1088
Hydroelectric power 9:865
Impulse 9:875
Train, railroad 18:1764-1765
Monarch see **BUTTERFLIES**
MONEL METAL 11:1088
Nickel 12:1148
MONERA 11:1088
MONGOLISM 11:1088-1089
Mongoloid see **EVOLUTION OF MAN**
MONGOOSE 11:1089
illus. 11:1089
MONKEY 11:1089
Ape 2:121
Gorilla 8:789
illus. 11:1089
Jungle 10:926
Lemur 10:952
Marmoset 11:1022
New World 11:1089
Old World 11:1089
Primates 14:1362-1363
MONOCOTYLEDON 11:1090
Angiosperm 1:81-82
Dicotyledon 6:580
Grasses 8:793
illus: 14:1324; fruit 11:1090;
  Indian cucumber-root 11:1090
Leaves 10:948-949
Palm 13:1240

MONOECIOUS 11:1090
Dioecious 6:516
Monomial 1:60
MONONUCLEOSIS 11:1090
Blood 3:268-269
cause 11:1090
treatment 11:1090
MONORAIL 11:1091
MONTREME 11:1091
Duckbill 6:531
Mammalia 11:1011-1012
MONSOON 11:1091
map 11:1091
Month see **CALENDAR; EARTH;
MOON**
MOON 11:1092-1094
Apollo 11:1094
atmosphere 11:1094
craters 11:1093
Gravity 8:794-795; 11:1094
illus. 11:1092, 1093
Mercury (planet) 11:1044-1046
Meteor 11:1052-1053
Moon, phases of 11:1094-1095
motion 11:1092
National Aeronautics and Space
Administration 11:1094
Satellite, natural 16:1508
Solar system 16:1575-1578
surface 11:1092-1093
Tektites 18:1724
MOON, PHASES OF 11:1094-1095
exp. 11:1094
first quarter 11:1095
illus. 11:1094-1095
Measurement 11:1033-1036
third quarter 11:1095
Venus 19:1810-1811
waning period 11:1095
waxing period 11:1095
Moonflower see **MORNING GLORY**
Moonstone see **FELDSPAR**
MOOR 11:1095
Moose, illus. 1:84
Moose see **DEER FAMILY**
MORAINE 11:1095
Glacial ages 8:779
ground 11:1095
*International Geophysical Year:
Antarctica* 9:890-891
lateral 11:1095
medial 11:1095
terminal 11:1095
Moropus, illus. 14:1360
MORDANT 11:1096
MOREL 11:1096
MORNING GLORY 11:1096
MORPHINE 11:1096
Drugs 6:530
Narcotics 12:1130
MORPHOLOGY 11:1096
MORSE, SAMUEL FINLEY BREESE
11:1097
Cable 4:320
illus. 11:1097
telegraph 11:1097; 18:1724
Mosaic virus see **VIRUS**
**MOSELEY, HENRY GWYN-
JEFFREYS** 11:1097
MOSQUITO 12:1107
anopheles, illus. 11:1009
DDT 12:1107
disease carrier 12:1107
food 1:83
illus.: body parts 12:1107; life
cycle 12:1107
Malaria 11:1009
reproduction 12:1107
Yellow fever 19:1889

MOSS 12:1108-1109
classification 12:1108
Club moss 5:411
exp. 12:1108
illus.: 4:308; 7:607; 14:1324,
1326; 18:1763; reproduction
12:1109
Peat 13:1258
Plants, classification of 14:1322-
1327
reproduction 12:1108
MOSSBAUER, RUDOLF 12:1109
MOTHS 12:1110
Butterflies 4:317
Caddis fly 4:321
Canker worms 4:333
Cocoon 5:417
Cutworm 5:471
food 1:83
illus.: io moth 12:1110; luna
12:1110; Promethea 12:1110;
silkworm 12:1110; Sphinx
12:1110
Metamorphosis 11:1052
Protective coloration 14:1375-
1376
reproduction 12:1110
MOTION 12:1111-1112
circular 12:1111
formula 12:1111, 1112
illus: linear 12:1111; uniform
12:1111
Inertia 9:877
linear 12:1111
Momentum 11:1088
Projectile 14:1371
Thermodynamics 18:1741-1742
uniform 12:1111
vector 12:1111
velocity 12:1111
Motion, perpetual see **PERPETUAL
MOTION MACHINE**
MOTION PICTURES 12:1112-1114
Camera 4:329
illus.: camera 12:1112; kineto-
graph 12:1113; phenakistoscope
12:1113; sound track 12:1114;
zoetrope 12:1113
Persistence of vision 12:1112;
13:1269
projector 12:1112, 1113; 14:1372-
1373
Sound recording 16:1592
sound track 12:1113
MOTOR 12:1114-1116
Commutator 5:429
Dynamometer 6:537
electric 12:1114
Engine 7:619-623
exp. 12:1115
Horsepower 9:856
illus.: automobile 12:1114; direc-
tion of current 12:1116
rotary 12:1115
Mouflon, illus. 7:643
Mt. Everest see **ASIA**
Mount Rainier see **NORTH AMERICA**
Mountain environment, illus. 6:552
Mountain goat see **GOAT**
Mountain laurel see **LAUREL;
RHODODENDRON**
Mountain lion see **CAT FAMILY**
Mountain sheep, illus. 12:1159
MOUNTAINS 12:1116-1117
continental drift 12:1117
Earthquake 6:547
Escarpment 7:636
Faulting 7:673
illus.: 12:1116; Alps 12:1116

Orogeny 13:1224
Mountains, elevations of 1:66
Mourning dove see **DOVE**
MOUSE 12:1117
illus.: 15:1475; grasshopper
12:1117; house 12:1117; jumping
12:1117; lemming 12:1117; white-
footed 12:1117
Rodent 15:1474-1475
MOUTH 12:1117
MUCILAGE 12:1117
MUCUS 12:1117
Mucous glands 6:511
MUCOUS MEMBRANE 12:1117
Infection 9:877
Palate 13:1236
Mud hen see **COOT**
Mud puppy see **SALAMANDER**
MULBERRY 12:1118
illus. 12:1118
MULCH 12:1118
Lily 10:964-965
MULE 12:1118
Mule deer see **DEER FAMILY**
Mullein see **WILD FLOWERS**
MULLER, PAUL HEEMAN 12:1118
MULLER, HERMANN J. 12:1118
MULLET 12:1118
illus. 12:1118
Multicellular organisms see
**ANIMALS, CLASSIFICATION OF;
EVOLUTION; PLANTS,
CLASSIFICATION OF**
Multinomial 1:60
MULTIPLE BIRTH 12:1119
fraternal twins 12:1119
identical twins 12:1119
illus: dog 12:1119; human 12:1119
Multiple fruits see **FRUIT**
MULTIPLE SCLEROSIS 12:1119
Paralysis 13:1245
Sclerosis 16:1515
Multiple star see **STARS**
MUMPS 12:1119
MUNITIONS 12:1119
MURRE 12:1119
illus. 12:1119
MUSCLE SYSTEM 12:1120-1122
all-or-none law 12:1121
Anatomy 1:76
arthropods 12:1120
Atrophy 2:174
fatigue 12:1122
function 12:1121-1122
illus: cardiac 12:1122; human
12:1121; planaria 12:1120; skel-
etal 12:1122; smooth 12:1122
Joints, skeletal 10:924-925
Muscle tissue 12:1122-1123
Muscular dystrophy 12:1123
myocytes 12:1122
Nervous system 12:1141-1145
rhythm 12:1122
Physiology 13:1289-1291
structure 12:1120-1121
tonus 12:1122
vertebrates 12:1120
MUSCLE TISSUE 12:1122-1123
Animals, classification of 1:95
cardiac 12:1123
Fiber 7:678
Fibrous tissue 7:679
Histology 9:846
illus. 9:847
Kinesthetic sense 10:934
Muscle system 12:1120-1122
Muscular dystrophy 12:1123
smooth 12:1122-1123
voluntary muscles 12:1122

MUSCULAR DYSTROPHY 12:1123
  Paralysis 13:1245
MUSHROOMS 12:1123-1124
  edible 12:1124
  exp. 12:1123
  growing 12:1124
  illus.: Brick top 12:1124; parts
    12:1123; Russula 12:1124
  poisonous 12:1124
  Toadstool 18:1755
MUSICAL INSTRUMENTS 12:1124-
  1126
  brass 12:1125
  edge-tone 12:1125
  electronic 12:1125
  exp. 12:1126
  illus: double reed 12:1125; flute
    12:1125; piccolo 12:1125;
    pipe organ pipe 12:1125;
    trombone 12:1125; trumpet
    12:1125
  Oscillator 13:1224-1225
  Overtones 13:1229-1230
  Percussion 13:1264
  Resonance 15:1452-1453
  stringed 12:1124-1125
  vibrations 12:1124; 19:1813
  wind 12:1125
  woodwind 12:1125
  voice 12:1126
MUSK 12:1126
Musk ox see **OXEN**
Muskmelon see **MELON**
MUSKRAT 12:1127
  characteristics 12:1127
  habitat 12:1127
  illus. 12:1127
MUSSEL 12:1127
  illus. 12:1127
MUSTANG 12:1127
MUSTARD 12:1127-1128
Mustard gas 4:373
MUTATION 12:1128
  Hemophilia 9:834
MUTISM 12:1128
Mutualism see **BALANCE OF
  NATURE**
MYELITIS 12:1128
MYNA 12:1128
  illus. 12:1128
Myocytes 12:1120
Myopia see **NEARSIGHTEDNESS**
MYRTLE 12:1128
  illus. 12:1128
MYXEDEMA 12:1128
Myxomycophya 18:1739
NADIR 12:1129; 19:1891
  illus. 12:1129
NAIL 12:1129
  Claw 4:392
  keratin 12:1129
  illus.: bear 12:1129; cow 12:1129;
    fowl 12:1129; horse 12:1129;
    human 12:1129
  Skin 16:1556-1557
  Skin modification 16:1558
Nanometer 5:423; 17:1643
Naptha see **PETROLEUM**
Naphthalene see **CHEMISTRY**
NARCISSUS 12:1129
  illus. 12:1129
NARCOTICS 12:1130
  Addiction 1:25
  Daffodil 5:475
  drug addict 12:1130
  Drugs 6:530
  Economic botany 6:554
  Morphine 11:1096
  Opium 13:1212-1213

Paregoric 13:1249
Plants, medicinal 14:1328-1329
Psychedelic 14:1380
uses 12:1130
withdrawal sickness 12:1130
Narwhal see **WHALE**
NASTURTIUM 12:1130
  illus. 12:1130
National Aeronautics and Space
  Administration 2:156, 157; 3:292;
  11:1094
NATURAL BRIDGE 12:1130-1131
  illus. 12:1131
  Bridges 3:294-296
  formation 12:1130-1131
  River 15:1459-1460
NATURAL GAS 12:1131, 13:1207-
  1208
  British Thermal Unit 3:297
  Butane 4:317
  Europe 7:645
  Fossil fuels 8:719
Natural number see **ALGEBRA**
NATURAL RESOURCES 12:1131-
  1133; 13:1207-1208
  agricultural 12:1132
  Australia 2:177-181
  conservation 12:1133; 5:439
  distribution 12:1132
  energy 12:1133
  Europe 7:645
  illus.: animal life 12:1132; min-
    eral deposits 12:1132; trees
    12:1131; sunlight and soil
    12:1132; water 12:1132
  *International Control of Natural
    Resources* 9:888
  Mineral 11:1065-1067; 12:1132
  nonrenewable 12:1131
  North America 12:1156-1160
  renewable 12:1131
  South America 16:1597
  water 12:1131
Natural selection see **EVOLUTION**
Natural science see **BIOLOGY;
  BOTANY; CHEMISTRY; PHYSICS;
  ZOOLOGY**
NATURALIST 12:1133
NATURE 12:1133
Nauplius 10:943
NAUSEA 12:1133
NAUTICAL MILE 12:1133
NAUTILUS 12:1133
  illus. 12:1133
Nautilus submarine see **SUBMARINE**
NAVIGATION 12:1134-1135
  Astrolabe 2:154
  astro-navigation 12:1135
  Beacon 3:235
  celestial 12:1134-1135
  Compass 5:430
  Dead reckoning 5:485; 12:1134
  Direction finder 6:517
  electronic 12:1135
  Geography 8:762
  illus.: early navigators 12:1135;
    ground control 12:1134; instru-
    ments 12:1134; use of land-
    marks 12:1134
  Measurement 11:1036
  measurement of speed 12:1135
  measurement of time 12:1135
  pilotage 12:1134
Neanderthal man see **EVOLUTION
  OF MAN**
Neaps see **TIDE**
NEARSIGHTEDNESS 12:1136
  Astigmatism 2:153-154
  cause 12:1136

correction 12:1136
Eye 7:664-667
illus.: 12:1136
Optometry 12:1215-1217
NEBULA 12:1136
  Laplace, Pierre Simon, Marquis de
    10:942
  Milky Way 11:1062
  Nova 12:1161
  Orion 13:1224
NECTAR 12:1136
NECTARINE 12:1136
NEEL, LOUIS EUGENE 12:1137
Negative integer 1:60
Negroid see **EVOLUTION OF MAN**
NEMATHELMINTHES 12:1137-
  1138
  Annelida 2:107-108
  Ascaris 2:144
  body structure 12:1138
  Eelworm 6:558
  habitat 12:1137-1138
  Hookworm 9:852
  illus.: ascaris 12:1137; Nematoda
    12:1138
  locomotion 12:1137
  parasitic 12:1137
  Pinworm 12:1197
  Skeleton 16:1552-1555
  Trichina 18:1772
  Worm 19:1881-1882
NEMATOCYST 12:1138
  Hydroid colony 9:867
  Nematoda illus. 12:1138
Nemertean ribbon worm, illus.
  19:1881
NEODYMIUM 12:1138
  Praseodymium 14:1356
Neolithic see **STONE AGE**
NEON 12:1138
NEPHRIDIA 12:1138
  Earthworm 6:548
  Kidney 10:932-933
NEPHRITIS 12:1138-1139
  causes 12:1138
  treatment 12:1139
NEPTUNE 12:1139-1140
  atmosphere 12:1140
  discovery 12:1139
  illus. 12:1139
  orbital path 12:1139
  Pluto 14:1338-1340
  satellites 12:1140
  size 12:1139
  Uranus 18:1789-1790
NEPTUNIUM 12:1140
NERNST, WALTHER H. 12:1140
NERVE CELL 12:1140-1141
  axon 12:1140-1141
  Autonomic nervous system
    2:189-190
  Cells 4:359-360
  cyton 12:1140
  Fiber 7:678
  Histology 9:846
  illus. 12:1141
  Impulse 9:875
  myelin 12:1141
  nucleus 12:1140
  Pain 13:1235
  Physiology 13:1289-1291
  Spinal cord 17:1648-1649
NERVOUS SYSTEM 12:1141-1145
  Anatomy 1:76
  Autonomic nervous system
    2:189-190
  Barbiturates 3:225
  Brain 3:289
  cell 12:1141

central nervous system: auto-
nomic system 12:1144; brain
12:1142-1144; spinal cord
12:1144
Cerebellum 4:366
Cerebrum 4:367
Dale, Sir Henry H. 5:478
Echinodermata 6:550
Electroencephalograph 6:574-
575
Epilepsy 7:631
exp.: nerve endings on skin
12:1142
Eye 7:667
Ganglion 8:750
Hiccough 9:844
Histology 9:846
Homeostasis 9:851
illus. 12:1143
Impulse 9:875
Medulla oblongata 11:1041
Meninges 11:1043
Midbrain 11:1058
Multiple sclerosis 12:1119
Muscle system 12:1120-1122
Myelitis 12:1128
Nerve cell 12:1140-1141
Paralysis 13:1245
Pineal gland 13:1296
Pituitary gland 14:1310
Physiology 13:1289-1291
Poliomyelitis 14:1346
Psychology 14:1380-1381
Receptors 15:1438
reflexes 12:1142
Sense organs 16:1528-1529
Spinal cord 17:1648-1649
Stimulant 17:1673
Stimulus 17:1673
Nests see **BIRD NESTS**
NETTLE 12:1145
Hop 9:852
illus.: false nettle 12:1145
Neurohormone see **ATROPINE;
BIOCHEMISTRY**
NEUTRALIZATION 12:1145
Hydrolysis 9:867
illus. 12:1145
NEUTRINO 12:1145
NEUTRON 12:1145-1146
illus. 12:1145
Nuclear reactor 12:1166-1168
NEUTRON STAR 12:1146
Neutron 12:1146
NEWT 12:1146-1147
habitat 12:1146
illus.: 12:1146; 15:1443
reproduction 12:1146-1147
Salamander 15:1489-1490
NEWTON, SIR ISAAC 2:166;
12:1147
Centrifugal and centripetal forces
4:364
Color 5:423
Copernicus, Nicolaus 5:447
Corpuscular theory 5:449
Gravity 8:794
illus. 12:1147
Kepler, Johannes 10:931
Mathematics 11:1029-1030
Mechanics 11:1037-1038
*Newton's Law of Universal Grav-
itation* 8:794
Newton's Laws of Motion 8:710-
711; 9:877; 10:922
Resistance 15:1452
Spectrum 17:1643
Niagara Falls see **NORTH AMERICA**
NICHE 12:1148

NICKEL 12:1148
Metal 11:1049-1051
Monel metal 11:1088
Nickel-plating see
ELECTROPLATING
NICOLLE, CHARLES JULES HENRI
12:1148
Nicotiana, illus. 12:1149
NICOTINE 12:1148
Tobacco 18:1756
Nictitating membrane see **FROG**
Night see **DAY AND NIGHT; EARTH**
NIGHT-BLOOMING PLANTS
12:1148-1149
illus.: cereus 12:1149; jasmine
12:1149; nicotiana 12:1149
Nocturnal habits 12:1154-1155
NIGHTHAWK 12:1149
illus. 12:1149
NIGHTINGALE 12:1149
illus. 12:1149
Nightshade see **WILD FLOWERS**
Nimbo-stratus see **CLOUDS**
Nimbus see **CLOUDS**
NIOBIUM 12:1149
Niter see **SALTPETER**
Niton see **RADON**
NITRATE 12:1150
NITRATION 12:1150
NITRIC ACID 12:1150
NITROGEN 12:1150
ammonia 12:1150
Nitrogen cycle 12:1150-1151
Protein 14:1376-1377
saltpeter 12:1150
NITROGEN CYCLE 12:1150-1151
combine with oxygen 12:1151
Decomposer organism 5:486
Fallow 7:670
Fertilizer 7:678; 12:1151
illus. 12:1151
legumes 12:1151
release of nitrogen 12:1150-1151
root nodules 12:1151
Soil testing 16:1572
NITROGLYCERIN 12:1151
dynamite 12:1151
Gunpowder 9:811
NITROUS ACID 12:1151
Nits 10:978
NOBEL PRIZE 12:1154
winners—1901-1977, chart
12:1152-1153
NOBELIUM 12:1154
NOCTURNAL HABITS 12:1154-
1155
adaptation 12:1155
illus.: bear 12:1155; desert
animals 12:1155; skunk 12:1155
Kiwi 10:935
Mouse 12:1117
Sleep 16:1560
Nodal tissue 9:825
NODE 12:1155
Bud 4:309
NOISE 12:1155
NONMETAL 12:1155
NORMALITY 12:1155
NORTH AMERICA 12:1156-1160
Climate 4:394-397; 12:1158-1160
Continent 5:444
Geography 8:761-763
Geologic time table 8:765
Geology 8:768-769
illus.: beaver 12:1159; chipmunk
12:1159; Labrador duck 12:1159;
manatee 12:1159; mountain sheep
12:1159; mule deer 12:1159;
puma 12:1159

land forms: Appalachian area
12:1157; Cordillera 12:1158;
Coastal Plain 12:1158; Great
Plains 12:1158; Laurentian
Upland 12:1156
map 12:1157; temperature and
rainfall 12:1156; vegetation
12:1156
Natural resources 12:1131-1133;
12:1160
plants and animals 12:1160
Plateau 14:1335
rivers and drainage: Great Lakes
12:1158; Missouri-Mississippi
system 12:1158
NORTH ATLANTIC DRIFT 12:116C
Currents, ocean 5:469
Gulf Stream 9:810
Sea level 16:1517
North Equatorial Current 5:469
North Equatorial Drift 5:469
North Pole see **MAGNET; POLES,
NORTH AND SOUTH**
North Star see **POLARIS; URSA
MAJOR AND URSA MINOR**
Northern Cross see **CYGNUS**
Northern Lights see **AURORA
BOREALIS**
NOSE 12:1161
external 12:1161
illus.: anteater 12:1161; dog
12:1161; elephant 12:1161;
human, cross section 12:1161;
salamander 12:1161
Sense organs 16:1528-1529
Smell 16:1562
NOTOCHORD 12:1161
Animals, classification of 1:95
Chordata 4:383
Embryology 6:595
NOVA 12:1161
Star, double 17:1659
Stars 17:1660-1662
NOVOCAINE 12:1161
NUCLEAR ENERGY 12:1162-1164
Bomb 3:281-282
Charged particles 4:370
Energy 7:616
Energy crisis 7:618
Engine 7:619-621
fission 12:1162-1163
fusion 12:1163
illus.: fission 12:1162; fusion
12:1163; power station 12:1164;
submarine 12:1162
Isotope 10:978
mass and energy 12:1163-1164
Neutrino 12:1145
Neutron 12:1145-1146
Nuclear reactor 12:1166-1168;
12:1162
Nuclear science 12:1170-1175
Physics 13:1287-1288
Plutonium 14:1340
radioactive decay 12:1162
Radioactivity 15:1422-1423
Rocket engine 15:1463-1467
Thermonuclear reaction 18:1744
Uranium 18:1788-1789
Volt 19:1823-1824
Weapons 19:1838-1841
NUCLEAR PARTICLES 12:1164-
1165
baryons 12:1164
bosons 12:1165
Cloud chamber 5:408
illus.: carbon family of isotopes
12:1165
leptons 12:1165

Meson 11:1046; 12:1164
Nuclear energy 12:1162-1164
Nuclear reactor 12:1166-1168
Nuclear science 12:1170-1175
Particle detector 13:1252
quarks 12:1165
Radium 15:1424-1425
smashing 12:1165
12 conservation laws 12:1165
NUCLEAR REACTOR 12:1166-1169
Accelerators (particle) 1:17-18
design 12:1167
equations 12:1168
Geiger counter 8:758
Generator 8:761
Graphite 8:792
history 12:1166
illus.: Argonne National Laboratory
12:1168-1170; first 12:1166
Lunar base 10:980
moderators 12:1167
Neutron 12:1146
Nuclear energy 12:1162-1164
Pharmacology 13:1272-1274
Radiation, protection from
15:1412-1413
radioisotopes 12:1167
Rocket engine 15:1463-1467
Uranium 18:1788-1789
NUCLEAR SCIENCE 12:1170-1175
Accelerators (particles) 1:17
Americium 1:71
Antimatter 2:117
atomic structure 12:1171-1172
Bohr theory 3:278
Californium 4:324-325
Chain reaction 4:368
Chemical change 4:371-372
Chemistry 4:374-375
determining age of wood 12:1174
effect on heredity 12:1174
Elements 6:586-589
Fission 7:688
Fuel 8:738-740
Geiger counter 8:758
Heavy water 9:830-831
illus.: Argonaut test reactor
12:1171; drinking radioactive
iodine 12:1173; natural uranium
12:1172; radioactive bufagin
12:1173; spontaneous disintegra-
tion of radioisotope 12:1174;
use in tracing motion of dif-
ferent cells 12:1174
Isotope 10:918; 12:1172-1173
Matter 11:1031
matter and energy 12:1171
Meson 11:1046
Microscope, electron 11:1057
Molecular theory 11:1083
mutants 12:1174
Neptunium 12:1140
Neutrino 12:1145
Neutron 12:1146
newer uses of nuclear energy
12:1173
Nuclear energy 12:1162-1164
nuclear fission 12:1170-1172
Nuclear reactor 12:1166-1168
Potassium 14:1354
Proton (elementary particle)
14:1377
Radiation 15:1407-1409
Radiation, protection from
15:1412-1413
Radiation, uses of 15:1414-1415
radioactive pollution 12:1175
Radioactivity 15:1422-1423

radioisotopes 12:1173
Ray, cosmic 15:1434
Rutherford, Ernest 15:1486-1487
Transmutation of elements 18:1769
treatment of cancer 12:1174
U.S. Atomic Energy Commission
12:1175
Universe 18:1786-1788
Uranium 18:1788-1789
Nuclear science glossary 12:1176-1177
NUCLEIC ACID 12:1178
illus.: deoxyribonucleic acid
12:1178; ribonucleic acid 12:1178
Nucleolus see **CELL; HISTOLOGY**
Nucleon see **NUCLEAR PARTICLES;**
NUCLEAR SCIENCE
NUCLEOPROTEIN 12:1178-1179
deoxyribonucleic acid 12:1178
heredity 12:1179
nucleotide 12:1178
Protein 14:1376-1377
Purine 14:1388
Pyrimidine 14:1388-1389
ribonucleic acid 12:1178
Virus 19:1816-1817
Nucleotides 4:385
Nucleus see **ATOM; NUCLEAR**
PARTICLES; NUCLEAR SCIENCE
Nudibranch illus. 11:1085
NUMERICAL SYSTEMS 12:1179-1183
Computer 5:434-436
illus.: early 12:1179
non-positional: ciphered numeral
systems 12:1181; multiplicative
systems 12:1181; simple grouping
systems 12:1180
positional systems 12:1181-1183
Zero 19:1891-1892
Nursery see **HORTICULTURE**
NUTCRACKER 12:1183
illus. 12:1183
NUTHATCH 12:1183
Bird houses 3:258
illus. 12:1183
NUTMEG 12:1183
illus. 12:1183
Mace 10:988
NUTRITION 12:1184
Hygiene 9:869
illus.: food groups 12:1184
Obesity 12:1187
Physiology 13:1289-1291
Protein 14:1376-1377
Vitamin 19:1818
Vitamin deficiency 19:1818
NUTS 8:735; 12:1184-1185
Almond 1:64
Beech 3:241
Hickory 9:844
illus.: almond 12:1185; Brazil
nut 12:1185; chestnut 12:1185;
English walnut 12:1185; pecan
12:1185
uses 12:1185
varieties 12:1185
NYLON 12:1185
Forest products 8:713
Parachute 13:1244
Nymph see **METAMORPHOSIS**
OAK 12:1186
Beech 3:241
Hardwood 9:820
illus. 12:1186
OARFISH 12:1186
illus. 12:1186
OASIS 12:1186
illus. 12:1186

OATS 12:1186
Cereal grains 4:366
illus. 12:1186
OBESITY 12:1187
Fat, adipose tissue 7:672
harmful effects 12:1187
hypothalamus 12:1187
Oblate spheroid 6:541
OBSERVATORY 12:1187
illus. 12:1187
Planetarium 14:1312-1313
Telescope 18:1728-1730
Obsidian 8:781, 10:945
Occipital lobe see **BRAIN**
OCEAN 12:1188-1190
divisions 12:1188-1189
features 12:1189
illus.: effect of depth of primary
colors of spectrum on animal life
12:1190; importance 12:1189;
map 12:1188
importance 12:1189-1190
International Hydrological Decade
9:894-895
Isotope 10:919
Marine biology 11:1019-1021
Mid-Atlantic Ridge 11:1058
Oceanography 12:1190-1195
origin 12:1188
Pelagic 13:1259
Sand 15:1493
Sea 16:1516
Sea water 16:1519-1520
seasons 12:1189
Tsunami 18:1775
Water desalinization 19:1833
Ocean currents see **CURRENTS,**
OCEAN; INTERNATIONAL
GEOPHYSICAL YEAR; OCEAN;
OCEANOGRAPHY
Ocean life see **MARINE BIOLOGY**
Ocean perch, illus. 11:1021
OCEANOGRAPHY 12:1190-1195
Balance of nature 3:220
Bathysphere and bathyscaphe
3:230-231
Currents, ocean 5:467-471
Deep-sea diving 5:488
Depth sounding 5:493-494
Grand Banks 8:791
Glomar Challenger 8:783
Gulf Stream 9:809-810
illus.: diving apparatus 12:1194;
diving records 12:1192; ocean re-
search 12:1191; study of spec-
imens 12:1193
International Geophysical Year:
the Solid Earth 9:894
International Oceanographic
Decade 9:896
Island 10:917
Marine biology 11:1019-1021
methods of study: diving apparatus
12:1195; measuring instruments
12:1194; sampling apparatus
12:1193
Moho 11:1080-1081
origin 12:1190-1191
Photography 13:1281-1282
Piccard, Auguste 13:1292
Plankton 14:1313
Sea 16:1516
Sea level 16:1517
Sonic barrier 16:1584
subjects of study 12:1191-1192
Submarine 17:1680
Tide 18:1750-1751
Ocelot see **CAT FAMILY**
OCHOA, SERVERO 12:1195

OCTOPUS 12:1195-1196
body structure 12:1196
Cuttlefish 5:471
illus.: 1:85; 12:1195
Marine biology 11:1019-1021
Mollusca 11:1084-1086
Nautilus 12:1133
locomotion 1:87
Squid 17:1655
OERSTED, HANS CHRISTIAN
12:1196
aluminum 1:68
Induction 9:876
Offset see **PRINTING**
OHM 12:1196
Electricity 6:566
Resistance 15:1452
Volt 19:1823-1824
OHM, GEORG SIMON 12:1196
illus. 12:1196
OHMMETER 12:1197
illus. 12:1197
Ohm 12:1196
Ohm, Georg Simon 12:1196
Ohm's Law see **RESISTANCE**
OIL 12:1197
exp. "oil drop" 11:1063
fossil fuels 13:1207
OIL GLAND 12:1197
Cyst 5:474
Gland 8:780
illus. 12:1197
Oil 12:1197
OIL WELL 13:1207-1208
exploration 13:1208
fields 13:1207
formation 13:1207
illus.: 13:1207; 13:1271
natural gas 13:1208
oil pools 13:1207
oil reservoirs 13:1207-1208
Petroleum 13:1270
OINTMENT 13:1208
Okapi see **GIRAFFE**
OKRA 13:1208
Hibiscus 9:843-844
illus. 13:1208
Oleander see **WILD FLOWERS**
Olfactory see **NOSE**
Oligocene see **CENOZOIC ERA;
GEOLOGIC TIME TABLE**
OLIVE 13:1208
Ash 2:145
illus.: 13:1208; 7:644
Jasmine 10:920
OLIVINE 13:1209
Ommatidia 7:668
OMNIVORE 13:1209; 3:216
Herbivore 9:836-837
Raccoon 14:1396
Omnivorous see **ANIMALS,
CLASSIFICATION OF; BALANCE
OF NATURE**
ONION 13:1209
ONNES, HEIKE KAMERLINGH
13:1209
ONYX 13:1209
illus. 13:1209
Quartz 14:1391-1392
OPAL 13:1209-1210
illus. 13:1210
OPAQUE 13:1210
illus. 13:1210
Mirror 11:1017
OPEN HEARTH PROCESS 3:247-
248; 13:1210-1212
basic oxygen furnace (BOF)
13:1211
charge 13:1210

converter 13:1210
illus. 13:1211
melting of charge 13:1211
Siemens regenerative process
13:1211
Steel 17:1666-1668
OPEN PIT MINE 13:1212
strip mining 13:1212
Operation Blue Book 18:1786
Operation see **SURGERY**
OPHTHALMOSCOPE 13:1212
Opiate see **NARCOTICS; OPIUM**
OPIUM 13:1212-1213
Drugs 6:529-530
illus. 13:1212
Morphine 11:1096
Narcotics 12:1130
Paregoric 13:1249
Plants, medicinal 14:1328-1329
Poppy 14:1349
OPPOSUM 13:1213
characteristics 13:1213
classification 13:1213
illus. 11:1026
Marsupial 11:1026
OPPENHEIMER, J. ROBERT
13:1213-1214
Optic nerve see **EYE; NERVOUS
SYSTEM**
OPTICAL ILLUSION 13:1214
illus. 13:1214
OPTICAL INSTRUMENTS 7:664-
667; 13:1214-1215
binoculars 3:250-251
eyeglasses 13:1214
illus. binoculars 13:1215; camera
lens 13:1215; electron microscope
13:1215; microscope 13:1214;
polarized lens 13:1215; telescope
13:1215
Lens, man-made 10:952-952
Microscope, electron 11:1057
Periscope 13:1265-1266
Photometer 13:1214, 1284
polarized light 13:1215
Range finder 15:1428
Optical masers see **LASERS**
OPTICS 13:1215
Huygens, Christian 9:861
OPTOMETRY 7:664-667; 13:1215-
1217
Astigmatism 2:153-154; 13:1217
emmetropia 13:1216
Farsightedness 7:671
Focus 8:708
history 13:1215-1216
hyperopia 13:1216
illus.: vision correction 13:1216,
1217
Lens, man-made 10:952-953
myopia 13:1216
Nearsightedness 12:1136
presbyopia 13:1217
refractive errors 13:1216
responsibilities 13:1216
strabismus 13:1217
visual training and orthoptics
13:1216
ORAL 13:1217
Orange see **CITRUS FRUITS**
ORANGUTAN 13:1217
Apes 2:121
characteristics 13:1217
diet 13:1217
illus. 13:1217
Primates 14:1362-1363
ORBIT 13:1217-1218
Asteroid 2:152
atoms 13:1218

celestial bodies 13:1217-1218
laws of orbital motion 13:1218
ORBITAL SYSTEMS 13:1218-
1220
artificial satellites 13:1218-
1220
east-west 13:1219
how achieved 13:1219
illus.: planets 13:1218; polar
and equatorial 13:1219; space
travel 13:1220
Perigee 13:1265
polar 13:1219
Orbit 13:1217-1218
radio and TV 13:1219
Satellite, man-made 16:1507-
1508
uses 13:1218
ORCHARD 13:1220
illus. 13:1220
ORCHID 13:1221
classification 13:1221
Epiphyte 7:631
illus. 13:1221
Jungle 10:926
propagation 13:1221
Order see **ANIMALS,
CLASSIFICATION OF; PLANTS,
CLASSIFICATION OF**
Ordovician see **GEOLOGIC TIME
TABLE; PALEOZOIC ERA**
ORE 13:1221
chemical compounds 13:1221
Flotation 7:692
Hematite 9:833
illus. 13:1221
Lode 10:977
native elements 13:1221
Open pit mine 13:1212
Reduction 15:1439
OREGANO 13:1222
illus. 13:1222
Marjoram 11:1022
ORGAN 13:1222
ORGANIC COMPOUNDS 13:1222-
1223
alcohols 13:1222
Amino acid 1:71
Benzene 3:245
benzene-ring 13:1223
Biochemistry 3:251
Carbon 4:337-338
Carbon life 4:341
Catalyst 4:352
Cells 4:360
Chemistry 4:373-377
Coal tar 5:414
Cytology 5:474
Elements in the human body 6:590
Enzymes 7:629-630
Ester 7:637
Ether 7:637
Ethylene 7:638
Fermentation 7:675
Formula 8:718-719
historical uses 13:1222
Hydrocarbons 9:864; 13:1222
illus.: benzene 13:1223
Matter 11:1031
Methane 11:1053
Nutrition 12:1184
Petroleum 13:1270
Phenols 13:1275
Plastics 14:1332-1334
properties 13:1222
Sulfa drugs 17:1684
Urea 18:1790
Uric acid 18:1791
uses 13:1223

ORGANIC ROCK 13:1223
ORGANISM 13:1223
ORIOLE 13:1223
  Bird nests 3:259
  illus. 13:1223
ORION 13:1224
  Canis Major and Canis Minor 4:333
  illus. 13:1224
  mythology 13:1224
  Scorpius 16:1515-1516
  Star, double 17:1658-1659
Orion, dogs of see **CANIS MAJOR
AND CANIS MINOR**
Ornithology see **BIRD**
Ornithopter see **AVIATION**
OROGENY 13:1224
ORYX 13:1224
  illus. 13:1224
OSAGE ORANGE 13:1224
OSCILLATOR 13:1224-1225
  Vacuum tube 18:1793-1794
OSCILLATORIA 13:1225
OSCILLOSCOPE 13:1225
  Cathode-ray tube 4:355
  dual-beam 13:1225
  dual-trace 13:1225
  illus. 13:1225
  long persistence 13:1225
Osier see **WILLOW**
OSLER, SIR WILLIAM 13:1225-
  1226
OSMIUM 13:1226
  Haber Process 9:814
OSMOSIS 13:1226-1227
  Absorption, physiological 1:16
  classic experiment 12:1226
  Diffusion 6:509
  exp. 13:1227
  Hypertonic solution 9:871
  Hypotonic solution 9:872
  illus. 13:1226
  Isotonic solution 10:918
  Liquid 10:968-970
  molecular movement 13:1226
  Permeability 13:1267-1268
  Root 15:1476-1477
Osmotic pressure 10:918
OSPREY 13:1227
  Bird nests 3:260
  illus. 13:1227
OSSIFICATION 13:1228
OSTRICH 13:1228
  Birds, flightless 3:261
  commensalism 13:1228
  illus. 13:1228
Ostwald process 1:72
OTTER 13:1228
  characteristics 13:1228
  diet 13:1228
  habitat 13:1228
  illus.: 7:643; 13:1228
  Weasel 19:1841-1842
Ova 3:207
OVARY 13:1229
  Dioecious 6:516
  Endocrine glands 7:610
  Gonad 8:787
  illus. 13:1229
  Ovum 13:1230
  Pituitary gland 14:1310
Oven bird see **WARBLER**
OVERTONES 13:1229-1230
  fundamental tone 13:1229
  illus. 13:1230
  Noise 12:1155
  Sound 16:1585-1590
  timbre 13:1229
  vibrations 13:1230
  Voice 19:1820-1821

OVIPAROUS 13:1230; 17:1639
OVOVIVIPAROUS 13:1230;
  17:1639
  Guppy 9:811
Ovulation see **ESTROUS CYCLE;
MENSTRUATION; MULTIPLE
BIRTHS**
OVUM 13:1230
  Eggs 6:559
  Ovary 13:1229
OWL 13:1230-1231
  Birds of prey 3:263
  characteristics 13:1230
  habitat 13:1230-1231
  illus. 1:84
Ox see **OXEN**
OXEN 13:1231
  characteristics 13:1231
  illus.: musk ox 13:1231
  varieties 13:1231
  Water buffalo 19:1831-1832
  Yak 19:1887
OXIDATION 13:1231-1232
  Bessemer process 3:248
  Coal gas 5:414
  Combustible 5:425
  Combustion 5:425
  exp. 13:1231
  Fire 7:683
  oxidation reduction 13:1231
  Oxide 13:1232
  Oxygen 13:1232-1233
  Praseodymium 14:1356
  Reduction 15:1439
  Rusting 15:1485
  Weathering 19:1858
OXIDATION NUMBER 13:1232
OXIDE 13:1232
  Anhydride 1:82
  illus. 13:1232
  Oxidation 13:1231-1232
Oxyacetylene torch see **ACETYLENE**
OXYGEN 13:1232-1233
  Carbon cycle 4:339
  Combustion 5:425
  compounds 13:1233
  illus.: preparation 13:1233
  molecular structure 13:1233
  Nitrogen cycle 12:1150-1151
  Oxidation 13:1231-1232
  Ozone 13:1234
  preparation 13:1233
  Priestley, Joseph 14:1362
  Protein 14:1376-1377
OXYGEN TENT 13:1233
Oxytocin 9:872
Oyashio Current 5:470
OYSTER 13:1234
  Animals, classification of 1:95
  characteristics 13:1234
  commercial production 13:1234
  illus. 13:1234
  Mussel 12:1127
  reproduction 13:1234
OYSTER PLANT 13:1234
  illus. 13:1234
OZONE 13:1234
  Bleaching agents 3:266
  harmful effects 13:1234
  properties 13:1234
Ozonosphere see **ATMOSPHERE**

Pacemaker see **HEART**
PACHYDERM 13:1235
  illus. 13:1235
Pacific albacore, illus. 11:1021
Pack rat, illus. 15:1475
PADDLEFISH 13:1235
  illus. 13:1235

PAHOEHOE LAVA 13:1235
  Volcano 19:1823
PAIN 13:1235
  Symptom 18:1713
PAINT 13:1236
  Color 5:423
  Dye 6:534-535
  enamel 13:1236
  oil 13:1236
  Pigment 13:1294
  Shellac 16:1534
  solvent base 13:1236
  vehicle 13:1236
  water 13:1236
Painted cup see **WILD FLOWERS**
PALATE 13:1236
  illus. 13:1236
Paleocene epoch 4:361
Paleolithic see **STONE AGE**
PALEONTOLOGY 13:1237-1238
  Animals, classification of 1:92
  Archeology 2:129-131
  Biology 3:253
  Cenozoic Era 4:361-362
  collecting fossils 13:1238
  Cuvier, Georges 5:472
  Earth, early development of
   6:545-547
  Evolution 7:654
  Evolution of man 7:654-659
  Fauna 7:673
  fields: paleobiochemistry 12:1237;
   paleobotany 13:1238; paleo-
   ecology 13:1238; paleoethnol-
   ogy 13:1238; paleogeography
   13:1238; paleontography 13:1238
  Flora 7:692
  Fossils 8:719-723
  Geologic time table 8:765
  Geology 8:768-769
  illus. 5:472; 13:1237, 1238
  Mammoth 11:1013
  Organic rock 13:1223
  paleoclimatology 13:1238
  Petrification 13:1270
  Prehistoric mammals 14:1359-
   1360
  Sediment 16:1523
  Trilobite 18:1772
  Zoology 19:1895-1896, 1897
PALEOZOIC ERA 13:1239
  Appalachian 13:1239
  Cambrian 13:1239
  Carboniferous 13:1239
  Devonian 13:1239
  illus.: animals 13:1239; corals
   13:1239
  Mesozoic Era 11:1047
  Mississippian 13:1239
  Ordovician 13:1239
  Pennsylvanian 13:1239
  Permian 13:1239
  Silurian 13:1239
PALLADIUM 13:1239
PALM 13:1240
  classification 13:1240
  Coconut 5:416
  Date 5:482
  illus.: date 13:1240; palmetto
   13:1240; royal 13:1240; tra-
   velers 13:1240; umbrella
   14:1331
  importance 13:1240
  Raffia 15:1425
Palmate venation see **LEAVES**
Palmer, Nathaniel 2:110
Palsy see **PARALYSIS**
Pampas see **SOUTH AMERICA**
Pampas grass, illus. 16:1593

Panama Canal see **SOUTH AMERICA**
PANCREAS 13:1240
  Diabetes 5:497
  Digestive system 6:510
  Endocrine glands 7:610
  Glandular tissue 8:780
  Histology 9:849
  illus. 13:1240
  Islets of Langerhans 10:917
  Mumps 12:1119
  Transplant 18:1770
PANDA 13:1241
  giant 13:1241
  illus. 13:1241
  lesser 13:1241
PANDANUS 13:1241
PANSY 13:1241
  illus. 13:1241; 19:1815
Panther see **CAT FAMILY**
PAPAYA 13:1241
  illus. 13:1241
  Plants, tropical 14:1329-1330
PAPER 13:1242
  Forest products 8:712
  illus.: manufacture 13:1242
  manufacture 13:1242
  Papyrus 13:1243
  Printing 14:1364-1370
  properties 13:1242
  sources of pulp 13:1242
Paper nautilus 2:134
PAPRIKA 13:1243
  Cayenne 4:357
  illus. 13:1243
  Pepper 13:1263
PAPYRUS 13:1243
  illus. 13:1243
  Paper 13:1242
PARACELSUS, PHILIPPUS AUREOLUS 13:1243
PARACHUTE 13:1244
  Nylon 12:1185
PARAFFIN 13:1244
  Forest products 8:713
  Microtome 11:1058
Paraffin series 9:864
PARAKEET 13:1245
  characteristics 13:1245
  Claw 4:392
  habitat 13:1245
  illus. 13:1245
  Parrot 13:1250
PARALLAX 13:1245
PARALLEL 13:1245
  Earth 6:544
Parallelism 7:634
PARALYSIS 13:1245
PARAMECIUM 13:1245-1246
  animal body structure 1:83
  digestive system 13:1246
  locomotion 13:1246
  Protozoa 14:1378-1379
  reproduction 13:1246
  Trichocyst 18:1772
PARASITES 3:209; 3:218-219; 13:1247-1249
  Ascaris 2:144
  Eelworm 6:558
  Epiphyte 7:631
  Filaria 7:680
  Flea 7:689
  Hobkworm 9:852
  illus.: cancerroot 13:1247; ergot on rye 13:1247; leech 13:1248; plant louse 13:1248; tapeworm 13:1247, 1248; tick 13:1248
  Infection 9:877
  Lamprey 10:941

  Liver fluke 10:973
  Malaria 11:1009
  Meningitis 11:1043
  methods of attack and defense 13:1248
  Microbe 11:1054
  Mold 11:1081-1082
  movement from host to host 13:248
  Nemathelminthes 12:1137-1138
  Pinworm 13:1297
  Plant diseases 14:1318-1319
  plants and animals 13:1247
  Platyhelminthes 14:1336-1337
  Protozoa 14:1378-1379
  Rot 15:1479
  Rust 15:1484
  saprophytes 13:1247
  scavengers 13:1247
  Tapeworm 18:1716-1717
  Tick 18:1749
  Trichina 18:1772
Parasympathetic see **AUTONOMIC NERVOUS SYSTEM**
Parathormone 13:1249
PARATHYROID 13:1249
  Endocrine glands 7:610
  function 13:1249
  overactivity 13:1249
  parathormone 13:1249
PARE, AMBROISE 13:1249
PAREGORIC 13:1249
PARICUTIN VOLCANO 13:1249
Paris green see **ARSENIC**
PARKINSON'S DISEASE 13:1250
  causes 13:1250
  symptoms 13:1250
PARROT 13:1250
  illus.: cockatoos 13:1250
  Lovebird 10:978
  Macaw 10:988
  Myna 12:1128
Parrot fever see **ANIMAL DISEASES; PARROT**
PARSEC 13:1250-1251
PARSLEY 13:1251
  Anise 2:107
  Celery 4:358
  Dill 6:513
  illus. 13:1251
PARSNIP 13:1251
PARTHENOCARPY 13:1251
  Fruit 8:736
PARTHENOGENESIS 13:1251-1252
  aphids 13:1251
  bees 13:1251
  Daphnia 5:481
  illus. 13:1251
  Reproduction, sexual 15:1446-1447
  rotifers 13:1251
Particle see **NUCLEAR PARTICLES**
PARTICLE DETECTOR 13:1252
PARTICULATE MATTER 13:1252
  Pollution 14:1347-1348
Partridge see **FOWL, GROUSE, QUAIL**
PARTURITION 13:1252
Pascal's Law 9:864
Pasqueflower see **WILD FLOWERS**
Passion flower see **PLANTS, TROPICAL**
Passion fruit 14:1330
PASTEUR, LOUIS 2:115, 118; 13:1252-1253
  Animal diseases 1:89
  bacteriology 3:210
  Leeuwenhoek, Anton van 10:950
  Medicine 11:1038-1040

  Pasteurization 13:1253
  Rabies 14:1395
  Sanitation 15:1495
PASTEURIZATION 13:1253
  Bacteriology 3:210-211
  Food preservation 8:709-710
  illus. 13:1253
  Milk 11:1061
  Pasteur, Louis 13:1252-1253
  Sanitation 15:1495
  Sterilization 17:1671
Patella see **SKELETON**
PATHOLOGY 13:1254-1255
  Biology 3:254
  Botany 3:284-285
  cellular 13:1254
  clinical 13:1254
  Diagnosis 5:497
  Disease 6:519
  Fever 7:678
  Fluoroscope 7:695-696
  Germ 8:773
  Germ theory 8:773
  history 13:1254
  Hypertrophy 9:871
  illus. 13:1254
  Internal medicine 9:887
  Surgery 17:1696-1697
  Swelling 18:1711
  Symptom 18:1713
  Vitamin deficiency 19:1818
Pauli, Wolfgang 7:660
PAULING, LINUS 13:1255
PAVLOV, IVAN PETROVICH 13:1255
  Psychology 14:1380-1381
Pawpaw see **PAPAYA**
PEA 13:1255
  illus. 13:1255
  Locoweed 10:976
  Mesquite 11:1047
  Mimosa 11:1064
PEACH 13:1255-1256
  illus. 13:1256
  Orchard 13:1220
PEACOCK 13:1256
  illus. 13:1256
Peafowl see **PEACOCK**
Peanuts see **LEGUME; NUTS**
PEAR 13:1256
  illus. 13:1256
  Orchard 13:1220
PEARL 13:1256-1257
  Albalone 1:13
  cultured 13:1257
  illus.: formation 13:1257
  mantle 13:1256
  Mussel 12:1127
  nacre 13:1257
  Oyster 13:1234
PEARY, ROBERT EDWIN 13:1257
  Amundsen, Roald 1:75
  Arctic 2:133
  illus. 13:1257
  Poles, North and South 14:1345
PEAT 13:1258
  Forest products 8:713
  illus.: sphagnum moss 13:1258
Pecan see **HICKORY; NUTS**
PECCARY 13:1258
  illus. 13:1258
  Pig 13:1293
PECTIN 13:1258
PEDIGREE 13:1258
  family tree 13:1258
PEEWEE 13:1259
  illus. 13:1259
PEGMATITE 13:1259
  Placer 14:1310

PEGASUS 13:1259
 illus. 13:1259
 mythology 13:1259
Peking man see **EVOLUTION OF MAN**
PELAGIC 13:1259
 illus. 13:1259
 Marine biology 11:1019-1021
 Ocean 12:1188-1190
 Oceanography 12:1190-1195
 Sargassum 15:1497
PELICAN 13:1260
 illus. 13:1260
Pellagra see **VITAMIN DEFICIENCY**
PELTIER, JEAN CHARLES ATHANASE 13:1260
PELVIS 13:1260
PENDULUM 13:1260-1261
 bob 13:1260
 Foucault 13:1261
 Galileo 8:746
 Huygens, Christian 9:861
 illus. 13:1260
 Motion 12:1111-1112
 Percussion 13:1264
 period 13:1260
 Rotation 15:1479
PENEPLAIN 13:1261
PENGUIN 3:261; 13:1261
 Antarctica 2:112
 characteristics 13:1261
 courtship 13:1261
 habitat 13:1261
PENICILLIN 13:1261-1262
 Antibiotic 2:115-116
 Fleming, Sir Alexander 7:689
 illus. 13:1261
 Mold 11:1081-1082
PENINSULA 13:1262
Penis see **REPRODUCTIVE SYSTEMS**
Pennsylvanian see **GEOLOGIC TIME TABLE; PALEOZOIC ERA**
PENUMBRA 13:1262
PEONY 13:1262
 Follicle (botanical) 8:709
 illus.: 13:1262; 18:1763
PEPEROMIA 13:1262
 illus. 13:1262
PEPPER 13:1263
 Cayenne 4:357
 chili 13:1263
 green and red 13:1263
 illus. 13:1263
 Paprika 13:1243
 white 13:1263
PEPPERMINT 13:1263
 Mint 11:1070
Pepsin see **ENZYMES**
Peptic ulcer see **ULCER**
Peptone 6:512
Perception see **EYE**
PERCH 13:1263
 illus. 13:1263
PERCUSSION 13:1264
 center of percussion 13:1264
 musical instruments 13:1264
 pendulum 13:1264
PERENNIAL 13:1264
 Bark 3:225
 Bitterroot 3:264
 Caladium 4:323
 Cambium 4:326
 Camomile 4:329
 Candytuft 4:332
 Daffodil 5:475
 Dahlia 5:475
 Delphinium 5:492
 Ferns 7:676

 Fittonia 7:688
 Forget-me-not 8:718
 Foxglove 8:727
 Gardening 8:752
 Hop 9:852
 Lily 10:964
 Mimosa 11:1064
 Philodendron 13:1275
 Plant 14:1314-1317
 Scabiosa 16:1510
 Shrub 16:1543
 Strawberry 17:1677
PERFUME 13:1264
 Essential oils 7:637; 13:1264
 fixatives 13:1264
 Forest products 8:712
 illus.: jasmine 13:1264; lavender 13:1264; violet 13:1264
 Lavender 10:946
PERICARDIUM 13:1265; 9:824
PERIGEE 13:1265
 illus. 13:1265
 Orbit 13:1217-1218
Perilymph 6:540
Period see **GEOLOGIC TIME TABLE**
Periodic law 11:1042
Periodic table see **ELEMENTS; MENDELEEV'S PERIODIC TABLE**
PERIPATUS 13:1265
 body structure 13:1265
 classification 13:1265
 diet 13:1265
 habitat 13:1265
 illus. 13:1265
 reproduction 13:1265
PERISCOPE 13:1265-1266
 gastroscope 13:1266
 observation of radioactive materials 13:1266
 Optical instruments 13:1214-1215
 submarine 13:1266
Peristalsis 6:511; 13:1266
PERITONEUM 1:14; 13:1266-1267
 Peritonitis 13:1267
PERITONITIS 13:1267
 causes 13:1267
 Peritoneum 13:1266-1267
 treatment 13:1267
PERIWINKLE 13:1267
 illus. 13:1267
 Snail 16:1564
Periwinkle (plant) see **VINCA**
PERMAFROST 13:1267
PERMEABILITY 13:1267-1268
 Isotonic solution 10:918
 magnetic 13:1267
 selective 13:1268
Peroxide see **OXYGEN**
PERPENDICULAR 13:1268
PERPETUAL MOTION MACHINE 13:1268
 illus. 13:1268
 second law of thermodynamics 13:1268
PERRIN, JEAN BAPTISTE 13:1268-1269
PERSEUS 13:1269
 illus. 13:1269
 mythology 13:1269
PERSIMMON 13:1269
 Ebony 6:548
PERSISTANCE 13:1269
PERSISTENCE OF VISION 13:1269
 Motion pictures 12:1112-1114
 Television 18:1730-1732
PERSPECTIVE 13:1269
Perspiration see **SWEAT GLANDS**
Peru (Humboldt) Current 5:470
PERUTZ, MAX F 13:1269-1270

PETREL 13:1270
 illus. 13:1270
PETRIFACTION 13:1270
 Paleontology 13:1237-1238
PETROLEUM 13:1270-1271
 Africa 1:36
 Asphalt 2:150
 Automobile 2:189
 British Thermal Unit 3:297
 Carbon cycle 4:339
 Coke 5:420
 Europe 7:645
 extraction 13:1270
 Forest products 8:713
 formation 13:1270
 Fossil fuels 8:719
 illus., oil well 13:1271
 Mineral 11:1065-1067
 Natural gas 11:1131
 Natural resources 12:1131-1133
 Oil 12:1197
 Oil wells 13:1207-1208
 Paraffin 13:1244
 products 13:1270
 sources 13:1270
 supply 13:1270
 Tar 18:1717
PETROLEUM JELLY 13:1272
Petrology see **ROCKS**
PETUNIA 13:1272
 illus. 13:1272
PEWTER 13:1272
pH ACIDS 13:1272
Phaeophyta 18:1739
PHARMACOLOGY 13:1272-1274
 Antibiotics 2:115-116
 branches: chemotherapy 13:1273; clinical 13:1273; pharmaco-dynamics 13:1273; toxicology 13:1273
 Chloroform 4:381
 Digitalis 6:513
 Drugs 6:528-530
 Herb 9:836
 history 13:1272
 illus. 13:1273, 1274
 Medicine 11:1038-1040
 methods of drug study 13:1273
 Morphine 11:1096
 Narcotics 12:1130
 nuclear energy isotopes 13:1274
 pharmacopoeias 13:1272
 Plants, medicinal 14:1328-1329
 scientific dosages 13:1273
 Sedative 16:1523
 Sulfa drugs 17:1684
PHARYNX 13:1274
 Sore throat 16:1584
Phases of the Moon see **EARTH; MOON, PHASES OF**
PHEASANTS 13:1274
 illus. 13:1274
PHENOLS 13:1275
Pheromones 1:88
PHILODENDRON 13:1275
 illus. 13:1275
Philosophers stone 1:56
PHLOEM 13:1275
 Annual rings 2:109
 Bark 3:225
 Birch 3:255
 Cambium 4:326
 Heartwood 9:826
 illus. 13:1275
PHLOX 13:1275
 illus. 13:1275
Phoebe see **PEEWEE**
Phonograph, illus. 6:556
PHOSPHATE 13:1276

PHOSPHORESCENCE 13:1276
  afterglow 13:1276
  illus.: lantern fish 13:1276
  Luminescence 10:980
PHOSPHORUS 13:1276-1277
  illus. 13:1277
  Matches 11:1028
  Phosphate 13:1276
  properties 13:1276
  uses 13:1276-1277
PHOTOCHEMICAL SMOG 13:1277
PHOTOCHEMISTRY 13:1277-1278
  blueprints 13:1278
  chemical production of light
   13:1278
  film 13:1277
  firefly 13:1278
  illus. 13:1278
  Light 10:959-963
  Photoelectricity 12:1278-1280
  photography 13:1277, 1281-1282
  photosynthesis 13:1277
PHOTOELECTRICITY 13:1278-
  1280
  cathode 13:1278-1280
  Electricity 6:572
  Electronics 6:581-585
  illus. 13:1278, 1279, 1280
  Light 10:959-963
  Motion pictures 12:1112-1114
  N-P-N junction transistor
   13:1280
  photoelectric relay 13:1279
  Photometer 13:1284
  photons 13:1278, 1284
  phototube 13:1279
  photovoltaic cell 13:1280
  Piezoelectric effect 13:1292
  solar cell 13:1280; 16:1574
  Sunshine recorder 17:1693-1694
  Telephotography 18:1727
  Television 18:1730-1732
  Transistors 18:1767-1768
  Vacuum tube 18:1793-1794
PHOTOGRAPHY 13:1281-1283
  Camera 4:328-329
  Color 5:422-423
  illus.: processes 13:1283; tele-
   scopic 13:1282
  Land, Edwin Herbert 10:941
  Microfilm 11:1054
  Motion pictures 12:1112-1114
  photographic process: camera
   13:1281; film 13:1281; light
   source 13:1281; negative
   13:1281; prints 13:1281
  photographic theory: color pho-
   tography 13:1282; photographic
   reversal 13:1282
  Printing 14:1364-1370
  Projector 14:1372-1373
  Radiograph 15:1423
  Telephotography 18:1727
  variations: aerial 13:1282; art
   13:1282; astronomical 13:1282;
   high-speed 13:1282; photoen-
   graving 13:1282; photomicro-
   graphy 13:1282; spectrography
   13:1282; underwater 13:1282
  Xerography 19:1884
PHOTOMETER 13:1284
  Candela 4:332
  Colorimeter 5:424
  illus. 13:1284
  Optical instruments 13:1214
  Photography 13:1281-1282
PHOTON 13:1284
  Quantum mechanics 14:1390-1391
  Photoelectricity 13:1278-1280

Photoperiodism 7:694
PHOTOSPHERE 13:1284
PHOTOSYNTHESIS 13:1285
  Biomass 3:254
  Botany 3:284
  Bulbs 4:314
  Carbon cycle 4:339
  Cells 4:360
  Chlorophyll 4:382
  equation 13:1285
  food storage 13:1285
  Fuel 8:738
  Homeostasis 9:851
  illus. 13:1285
  Leaves 10:948
  Light 10:959-963
  Metabolism 11:1048
  Photochemistry 13:1277-1278
  Plant 14:1314-1317
  Plants, insectivorous 14:1328
  Venus's flytrap 19:1811
Photosynthetics 3:209
Phototropism see **TROPISM**
Phyla 1:92
PHYLOGENY 13:1286
PHYSICAL STATES AND CHANGES
  13:1286-1287
  Diffusion 6:509
  Evaporation 7:646
  Gas 8:756; 13:1286
  Heat of fusion 9:828-829
  Heat of reaction 9:829
  heating 13:1287
  illus. 13:1286
  Kinetic theory 10:934
  Latent heat 10:944
  Liquid 10:968-970; 13:1286
  Matter 11:1031
  solids 13:1286; 16:1581
  Substances, properties of 17:1681-
   1682
PHYSICS 13:1287-1288
  areas of study: biophysics
   13:1288; electricity 13:1288;
   heat 13:1288; light 13:1288;
   mechanics 13:1288; nuclear
   energy 13:1288; radiation
   13:1288; sound 13:1288
  Biophysics 3:255
  Filter 7:681
  illus. 13:1287, 1288
  Mechanics 11:1037-1038
  Nuclear science 12:1170-1175
  Oersted, Hans Christian 12:1196
  Physical states and changes
   13:1286-1287
  Physiology 13:1289-1291
  scientific method 13:1287
PHYSIOLOGY 13:1289-1291
  adaptation 13:1290-1291
  Anatomy 1:76; 13:1289
  Animal 1:83
  Animals, classification of 1:91-96
  Botany 3:184-285
  circulation 13:1290
  digestion 13:1289-1290
  elimination 13:1290
  excretion 13:1290
  Galen 8:745
  illus.: discoveries 13:1289, 1291
  Medicine 11:1038-1040
  metabolism 13:1290
  Pathology 13:1254-1255
  Pharmacology 13:1272-1274
  respiration 13:1290
  Scar 16:1511
  Virchow, Rudolf 19:1815
  Vitamin 19:1818
  Zoology 19:1895-1896, 1897

PHYSIOTHERAPY 13:1291-1292
PICCARD, AUGUSTE 13:1292
  Bathysphere and bathyscaphe
   3:230-231
Piccard, Jacques see **BATHY-
  SPHERE AND BATHYSCAPHE**
PICCARD, JEAN 13:1292
Pickerel see **PIKE**
Pickle see **CUCUMBER**
PICKLING 13:1292
Picric acid see **CARBOLIC ACID**
PIEZOELECTRIC EFFECT 5:462;
  13:1292
  Electricity 6:563-572
  illus. 13:1292
  Tourmaline 18:1762
PIG 13:1293
  breeding 13:1293
  characteristics 13:1293
  illus. 13:1293
  uses 13:1293
Pig iron see **IRON**
PIGEON 13:1393
  Dove 6:526
  illus. 13:1393
PIGMENT 13:1294
  Acetic acid 1:19
  Paint 13:1236, 1294
  skin 13:1294
  Xanthophyl 19:1884
Pika see **RABBIT**
PIKE 13:1294
  illus. 13:1294
Pile, atomic see **ACCELERATORS;
  NUCLEAR REACTORS; NUCLEAR
  SCIENCE**
Pilot see **AVIATION**
PILOT FISH 13:1295
  illus. 11:1021; 13:1295
Pimento 1:64
PIMPLE 13:1295
PINE 13:1295-1296
  Balsam 3:223
  Cedar 4:357
  characteristics 13:1295
  Evergreen 7:646
  Fir 7:683
  illus. 13:1295; 18:1763
  Juniper 10:927
  spruce 17:1654
  varieties 13:1296
PINEAL GLAND 13:1296
  Endocrine glands 7:610
  illus. 13:1296
PINEAPPLE 13:1296-1297
  illus. 13:1297
Pinkeye see **CONJUNCTIVITIS**
PINKS 13:1297
  illus. 13:1297
Pinnipedia 11:1012
Pinna see **EAR**
Pinnate venation see **LEAVES**
PINWORM 13:1297
  illus. 13:1297
  Parasites 13:1247-1249
Piranha see **TROPICAL FISH**
PISCES (ANIMAL) 14:1307-1308
  Chordata 4:383-385
  classification 14:1307
  digestive system 14:1308
  fins 14:1308; 7:682
  Fish 7:686-687
  fishlike mammals 14:1307
  Flounder 7:692
  Flying fish 8:707
  illus.: 14:1307; scales 14:1308
  jawed fish 14:1307
  jawless 14:1307
  Lamprey 10:941

Perch 13:1263
Pike 13:1294
scales 14:1307
Shark 16:1533
Spawning 17:1639
Swordfish 18:1712
Whitefish 19:1868
PISCES (CONSTELLATION)
14:1308
illus. 14:1308
Pistachio see **NUTS**
PISTIL 14:1308-1309
illus. 14:1309
Pollination 14:1346-1347
Stigma 17:1672
Piston see **AUTOMOBILE; ENGINE**
Pitch 2:150
Pitch see **RESONANCE; SOUND**
PITCHBLENDE 14:1309
Curie, Pierre and Marie 5:465-466
illus. 14:1309
Uranium 18:1788-1789
PITCHER PLANT 14:1309
illus. 14:1309
Plants, insectivorous 14:1328
PITH 14:1309
Pitot tube see **ALTIMETER**
PITUITARY GLAND 14:1310;
16:1549
Acromegaly 1:24
Adrenal glands 1:27-28
anterior lobe 14:1310
Cretin 5:456
Diabetes 5:497
Endocrine glands 7:610
Giant 8:775
Glandular tissue 9:871
growth hormone 14:1310
hypothalamus 9:872
illus. 14:1310
intermediate lobe 14:1310
Lactogen 10:938
Menstruation 11:1044
Midget 11:1059
Obesity 12:1187
Ovary 13:1229
posterior lobe 14:1310
Puberty 14:1383
Thyroid 18:1749
PLACER 14:1310
PLAIN 14:1310-1311
Mountains 12:1116
PLANARIA 14:1311
body structure 14:1311
digestive system 14:1311
excretion 14:1311
illus.: reproductive system
15:1448
Platyhelminthes 14:1336-1337
regeneration 14:1311
reproductive system 14:1311;
15:1447-1448
Plane 14:1312
illus. 14:1312
PLANET 14:1312
Asteroid 2:152
Comet 5:426
giant 14:1312
Gravity 8:794
Interstellar communication 10:907-
909
Jupiter 10:928-929
light 14:1312
Mars 11:1023-1025
Neptune 12:1139
orbits 14:1312
Revolution 15:1456
Solar system 16:1575-1578
terrestrial 14:1312

Venus 19:1810-1811
PLANETARIUM 14:1312-1313
Adler Planetarium 14:1312
illus. 14:1312
projector 14:1312
Planetoid see **ASTEROID**
PLANKTON 14:1313
Coral 5:448
illus. 14:1313
Larva 10:943
Ocean 12:1188-1190
Oceanography 12:1190-1195
Pelagic 13:1259
Sardine 15:1497
PLANT 14:1314-1317
adaptation 14:1316-1317
Albino 1:55
Annual 2:108-109
Botany 3:284-285
Bud 4:309-310
Capsule 4:336
cellular structure 14:1314
Corm 5:448
Dioecious 6:516
Evergreen 7:646
Flora 7:692
Gametophyte 8:749
Gardening 8:751-753
Germination 8:774
Gland 8:780
Herb 9:836
Horticulture 9:856-857
illus.: cell 14:1314; parts
14:1315; roots 14:1317; seed
dispersal 14:1316-1317
Leaves 10:949
Life, characteristics of 10:958
locomotion 14:1317
Metabolism 11:1048; 14:1314
Plant tissues 14:1320
Plants, classification of
14:1322-1327
Pollen 14:1346
reproduction 14:1316
Seed 16:1524-1525
Seed dispersal 16:1526
Stem 17:1668
Sugar 17:1683
Transpiration 18:1769
Tropism 18:1774
PLANT DISEASES 14:1318-1319
bacteria 14:1318
Blight 3:267
Disease 6:519
Gardening 8:751-753
illus.: apple cedar rust 14:1318;
potato blight 14:1319
plant pathologists 14:1318
Plant pests 14:1319-1320
prevention 14:1318
Rot 15:1479
Rust 15:1484
symptoms 14:1318
viruses 14:1318
PLANT PESTS 14:1319-1320
biting insects 14:1319
borers 14:1320
illus.: boll weevil 14:1319;
caterpillar 14:1319; corn borer
14:1320; scale insects 14:1319
Moths 12:1110
Rot 15:1479
sucking insects 14:1319
PLANT TISSUES 14:1320
Cells 4:359-360
Cortex 5:449
Embryophyta 7:607-608
Grafting 8:790
Heartwood 9:826

illus.: chart 14:1320-1321
Leaves 10:949
Meristem 11:1046
Phloem 13:1275
Pith 14:1309
Plant 14:1314-1317
Plants, classification of
14:1322-1327
Root 15:1476-1477
Vascular bundle 18:1797
Plants, aquarium see **AQUARIUM;
TROPICAL FISH**
PLANTS, CLASSIFICATION OF
14:1322-1327
acacia 14:1331
Algae 1:58-59; 14:1322
angiosperms 14:1327
bacteria 14:1322
Botany 3:284-285
chart 14:1323
Embryophyte 7:607-608
Evergreen 7:646
Evolution 7:647-654
Ferns 7:676; 14:1327
fungi imperfecti 14:1326
Fungus 8:741-742; 14:1326
Gymnosperm 9:813; 14:1327
history 14:1322
horsetails 14:1326-1327
illus.: algae 14:1322, 1324;
angiosperm 14:1237; bacteria
14:1322, 1325; dicotyledon
14:1324; fern 14:1325, 1327; fun-
gus 14:1322, 1325; gymnosperm
14:1327; lichen 14:1324, 1326;
liverwort 14:1326; mold 14:1322;
monocotyledon 14:1324; moss
1324, 1326
Leaves 10:949
Legume 10:951
lichen 14:1326
Linnaeus, Carolus 10:967
mold 14:1323
Morphology 11:1096
Moss 12:1108-1109
mosses and liverworts 14:1326
Mushrooms 12:1124
Phylogeny 13:1286
Plant 14:1314-1317
Seed 16:1524-1525
Spermatophyte 17:1645
Thallophytes 18:1739
Theophrastus 14:1322
Tracheophytes 18:1763
Wild flowers 19:1870-1873
PLANTS, INSECTIVOROUS
14:1328
illus., Venus's flytrap 14:1328
Pitcher plant 14:1309, 1328
Sundew 14:1328
Venus's flytrap 14:1328; 19:1811
Wild flower 19:1870-1871, 1872-
1873
PLANTS, MEDICINAL 14:1328-
1329
adrenalin 14:1328
atropine 14:1328
belladonna 14:1328
caffeine 14:1328
castor bean 14:1329
coca 14:1329
digitalis 14:1329
Economic botany 6:554
illus.: cinchona 14:1328; coffee
14:1328; poppy 14:1328
poppy 14:1329, 1349-1350
quinine 14:1328; 1393
Wild flower 19:1870-1873
wintergreen 14:1328-1329

PLANTS, SUCCULENT 14:1329
  illus. 14:1329
  Peperomia 13:1262-1263
  Sedum 16:1524
  Wild flower 19:1870-1871; 1872-1873
PLANTS, TROPICAL 14:1329-1331
  Croton 5:458
  export 14:1329-1330
  Fittonia 7:688
  food: breadfruit 14:1330; durian 14:1330; jackfruit 14:1330; mango 14:1330; papaya 14:1330; passion fruit 14:1330
  garden: bleeding-heart 14:1330; clematis 14:1330; lantana 14:1330; lotus 14:1330; oleander 14:1330; spider plant 14:1330; water lillies 14:1330; bird of paradise 14:1330
  Gardenia 8:750
  Greenhouse 8:796-797
  Guava 9:808
  illus.: acacia 14:1331; bouganvillea 14:1331; breadfruit 14:1331; hibiscus 14:1331; passion flower 14:1331; tree fern 14:1331; umbrella palm 14:1331
  Jungle 10:926-927
  Mangrove 11:1014
  Mimosa 11:1064
  Myrtle 12:1128
  Night-blooming plants 12:1148-1149
  ornamental: bouganvillea 14:1330; climbing pothos 14:1331; eucalyptus 14:1331; wooden rose 14:1330-1331
  Palm 13:1240
Plasma see **BLOOD**
Plasma membrane see **CELL**
PLASTER 14:1332
PLASTER OF PARIS 14:1332
PLASTICS 14:1332-1334
  Fat 7:672
  foamed plastics 14:1334
  Forest products 8:713
  glyptals 14:1334
  illus.: molecular structures 14:1333; roof of Climatron at Missouri Botanical Garden 14:1333
  ion exchange resins 14:1334
  phenolic resins 14:1333-1334
  Polymer 14:1348; 14:1332-1333
  Rubber, synthetic 15:1482
  thermoplastic 14:1332
  Veneer 19:1809
PLASTIC SURGERY 14:1332
PLASTID 14:1334
  Cells 4:360
  illus.: potato tuber 14:1334; spirogyra 14:1334
PLATE TECTONICS 14:1334-1335
  Continental drift 5:444
  illus.: map 14:1335
  International Geophysical Year: the Solid Earth 9:894
  Oceanography 12:1190-1195
  Orogeny 13:1224
  Trench, deep-ocean 18:1771
  Volcano 19:1822
PLATEAU 14:1335
  Mesa 11:1046
Platelets see **BLOOD;**
  CIRCULATORY SYSTEM
PLATINUM 14:1335-1336
  Iridium 10:913

PLATYHELMINTHES 14:1336-1337
  alternation of host 14:1336-1337
  Annelida 1:107-108
  bilateral symmetry 14:1337
  habitat 14:1336
  illus. 14:1337
  life cycle 14:1336
  Liver fluke 10:973
  locomotion 14:1336
  Nemathelminthes 12:1137-1138
  planaria 14:1336
  Skeleton 16:1552-1555
  Tapeworm 18:1716-1717
  Worm 19:1882
Platypus see **DUCKBILL**
Pleiades see **TAURUS**
Pleistocene see **CENEZOIC ERA;**
  GEOLOGIC TIME TABLE
PLEURISY 14:1337
  Lung 10:983-984
  Pneumonia 14:1341
Plexus see **NERVOUS SYSTEM**
Pliocene see **CENEZOIC ERA;**
  GEOLOGIC TIME TABLE
PLOVER 14:1338
  illus. 14:1338
  Killdeer 10:933
PLUM 14:1338
  illus. 14:1338
  Orchard 13:1220
PLUMERIA 14:1338
  illus. 14:1338
PLUMULE 14:1338
  Radicle 15:1416
  Seed 16:1524-1525
PLUTO 14:1338-1340
  discovery 14:1339
  illus.: orbit 14:1339
  orbit 14:1339
  Planet 14:1312
  Uranus 18:1790
PLUTONIUM 14:1340
PLYWOOD 14:1340
  Forest products 8:712
PNEUMATICS 14:1340
PNEUMONIA 14:1341
  bronchial 14:1341
  bronchitis 3:297
  Bubonic plague 4:308
  causes 14:1341
  illus.: lung 14:1341
  Infection 9:878
  Leukemia 10:956
  lobar 14:1341
  Lung 10:983-984
  Pleurisy 14:1337
  symptoms 14:1341
Poi see **TARO**
POINCIANA 14:1341
  dwarf 14:1341
  illus. 14:1341
  royal 14:1341
POINSETTIA 14:1342
  illus. 14:1342
Pointer, illus. 6:522
POISON 14:1342
  Arsenic 2:138
  Botulism 3:286
  Carbon life 4:341
  Carbon monoxide 4:342
  Curare 5:464-465
  irritant 14:1342
  nerve 14:1342
  Strychnine 17:1679
POISON GLAND 14:1343
  illus. 14:1343
  Venom 19:1809
POISON IVY 14:1343
  illus. 14:1343

POISON OAK 14:1343
  illus. 14:1343
  Poison ivy 14:1343
  universal antidote 14:1342
Poison sumac see **SUMAC**
Pokeweed see **WILD FLOWERS**
Polar bear see **BEAR**
Polar climate see **CLIMATE**
POLAR EASTERLIES 14:1344
  illus. 14:1344
Polar regions see **ANTARCTICA;**
  ARCTIC; EARTH; POLES, NORTH
  AND SOUTH
POLAR WANDERING 14:1344
Polaris see **MISSILE; SUBMARINE**
POLARIS 14:1344
  Cassiopeia 4:347
  Cepheus 4:365
  illus. 14:1344
POLARIZATION 14:1345
Polaroid see **LAND, EDWIN**
POLE (GENERAL) 14:1345
Pole, magnetic see **MAGNET;**
  ELECTRICITY
Polecat see **WEASEL**
POLES, NORTH AND SOUTH
  14:1345
  Antarctica 2:112
  Compass 5:430
  Earth 6:543
  exploration 14:1345
  illus. 2:112; 14:1345
  International Geophysical Year: Glaciers 9:892-893
  Magnet 10:997
  Meridian 11:1046
  Peary, Robert Edwin 13:1257
POLIOMYELITIS 14:1346
  Atrophy 2:174
  bulbar 14:1346
  Iron lung 10:915
  Myelitis 12:1128
  nonparalytic 14:1346
  Paralysis 13:1245
  paralytic 14:1346
  Sabin vaccine 14:1346
  Salk, Jonas Edward 15:1490-1491; 14:1346
POLLEN 14:1346
  Allergy 1:62
  Hay fever 9:823
POLLINATION 14:1346-1347
  breeding 3:293
  cross-pollination 14:1347
  Flower 7:694
  illus. 14:1347
  Nectar 12:1136
  Ovum 13:1230
  Pistil 14:1308-1309
  self-pollination 14:1347
  Stigma 17:1672
Pollutants 9:830
POLLUTION 9:895; 14:1347-1348
  Biodegradable 3:252
  Leaching 10:947
  Mercury (element) 11:1044
  Plankton 14:1313
POLONIUM 14:1348
  Curie, Pierre and Marie 5:466
POLYCOTYLEDON 14:1348
Polygon see **GEOMETRY**
POLYMER 14:1348
  Nylon 12:1185
  Polymorphism 9:867
POLYPS 14:1348
POME 14:1348
  Fruit 8:736
  illus. 14:1348
POMEGRANATE 14:1348

POMPANO 14:1349
 illus. 14:1349
POND 14:1349
Ponderosa pine, illus. 9:812
Pons see **BRAIN; NERVOUS SYSTEM**
Pontoon bridge see **BRIDGES**
POPCORN 14:1349
POPLAR 14:1349
 Aspen 2:150
POPPY 14:1349-1350
 illus. 13:1212; 14:1328
 morphine 14:1349
 Narcotics 12:1130
 opium 14:1349
POPPY SEED 14:1350
Pore see **SKIN; SWEAT GLAND**
PORCELAIN 14:1350
 feldspar 14:1350
 kaolin 14:1350
PORCUPINE 7:643; 14:1350
 characteristics 14:1350
 diet 14:1350
 ilus. 14:1350
 Mammalia 11:1011-1012
 protection 1:87
 reproduction 14:1350
 Rodent 15:1474-1475
 species 14:1350
PORIFERA 14:1351-1352
 body structure 14:1351
 characteristics 14:1351
 Digestive system 6:510
 habitat 14:1351
 illus. 14:1351, 1352
 Marine biology 11:1019-1021
 mesenchyme cells 14:1351
 Skeleton 16:1552-1555
 Spicule 17:1646
POROSITY 14:1352
PORPOISE 14:1352
 Cetacea 4:368
 Dolphin 6:524
 habitat 14:1352
 illus.: 4:368; 14:1352
 reproduction 14:1352
PORTER, RODNEY R. 14:1352-1353
Portuguese man-of-war see **MAN-OF-WAR, PORTUGUESE**
PORTULACA 14:1353
Positive integers 1:60
POSITRON 6:579; 14:1353
POSTERIOR 14:1353
POSTURE 14:1353
 illus. 14:1353
POTASH 14:1354
POTASSIUM 14:1354
 dating 14:1354
 Davy, Sir Humphry 5:483
 properties 14:1354
 uses 14:1354
POTATO 14:1354
 illus. 14:1354
 Stem, underground 17:1668-1669
 Tuber 18:1775
POTENTIAL 14:1354
POTENTILLA 14:1355
 illus. 14:1355
Poultry see **CHICKEN; FOWL**
Pound see **FOOT-POUND; MEASUREMENT**
POWELL, CECIL FRANK 14:1355
POWER 14:1355
 Dynamometer 6:537
 Electricity 6:568
 Energy 7:612-617
 formula 14:1355
 Machinery 10:989-991
 measurement 14:1355

PRAIRIE 14:1355-1356
 illus. 14:1355
Prairie chicken see **GROUSE**
PRAIRIE DOG 14:1356
 illus. 1:84
 Rodent 15:1474-1475
Prairie wolf see **COYOTE**
PRASEODYMIUM 14:1356
PRAYING MANTIS 14:1356
 illus. 14:1356
Pre-Cambrian see **GEOLOGIC TIME TABLE**
Precious stones see **GEM**
PRECIPITATION (CHEMICAL) 14:1357
 coagulation 14:1357
 colloids 14:1357
 factors affecting 14:1357
 Reagent 15:1437
PRECIPITATION (WEATHER) 14:1358
 adiabatic cooling 14:1358
 Air masses 1:46
 Hail 9:816; 14:1358
 measurement of 14:1358
 temperature inversions 14:1358
 Thunderstorm 18:1747
 Vapor 18:1796
 water cycle 14:1358; 19:1832-1833
 Weather 19:1843-1846
PREDATOR-PREY 14:1358-1359
PREGL, FRITZ 14:1359
PREGNANCY 14:1359
 Abortion 1:14
 Fetus 7:678
 Hypertrophy 9:871
 Lactogen 10:938
 Reproductive systems 15:1447-1448
PREHENSILE 14:1359
PREHISTORIC MAMMALS 14:1359-1360
 characteristics 14:1359
 Dinosaur 6:514-516
 elephant family 14:1360
 giant ground sloth 14:1360
 horse family 14:1360
 illus.: moropus 14:1360; prehistoric horse 14:1360
 mammoths 14:1360
 mastodons 14:1360
Prehistoric man see **EVOLUTION OF MAN; STONE AGE**
PRELOG, VLADIMIR 14:1360
Presbyopia see **OPTOMETRY**
Prescription see **DRUGS**
PRESERVE 14:1361
 Forestry 8:716-717
 illus. 14:1361
 National Audubon Society 14:1361
 United States government 14:1361
PRESSURE 14:1361
 Air pressure 1:47
 illus. 14:1361
 Machinery 10:989-991
 Turbine 18:1778-1779
PRESSURE GAUGE 14:1361
PRICKLY HEAT 14:1362
Prickly pear see **CACTUS**
PRIESTLEY, JOSEPH 14:1362
 Botany 3:284
 Oxidation 13:1231-1232
 Oxygen 13:1232-1233
Primary color see **COLOR**
PRIMATES 14:1362-1363
 Ape 2:121
 characteristics 14:1362

 classification: Aye-aye 14:1362; baboon 14:1362; capuchin monkey 14:1362; lemur 14:1362; man 14:1363; manlike apes 14:1363; marmoset 14:1362; tarsier 14:1362
 illus.: gorilla 14:1363; lemur 14:1363; man 14:1363; tarsier 14:1363
 Lemur 10:952
 Mammalia 11:1011-1012
 Marmoset 11:1022
 Monkey 11:1089
Prime meridian see **TIME ZONES**
PRIMROSE 14:1363
 illus. 14:1363
PRINTED CIRCUIT 14:1364
PRINTING 14:1364-1370
 electrostatic 14:1368
 first printing press 14:1365, 1368
 history 14:1364-1365
 illus.: Gutenberg press 14:1365; letterpress 14:1366; lithography 14:1367; mounting, cutting, folding 14:1369; rotogravure 14:1366; wood block 14:1364
 Ink 9:880
 intaglio 14:1369-1370
 invention of movable type 14:1365
 offset 14:1367
 Paper 13:1242
 planographic 14:1369
 relief: four-color process 14:1368; half-tone process 14:1368; letterpress 14:1368
 Xerography 19:1884
Printing press, illus. 5:427
PRISM 14:1370
 Color 5:422
 Dispersion 6:519
 Lens, man-made 10:952-953
 Optical instruments 13:1214-1215
 Periscope 13:1266
 polarization of light 14:1370
 Rainbow 15:1427
 spectrum 14:1370
 White light 19:1867
PRIVET 14:1370
PROBABILITY 14:1370
 Statistics 17:1664-1665
PROBOSCIS 14:1370
PROCYON 14:1370-1371
PRODUCER 14:1371
 Plankton 14:1313
PROGESTERONE 14:1371;
PROJECTILE 14:1371
 Ballistics 3:221
 illus. 14:1371
 Missile 11:1071-1075
 Munitions 12:1119
 trajectories 14:1371
PROJECTION 14:1371
 Cartography 4:346
 Surveying 18:1707
PROJECTOR 14:1372-1373
 illus.: lantern-slide 14:1372; light sources 14:1373; opaque 14:1372
 lantern-slide 14:1372
 lens arrangement 14:1372
 Lens, man-made 10:952-953
 light-gathering 14:1372
 Motion pictures 12:1112-1114
 movie 14:1372
 opaque 14:1372
PROMETHIUM 14:1373
Pronghorn see **ANTELOPE; DEER FAMILY**

Prop roots see **BANYAN;**
PANDANUS
PROPAGATION 14:1373-1374
Apple 2:123
Begonia 3:244
bulbs 14:1373
Camellia 4:327
corm 14:1373
cuttings 14:1373
Forsythia 8:719
Germination 8:774
Grafting 8:790
illus. 14:1374
layering 14:1374
Lilac 10:964
Myrtle 12:1128
Plant 14:1314-1317
rhizome 14:1373
root 14:1373
Runner 15:1484
seed 14:1373
tuber 14:1373
Propane **METHANE;**
HYDROCARBON
Prophase see **MITOSIS AND**
MEIOSIS
PROPORTION 14:1374
Prostate gland see **REPRODUCTIVE**
SYSTEMS
PROTACTINIUM 14:1374
Actinium 1:24
Hahn, Otto 9:815
PROTECTIVE COLORATION
14:1375-1376
Adaptation 1:24-25
Camouflage 4:329
countershading 14:1376
Ducks 6:532
Herbivore 9:837
illus.: 19:1842; arctic fox
14:1375; bittern 14:1375; buf-
falo treehopper 14:1375; bush
katydid 14:1375; chameleon
14:1375; fawn 14:1375; flounder
14:1375; ichneumon fly 14:1375;
leopard 14:1375; mason wasp
14:1375; monarch butterfly
14:1375; io moth 14:1375; under-
wing moth 14:1375; walking stick
14:1375; weasel 14:1375; zebra
14:1375
Mimicry 11:1064; 14:1376
patterning 14:1376
Quail 14:1390
Toad 18:1755
Walking stick 19:1827
warning coloration 14:1376
Protective equipment of animals,
illus. 1:187
PROTEIN 14:1376-1377
Albumin 1:56
Alfalfa 1:57
Amino acid 1:71
Animal digestion 1:86
Digestive system 6:512
Elements in the human body 6:590
Gelatin 8:758
Gene 8:760
Kidney 10:932-933
Metabolism 11:1048
Nitrogen 12:1150
Purine 14:1388
Urea 18:1790
Uric acid 18:1791
PROTEROZOIC ERA 14:1377
illus. 14:1377
land forms 14:1377
plants and animals 14:1377
Protoceratops 6:515

PROTON (ELEMENTARY
PARTICLE) 14:1377
Proton number see **ATOMIC**
NUMBER IN NUCLEAR GLOSSARY
Protoplasm 1:83; 14:1378
Biochemistry 3:251
Cells 4:359-360
PROTOZOA 14:1378-1379
Ameba 1:70
animal body structure 1:83
Animals, life span 1:97
Cells 4:359-360
digestion 14:1379; 6:510
Euglena 7:639
Germ theory 8:773
habitat 14:1378
illus. 14:1379
Marine biology 11:1019-1021
Microbe 11:1054
movement 14:1378-1379
Paramecium 13:1245-1246
Parasites 13:1247-1249
parts of the body 14:1379
self-preservation 14:1379
Skeleton 16:1552-1555
Stentor 17:1670
Volvox 19:1825-1826
Vorticella 19:1826
Proxima Centauri 4:363; 17:1661
Prune (fruit) see **PLUM**
PRUNING 14:1380
illus. 14:1380
PSEUDOPODIA 14:1380; 1:70;
1:86; 3:269
Migratory cells 11:1061
Psilophyta 18:1763
Psilotum 18:1763
Psittacosis 13:1250
PSYCHEDELIC 14:1380
history 14:1380
lysergic acid diethylamide (LSD)
14:1380
medical uses 14:1380
PSYCHOLOGY 14:1380-1381
Biology 3:254
confusion with psychiatry 14:1381
fields: clinical 14:1381; coun-
seling 14:1381; educational
14:1381; experimental 14:1381;
industrial 14:1381; learning
14:1381; physiological 14:1381;
social 14:1381
Freud, Sigmund 8:730
illus.: chimpanzee 14:1381
Instinct 9:884
Memory 11:1042
Pavlov, Ivan Petrovich 13:1255
Psychosomatic illness 3:252
PSYLLIUM 14:1382
illus. 14:1382
Ptarmigan see **GROUSE**
PTERODACTYL 14:1382
illus. 14:1382
Pterophyta 18:1763
PTOLEMY 14:1382-1383
Copernicus, Nicolaus 5:446
PTOMAINE 14:1383
PUBERTY 14:1383
Acne 1:22
Adolescence 1:27
female 14:1383
illus. 14:1383
male 14:1383
Puff adder see **SNAKES**
PUFFIN 14:1384
illus. 14:1384
Pulley see **MACHINES, SIMPLE**
PULSARS 14:1384
Star, variable 17:1659

PULSE 14:1384
Pulselogia 8:746
Puma, illus. 12:1159
PUMP 14:1384-1385
centrifugal 14:1385
force 14:1384
history 14:1384
illus.: bicycle 14:1385; centrifugal 14:1385; deep well (force)
14:1385; human heart 14:1385;
lift 14:1385
lift 14:1384
Machinery 10:989-991
mercury vapor 14:1385
purposes 14:1384
Refrigeration 15:1441-1442
suction 14:1384
well 19:1862
PUMPKIN 14:1386
illus. 14:1386
Pupa see **METAMORPHOSIS**
Pupil see **EYE**
Pure culture see **BACTERIOLOGY**
Pure substance 4:374
PURIFICATION 14:1386
aeration 14:1387
chemicals 14:1386
chlorination 14:1387
desalination 14:1387
Filter 7:681
filtration 14:1386-1387
illus. 14:1386-1387
settling 14:1386
PURINE 14:1388
Caffeine 4:322
Fischer, Emil 7:686
Nucleic acid 12:1178
Pyrimidine 14:1388-1389
Uric acid 18:1791
Purple finch, illus. 7:682
PUS 14:1388
PUSSY WILLOW 14:1388
illus. 14:1388; 16:1543
Pyloric sphincter 6:511
Pylorus see **DIGESTIVE SYSTEM**
Pyramid see **GEOMETRY**
Pyridoxine see **VITAMIN**
PYRIMIDINE 14:1388-1389
illus. 14:1388
Nucleic acid 12:1178
PYRITE 14:1389
illus. 14:1389
Mineralogy 11:1067-1069
PYROXINE 14:1389
illus. 14:1389
Pyrrophyta 18:1738-1739
PYTHAGORAS 14:1389
illus. 14:1389
Python see **SNAKES**
Quadruplets see **MULTIPLE BIRTHS**
QUAIL 14:1390
illus. 14:1390
QUANTUM MECHANICS 14:1390-
1391
history 14:1390
illus.: 14:1390, 1391
Planck's Constant 14:1391
Radiation 15:1407-1409
Photon 13:1284
Wave 19:1836-1837
QUARANTINE 14:1391
QUARRY 14:1391
illus. 14:1391
Open pit mine 13:1212
Quaternary see **CENEZOIC ERA;**
GEOLOGIC TIME TABLE
QUARTZ 14:1391-1392
Agate 1:37
Amethyst 2:161

illus.: 9:819; 11:1065; agate
14:1392; amethyst 14:1392; ci-
trine 14:1392; flint 14:1392;
jasper 14:1392; natural state
14:1392; rose quartz 14:1392
Onyx 13:1209
Opal 13:1209-1210
Pegmatite 13:1259
Pyrite 14:1389
QUARTZITE 14:1392
QUASAR 14:1392
Pulsars 14:1384
Telescope 18:1728-1730
Queen Anne's Lace see **WILD
FLOWERS**
Queen of knowledge 11:1029
Queen see **ANTS; BEES**
Quicklime see **LIME**
QUICKSAND 14:1392-1393
Quicksilver see **MERCURY
(ELEMENT)**
Quill see **FEATHER**
QUINCE 14:1393
illus. 14:1393
Orchard 13:1220
QUININE 14:1393
cinchona bark 14:1393
Forest products 8:713
illus. 14:1393
Malaria 11:1009
Plants, medicinal 14:1328-1329
South America 16:1593-1597
Quintuplets see **MULTIPLE
BIRTHS**
RABBIT 14:1394-1395
arctic hare 14:1394
cottontail 14:1395
illus.: breeding for fur color
14:1394; desert cottontail
5:495; domestic white (albino)
14:1395; pika 14:1394; snowshoe
rabbit 14:1394; tracks 1:90
pika 14:1395
protection 1:87
snowshoe hare 14:1394
Rabbit fever see **ANIMAL
DISEASES; RABBIT**
RABI, ISADOR ISAAC 14:1395
RABIES 14:1395
cause 14:1395
dumb 14:1395
furious 14:1395
sylvatic 14:1395
symptoms 14:1395
treatment 14:1395
urban 14:1395
virus 14:1395
RACCOON 14:1396
characteristics 14:1396
illus.: 14:1396; 1:84; tracks 1:90
reproduction 14:1396
RACE 14:1396
RADAR 14:1396-1397
Antenna (electronic) 2:114
Electronics 6:581-585
illus. 14:1397
kinds of indicators: A-range
14:1397; B-range 14:1397; Range
Height Indicator (RHI) 14:1396;
Plan Position Indicator (PPI)
14:1396
parts 14:1396
uses 14:1397
VHF 19:1813
Weather station 19:1856-1858
Radial symmetry see **ANIMALS,
CLASSIFICATION OF**
RADIANT ENERGY 14:1397
Candela 4:332

RADIATION 15:1407-1409
Charged particles 4:370
Einstein, Albert 15:1408
Elements 6:586-589
energy in motion 15:1407
Half-life 9:817
Heat barrier 9:828
illus.: control board of atomic
reactor 15:1408; Geiger counter
15:1409; in human body 15:1407;
strontium-90 15:1409
Isotope 10:918
Light 10:959-963
Luminescence 10:980
man-made high-energy radiation
15:1408
natural high-energy radiation
15:1408
Nuclear energy 12:1162-1164
Nuclear reactor 12:1166-1168
Pharmacology 13:1272-1274
Physics 13:1287-1288
quantum 15:1407
Quantum mechanics 14:1390-1391
Radiant energy 14:1397; 15:1407
Radiation, biological effects of
15:1410-1411
Radiation, protection 15:1412-
1413
Radiation, uses 15:1414-1415
Radioactive elements 15:1420-
1421
Radioactivity 15:1422-1423
Ray, alpha 15:1433
Ray, beta 15:1433
Ray, gamma 15:1434
Roentgen, Wilhelm Konrad 15:1476
Wave 19:1836-1837
**RADIATION, BIOLOGICAL
EFFECTS** 15:1410-1411
effect on heredity 15:1411
effect on life span 15:1410
illus.: kidney bean plants 15:1410
ionizing radiation 15:1410
Neutron 12:1145-1146
Radiation 15:1407-1409
Radiation, protection 15:1412-
1413
Radiation, uses 15:1414-1415
Ray, alpha 15:1433
Ray, beta 15:1433
Strontium 17:1679
RADIATION DETECTOR 15:1411
illus. 15:1411
Radiation 15:1407-1409
RADIATION, PROTECTION
15:1412-1413
detection devices 15:1413
illus.: 15:1412, 1413
kinds of unsafe radiation 15:1412
Radiation 15:1407-1409
Radiation, biological effects of
15:1410-1411
shielding devices 15:1412
Radiation sickness see **RADIATION,
BIOLOGICAL EFFECTS**
RADIATION, USES 15:1414-1415
illus.: cancer therapy 15:1414,
1415
in biology 15:1415
in chemistry 15:1415
in medicine 15:1415
Nuclear science 12:1170-1175
Radiation, biological effects
15:1410-1411
Radiation, protection 15:1412
tracers: in biology 15:1414-1415;
in chemistry 15:1414
treatment of cancer 15:1414

Radiator 5:437
RADICAL, CHEMICAL 15:1416
Ethyl 7:638
RADICLE 15:1416
illus. 15:1416
RADIO 15:1416-1418
Antenna (electronic) 2:114
Beacon 3:235
Beam antenna 3:235
Carrier wave 4:345
Communication 5:427-429
Condenser 5:438
development 15:1416
diode 15:1417
Electricity 6:571
Electronics 6:581-585
Fleming, Sir John A. 15:1417
Frequency 8:730
Henry, Joseph 9:835
illus.: 15:1417, 1418
Instrument landing system 9:885
Oscillator 13:1224-1225
Radio tube 15:1420
*Search for Extraterrestrial
Intelligence (SETI)* 16:1522
Short wave radio 16:1540-1541
Sonar 16:1584
Stereophonic sound 17:1670
Sound interference 16:1591
Telephone 18:1726
transmission 15:1418
triode 15:1417
VHF 19:1813
Vacuum tube 15:1487; 18:1793-
1794
Wave 19:1836-1837
Radio altimeter 1:66
Radio beacon see **BEACON**
RADIO TELESCOPE 15:1419
antenna 15:1419
illus.: 10:907; 15:1419
Interstellar communication 10:907-
909
Jupiter 10:928-929
Milky Way 11:1062
Observatory 12:1187
radio astronomy 15:1419
RADIO TUBE 15:1420
diode 15:1420
illus. 15:1420
rectifier 15:1420
triode 15:1420
Radio wave see **ELECTRO-
MAGNETIC SPECTRUM; RADIO**
RADIOACTIVE ELEMENTS
15:1420-1421
Actinium series 1:24; 15:1420
atomic structure 15:1420
Berkelium 3:245
Californium 4:324-325
Curium 5:466
discovery 15:1420
half-life 15:1421
illus. 15:1421
Neutron 12:1145-1146
Nuclear reactor 12:1166-1168
Pitchblende 14:1309
Plutonium 14:1340
Radon 15:1425
thorium series 15:1420
uranium-radium series 15:1420
Radioactive decay see **NUCLEAR
SCIENCE**
Radioactive fallout see **FALLOUT;
RADIATION, BIOLOGICAL
EFFECTS**
RADIOACTIVITY 15:1422-1423
Atom 2:172-174
Elements 6:586-589

illus. 15:1422
Moseley, Henry Gwyn-Jefferys
11:1097
Nuclear particles 12:1164-1165
properties 15:1422
Radium 15:1424-1425
Ray, alpha 15:1433
Ray, beta 15:1433
rays 15:1422
Rubidium-strontium dating method
15:1483
Rutherford, Ernest 15:1486-1487
Strontium 17:1679
Uranium 18:1788
Radioastronomy see **ASTRONOMY;**
RADIO TELESCOPE
RADIOGRAPH 15:1423
Radioisotopes see **RADIATION**
Radiolaria see **PROTOZOA**
RADIOSONDE 15:1424
Balloon 3:222
illus. 15:1424
Weather station 19:1856
Radiotherapy see **RADIATION,**
USES
RADISH 15:1424
illus. 15:1424
RADIUM 15:1424-1425
Curie, Pierre and Marie 5:466
Half-life 9:817
Pitchblende 14:1309
properties 15:1425
Radioactivity 15:1422-1423
Radius see **SKELETON**
RADON 15:1425
RAFFIA 15:1425
Palm 13:1240
RAGWEED 15:1425
illus. 15:1425
Rain see **PRECIPITATION; RAIN**
MAKING; WEATHER
RAIN GAUGE 15:1426
Gauge 8:756
RAIN MAKING 15:1426-1427
Clouds 5:409-410
exp. 15:1426
Precipitation (weather) 14:1358
RAINBOW 15:1427
Color 5:422-423
exp. 15:1427
Spectrum 17:1643
Raisin see **GRAPE**
Ram see **SHEEP**
Ram, the see **ARIES**
RAMIE 15:1428
illus. 15:1428
Ramjet see **JET PROPULSION**
RANGE FINDER 15:1428
illus. 15:1428
RAOULT'S LAW 15:1428-1429
RAPID 15:1429
illus. 15:1429
RAPTURES OF THE DEEP 15:1429
causes 15:1429
prevention 15:1429
symptoms 15:1429
RARE-EARTH ELEMENTS 15:429
Cerium 4:368
Dysprosium 6:537
Einsteinium 6:562
Europium 7:646
Erbium 7:646
Fermium 7:676
Gadolinium 8:744
Holmium 9:850
Lanthanum 10:942
Lutetium 10:985
Neodymium 12:1138
Praseodymium 14:1356

RAREFACTION 15:1430
RAREFIED AIR 15:1430
Sound interference 16:1591
RASPBERRY 15:1430
illus. 15:1430
RAT 15:1430-1431
Bubonic plague 4:308
characteristics 15:1430
habitat 15:1430
illus.: 7:643; 15:1430; kangaroo
rat 15:1431
Jerboa 10:922
RATIO 15:1431
illus. 15:1431
Rational number see **ALGEBRA**
Ratites 3:261
RATTAN 15:1431
illus. 15:1431
Rattlesnake see **SNAKES**
RAVEN 15:1431
Blue jay 3:272
illus. 15:1431
RAY 15:1432
characteristics 15:1432
habitat 15:1432
illus.: barndoor skate 15:1432;
devilfish 15:1432; stingaree
15:1432; torpedo ray 15:1432
Skate 16:1551
varieties 15:1432
RAY, ALPHA 15:1433
Helium 9:833
illus. 15:1433
Radium 15:1424-1425
RAY, BETA 15:1433
hyperthyroidism 15:1433
illus. 15:1433
RAY, COSMIC 15:1434
Compton, Arthur Holly 5:434
illus. 15:1434
primary 15:1434
theories 15:1434
RAY, GAMMA 15:1434
Electromagnetic spectrum 6:578
Nuclear science 12:1170-1175
Radiograph 15:1423
RAY, INFRARED 15:1434-1435
discovery 15:1435
illus. 15:1435
properties 15:1434-1435
RAY, ULTRAVIOLET 15:1435
beneficial effects 15:1435
Electromagnetic spectrum 6:578
illus. 15:1435
properties 15:1435
RAYON 15:1436
illus.: production 15:1436
viscose process 15:1436
Reaction see **CHEMICAL CHANGE;**
CHEMISTRY
Reactor see **NUCLEAR ENERGY**
REAGENT 15:1437
exp. 15:1437
REAL IMAGE 15:1437-1438
Real number see **ALGEBRA**
Recent see **GEOLOGIC TIME TABLE**
Reception see **RADIO**
RECEPTORS 15:1438
RECESSIVE 15:1438
Reckoning see **DEAD RECKONING**
Recording see **SOUND RECORDING**
Rectifier see **RADIO**
RECTUM 15:1438
RECYCLING 15:1438-1439
garbage 15:1438
illus. 15:1438
soil 15:1439
water 15:1438
Red adder see **SNAKES**

Red deer, illus. 7:643
Red dory, illus. 11:1021
Red eft 12:1146
Red jellyfish, illus. 5:418
REDBUD 15:1439
illus. 15:1439
Redi, Francesco 17:1652
REDUCING AGENT 15:1439
REDUCTION 15:1439
Oxide 13:1232
REDWOOD 15:1439-1440
REED 15:1440
REED, WALTER 15:1440
Yellow fever 19:1889
Reed mace see **CATTAIL**
REEF 15:1440; 10:917
illus. 15:1440
Refining see **METAL; PETROLEUM;**
SUGAR
REFRACTION 15:1441
illus. 15:1441
Lens, man-made 10:952-953
Rainbow 15:1427
REFRACTORY 15:1441
REFLECTION 15:1440
illus. 15:1440
Mirror 11:1070
Reflex action see **NERVOUS**
SYSTEM
REFRIGERATION 15:1441-1442
Ammonia 1:72
compressor 15:1441
dehumidifiers 15:1442
Food preservation 8:709-710
gas 15:1442
heat pump 15:1441
illus. 15:1441
Liquid air 10:970
Peltier, Jean Charles Athanase
13:1260
Rarefaction 15:1430
REGENERATION 15:1442-1443
Autotomy 2:190
Ctenophora 5:463
exp. 15:1442
illus.: crawfish 15:1443; earthworm
15:1443; newt 15:1443; sea
cucumber 15:1443; starfish
15:1443
Newt 12:1146-1147
Scar 16:1511
Spallanzani, Lazzaro 17:1638
Walking stick 19:1827
Regulus see **CONSTELLATION**
Reindeer see **DEER FAMILY**
Reindeer moss see **LICHEN**
REINFORCED CONCRETE 15:1443
RELAPSE 15:1443
RELATIVITY 15:1443-1444
Einstein, Albert 6:560-561;
15:1443
Energy 7:613
illus. 15:1444
law of equivilance of mass and
energy 15:1444
Mass 11:1027
Michelson 15:1443-1444
Universe 18:1786-1788
REPRODUCTION, ASEXUAL
15:1445
animal 1:87
budding 15:1445
Embryology 6:592-597
fission 15:1445; 7:688
fragmentation 15:1445
illus.: ameba 15:1445; hydra
15:1445; sphagnum 15:1445
Oscillatoria 13:1225
Paramecium 13:1245-1246

Parthenogenesis 13:1251-1252
Plants, classification of 14:1322-1327
Protozoa 14:1378-1379
Reproductive systems 15:1447-1448
spore formation 15:1445
REPRODUCTION, SEXUAL 15:1446-1447
cross-fertilization 15:1446-1447
dioecious 15:1446
Gamete 8:749
illus.: hydra 15:1446; insect 15:1446; zygote 15:1446
Mammalia 11:1011-1012
metagenesis 15:1446
monoecious 15:1447
Ovum 13:1230
parthenogenesis 15:1446
Parturition 13:1252
Plants, classification of 14:1322-1327
Pollen 14:1346
Pregnancy 14:1359
zygote 15:1446
REPRODUCTIVE SYSTEMS 15:1447-1448
Adrenal glands 1:27-28
Anatomy 1:76
Androgen 1:79
animal 1:87
Annelida 15:1447-1448
Arthropoda 15:1447-1448
Baby animals 3:207-208
Eggs 6:559
Embryology 6:592-597
Estrous cycle 7:637
Fertilization 7:678
flatworms 15:1447
Follicle (reproduction) 8:709
Gamete 8:749
Gonad 8:787; 15:1447
Gonorrhea 8:787
Heredity 9:837-841
human 15:1448
Hybridization 9:862
illus.: crayfish 15:1448; earthworm 15:1447; human, male 15:1448; human, female 15:1448; planaria 15:1448; starfish 15:1447
Liver fluke 10:973
Menstruation 11:1044
Mitosis and meiosis 11:1076-1078
Ovary 13:1299
Oviparous 13:1230
Parthenogenesis 13:1252
Physiology 13:1289-1291
Progesterone 14:1371
Puberty 14:1383
Reproduction, sexual 15:1446-1447
Spawning 17:1639
Testis 18:1736-1737
REPTILIA 15:1449-1450
Alligator 1:62
Chameleon 4:369
characteristics 15:1449
Chordata 4:383-385
crocodile 1:62
Dinosaur 6:516
evolution 15:1449
Gila monster 8:777
habitat 15:1449-1450
illus.: American alligator 15:1449; characteristics 15:1450; gopher tortoise 15:1449
Lizard 10:974-975
Marine biology 11:1019-1021

Pterodactyl 14:1382
Snakes 15:1564-1566
Turtle 18:1782
Venom 19:1809
RESEARCH 15:1450-1451
applied 15:1451
deductive 15:1450
illus.: examples 15:1451
inductive 15:1450
Invention 10:910
Science 16:1513-1514
scientific method 15:1450-1451
RESERVOIR 15:1451
RESIN 15:1452
Amber 1:69
Essential oils 7:637
Forest products 8:712
illus.: amber 15:1452
Plastics 14:1332-1334
RESISTANCE 15:1452
Ammeter 1:72
Ampere 1:72-73
friction 15:1452
gravity 15:1452
molecular forces 15:1452
Ohm's law 15:1452
RESOLUTION 15:1452
RESONANCE 15:1452-1453
exp. 15:1453
formula 15:1452
Voice 19:1821
Resources see **NATURAL RESOURCES**
Respirator 10:915
illus. 10:915
RESPIRATORY SYSTEM 15:1453-1455
amphibian 15:1455
Anatomy 1:76
Arthropoda 15:1453
Artificial respiration 2:143
Asphyxia 2:151
Asthma 2:153
Diaphragm 6:508
echinoderms 15:1454
exp.: constructing a respiratory model 15:1455
Expiration 7:663
Gill 8:777
Glycolysis 8:793
Hiccough 9:844
Histology 9:849
illus.: earthworm 15:1453; fish gills 15:1454; grasshopper 15:1454; human (anatomy) 15:1454; land snail 15:1454; salamander 15:1455; starfish 15:1454
Inspiration 9:884
Iron lung 10:915
Krebs, Sir Hans 10:937
Larynx 10:944
lower animals 15:1453
Lung 10:983-984
Mammalia 11:1011-1012
mollusks 15:1454
Nose 12:1161
Pharynx 13:1274
Physiology 13:1289-1291
Pneumonia 14:1341
vertebrates 15:1454
Voice 19:1820-1821
Resurrection plant see **WILD FLOWERS**
RESUSCITATION 15:1455
Retch see **VOMIT**
Reticulum see **RUMINANT**
Retina see **EYE**
RETROGRADE MOTION 15:1456

Retrorocket see **ASTRONAUT; ASTRONAUTICS; SPACE TRAVEL; SPACE VEHICLES**
Reverberation 1:22
REVOLUTION 15:1456
Revolver see **WEAPONS**
RH FACTOR 15:1456
Blood types 3:271
Transfusion 18:1766-1767
Rhea see **BIRDS, FLIGHTLESS**
RHENIUM 15:1456-1457
RHEOSTAT 15:1457
Rhesus monkey see **RH FACTOR**
RHEUMATIC FEVER 15:1457
Arthritis 2:140
Rheumatism see **ARTHRITIS**
RHINOCEROS 13:1235; 15:1457
characteristics 15:1457
illus.: 1:34; 15:1457
Mammalia 11:1011-1012
reproduction 15:1457
Rhizoid see **MOSS**
RHIZOME 15:1457-1458
Arrowroot 2:138
Bamboo 3:223
Begonia 3:244
Fern 7:676
Gardening 8:751-753
Ginger 8:777
Grasses 8:792-793
Hop 9:852
Plants, classification of 14:1322-1327
Stem, underground 17:1668-1669
RHODIUM 15:1458
RHODODENDRON 15:1458
Azalea 2:197
illus. 15:1458
Rhodophyta 18:1739
RHUBARB 15:1458
Rib see **SKELETON**
Rib grass see **WILD FLOWERS**
Riboflavin see **VITAMIN DEFICIENCY**
Ribonucleic acid, illus. 12:1178
Ribose see **NUCLEOPROTEIN**
RICE 15:1458-1459
Cereal grains 4:366
illus. 15:1458
RICHARDS, DICKENSON WOODRUFF 15:1459
RICHARDSON, SIR OWEN WILLANS 15:1459
RICHTER SCALE 15:1459
Rickets see **VITAMIN DEFICIENCY**
RIDGE 15:1459
Rifle see **WEAPONS**
RIFT VALLEY 15:1459
Rigel see **ORION; STARS**
RINGWORM 15:1459
Riptide see **TIDE**
RIVER 15:1459-1460
Delta 5:492
drainage basin 15:1459-1460
erosion 15:1460
Fiord 7:662
Flood 7:692
Forestry 8:716-717
gradient 15:1460
Groundwater 9:807-808
illus.: 15:1460; river system 15:1459
importance 15:1459
Island 10:917
natural bridge 15:1460
Sandbar 15:1494
speed 15:1460
Riverbank 4:369
Roadrunner, illus. 1:84

Roasting metal see **METAL**
ROBBINS, FREDERICK CHAPMAN
15:1460
ROBIN 15:1460
Bird houses 3:258
ROBINSON, SIR ROBERT 15:1461
ROBOT 15:1461
ROBOTICS 15:1461
ROCKET 15:1461-1463
Astronautics 2:157-165
Cosmonaut 5:450-451
engine 15:1462
Goddard, Robert Hutchings 8:785
guidance and control system
15:1463
history 15:1461
illus.: 15:1461, 1463
liquid-fuel 15:1465
Missile 11:1071-1075
propellant efficiency 15:1462
Rocket engine 15:1463-1467
Rocket propellants 15:1468-1469
Rocket sled 15:1470
Satellite, man-made 16:1507-1508
solid-fuel 15:1462
staging 15:1462
Submarine 17:1680-1681
Weapons 19:1838-1841
ROCKET ENGINE 15:1463-1467
Airplane 1:52
Aviation 2:191-197
electrostatic system 14:1464
energy sources 15:1464
Engine 7:619-623
illus.: chemical liquid engine
15:1465; chemical solid engine
15:1466; classification 15:1464;
nuclear heat exchanger propulsion
system 15:1467
ion 15:1467
liquid propellant 15:1465
Missile 11:1071-1075
Motor 12:1114-1116
nuclear 15:1466-1467
propulsion system 15:1463
reaction engine 15:1463
Rocket 15:1461-1463
Rocket propellant 15:1468-1469
Rocket sled 15:1470
solid propellant 15:1465-1466
thermonuclear system 15:1464
ROCKET PROPELLANT 15:1468-
1469
bipropellants 15:1468
Fuel 8:738-740
illus.: charts 15:1468, 1469
liquid 15:1468
Missile 11:1071-1075
monopropellants 15:1468
Rocket 15:1461-1463
Rocket engine 15:1463-1467
solid propellants 15:1469
ROCKET SLED 15:1470
development 15:1470
illus. 15:1470
use in testing 15:1470
ROCKS 15:1471-1474
Amethyst 1:71
Apatite 2:120
Archeozoic Era 2:132
Calcium carbonate 4:323
Crystal 5:461
Earth 6:541-545
Gem 8:759
Geology 8:768
igneous: basalt 15:1471; felsite
15:1471; granite 15:1471; peg-
matite 15:1471; porphyry
15:1471

illus.: basalt 15:1473; collecting
equipment 15:1471; conglomerate
15:1473; gasbro 15:1473; gneiss
15:1473; granite 15:1471;
15:1473; igneous 15:1473; limestone 15:1473; marble 15:1473;
metamorphic rocks 15:1473;
obsidian 15:1473; porphyry
15:1473; pumice 15:1473; rock
cycle 15:1472; schist 15:1473;
sedimentary 15:1473; slate
15:1473; syenite 15:1473
Intrusion 10:910
Lava 10:945
Lime (chemical) 10:965
Lode 10:977
metamorphic: gneiss 15:1472;
marble 15:1474; schist 15:1472,
1474; quartzite 15:1474; slate
15:1474
Mineral 11:1065-1067
North America 12:1156-1160
Open pit mine 13:1212
Organic rock 13:1223
Paleontology 13:1237-1238
Pegmatite 13:1259
Pumice 14:1384
Sand 15:1493
sedimentary: conglomerate
15:1472; limestone 15:1472;
sandstone 15:1472; shale
15:1472
Stratigraphy 17:1676-1677
Volcano 19:1822-1823
weathering 15:1474
Rocky Mountains see **NORTH
AMERICA**
RODENT 15:1474-1475; 19:1868
Capybara 4:336
Chinchilla 4:379
Chipmunk 4:380
Dormouse 6:526
Gopher 8:788
Groundhog 9:807
Guinea pig 9:808-809
habitat 15:1474
Herbivore 9:836-837
illus.: capybara 15:1475; charac-
teristics 15:1475; mice 15:1475;
pack rat 15:1475; squirrel
15:1474
Jerboa 10:922
Lemming 10:951
Mammalia 11:1011-1012
Marmot 11:1022
Mouse 12:1117
Muskrat 12:1127
Porcupine 14:1350
Prairie dog 14:1356
Rat 15:1430-1431
Squirrel 17:1655-1656
varieties 15:1475
Vole 19:1823
Rods and cones see **EYE**
ROE 15:1475
ROENTGEN, WILHELM KONRAD
15:1476
Curie, Pierre and Marie 5:465
Radioactive elements 15:1420-
1421
Radiograph 15:1423
X rays 19:1884-1886
Roller bearing see **BEARING**
Rook see **CROW**
ROOT 15:1476-1477
Absorption, physiological 1:15
adventitious 15:1476
aerial 15:1476
diffuse 15:1476

illus.: adventitious 15:1476;
aerial adventitious 15:1476
cross-section 15:1477; parasitic
15:1476; prop 15:1476; tap
15:1476
internal structure 15:1477
Plant 14:1314-1317
primary 15:1476
ROOTWORM 15:1477
ROPE 15:1477
ROSE 15:1477-1478
illus. 15:1478
ROSE-OF-SHARON 15:1478
ROSEMARY 15:1478
illus. 15:1478
Mint 11:1070
ROSEWOOD 15:1478
Ross, James 2:133
ROSS, SIR RONALD 15:1478-1479
ROT 15:1479
ROTATION 15:1479
Jupiter 10:928-929
ROTIFERA 15:1479-1480
body structure 15:1480
characteristics 15:1479
defenses 15:1480
habitat 15:1479
illus. 15:1480
locomotion 15:1479-1480
Parthenogenesis 13:1251-1252
reproduction 15:1480
Rotogravure see **PRINTING**
ROTOR 15:1481
Roundworm see **ASCARIS;
NEMATHELMINTHES**
RUBBER 15:1481-1482
Forest products 8:713
history 15:1481
Insulator 9:887
Latex 10:944
manufacture 15:1481-1482
properties 15:1481
Vulcanization 19:1826
RUBBER, SYNTHETIC 15:1482
illus.: 15:1481; chart 15:1482
RUBBER PLANT 15:1482
Rubella see **MEASLES**
RUBIDIUM 15:1483
**RUBIDIUM-STRONTIUM DATING
METHOD** 15:1483
RUBY 15:1483
illus. 15:1483
Mineral 11:1065-1067
Sapphire 15:1496
Rudder 1:52
Ruffed grouse see **FOWL; GROUSE**
RUMINANT 15:1483
illus.: stomach 15:1483
Oxen 13:1231
RUNNER 15:1484
illus. 15:1484
Rupture see **HERNIA**
Russula, illus. 12:1124
RUST 15:1484
Cedar 4:357
illus. 15:1484
Plant diseases 14:1319
RUSTING 15:1485
causes 15:1485
Combustion 5:425
Corrosion 5:449
exp.: prevention 15:1485
RUTABAGA 15:1485
illus. 15:1485
RUTHENIUM 15:1486
RUTHERFORD, ERNEST 15:1486-
1487
Atom 2:173
Bohr theory 3:278

Chemistry 4:373-377
illus.: 15:1486, 1487
Proton (elementary particle)
14:1377
Electron 6:579
RYE 15:1487
Cereal grains 4:366
illus. 15:1487
Saber-toothed tiger see **CAT FAMILY**
Sable see **WEASEL**
SACCHARIN 15:1488
Sacrum see **SKELETON**
Safrole see **SASSAFRAS**
SAGE 15:1488
illus. 15:1488
Mint 11:1070
Sage hen see **GROUSE**
Sage sparrow see **FINCH**
SAGEBRUSH 15:1488
illus. 15:1488
SAGITTARIUS 15:1488-1489
illus. 15:1489
Scorpius 16:1515-1516
Sago see **PALM**
Saguaro see **CACTUS**
Sahara Desert see **AFRICA**
Saint Lawrence Seaway see **NORTH AMERICA**
SAINT VITUS DANCE 15:1489
cause 15:1489
symptoms 15:1489
treatment 15:1489
SALAMANDER 15:1489-1490
characteristics 15:1489
exp.: caring for 15:1490
habitat 15:1489
illus.: ambystoma 15:1489; dusky salamander 15:1489; mud puppy 15:1489
Newt 12:1146-1147
Tadpole 18:1715
Saleratus see **SODIUM BICARBONATE**
Saliva see **SALIVARY GLANDS**
SALIVARY GLANDS 15:1490
Digestive system 6:510
Gland 8:780
illus. 15:1490
Mumps 12:1119
SALK, JONAS EDWARD 15:1490-1491
Poliomyelitis 14:1346
Vaccine 18:1792-1793
SALMON 15:1491
characteristics 15:1491
illus. 15:1491
spawning 15:1491
Salsify see **OYSTER PLANT**
SALT 15:1492
exp.: as a conductor of electricity 15:1492
Phosphate 13:1276
Water 19:1830-1831
SALTPETER 15:1492
Nitrogen 12:1150
Saltwater see **BRINE; OCEAN-OGRAPHY; SEA WATER**
SALVE 15:1493
Ointment 13:1208
SALVIA 15:1493
illus. 15:1493
Samara 8:734
SAMARIUM 15:1493
SAND 15:1493
illus. 15:1493
SAND DOLLAR 15:1493
illus. 15:1493
Sand dune see **DUNE**

Sand verbena see **WILD FLOWERS**
SANDALWOOD 15:1494
illus. 15:1494
SANDARAC 15:1494
SANDBAR 15:1494
illus. 15:1494
SANDBLAST 15:1494
Sandpaper see **ABRASIVE**
SANDPIPER 15:1494-1495
illus. 15:1494
Sandstone see **ROCKS**
SANDWORM 15:1495
body structure 15:1495
illus. 15:1495
SANITATION 15:1495
Sewage disposal 16:1530-1531
SANSEVIERIA 15:1495
illus. 15:1495
Sapodilla see **CHICLE**
Sapodilla tree 4:378
SAPONIFICATION 15:1496
SAPPHIRE 15:1496
illus. 15:1496
Mineral 11:1065-1067
SAPROPHYTE 15:1496
Nitrogen cycle 12:1150-1151
Parasites 13:1247
Rot 15:1479
SAPSUCKER 15:1496
SAPWOOD 15:1496
illus. 15:1496
Saran see **PLASTICS**
Sarcoma see **CANCER (DISEASE)**
SARDINE 15:1497
illus. 15:1497
SARGASSUM 15:1497
Currents, ocean 5:467-471
illus. 15:1497
Ocean 12:1188-1190
Pelagic 13:1259
Sea 16:1516
SASSAFRAS 15:1497
illus. 15:1497
SATELLITE, MAN-MADE 16:1507-1508
applications 16:1507
biosatellites 16:1507
illus.: 16:1507; 19:1846; 19:1857
International Geophysical Year: Atmosphere 9:891-892
lunar orbiter 16:1507
manned 16:1508
Orbital systems 13:1218-1220
orbiting observatories 16:1507
solar power stations 16:1508
space shuttles 16:1508
speed 16:1507
Viking Project 19:1814
SATELLITE, NATURAL 16:1508
illus., chart 16:1508
Moon, phases of 11:1094-1095
orbit 16:1508
retrograde motion 16:1508
Saturn 16:1509-1510
Solar system 16:1575-1578
Uranus 18:1789-1790
SATURATION 16:1508
SATURN 16:1509-1510
characteristics 16:1509
diameter 16:1510
distance from the sun 16:1510
illus. 16:1509
rings 16:1509
rotation and revolution 16:1509
satellites 16:1510
Sawfish see **RAY**
Saxifrage see **WILD FLOWERS**
SCAB 16:1510

SCABIOSA 16:1510
SCALE, ANIMAL 16:1510-1511
illus. 16:1511
Skin modification 16:1558
Scale insects, illus. 14:1319
Scale, musical see **MUSICAL INSTRUMENTS; OVERTONES; SOUND**
Scales see **BALANCE; WEIGHT**
Scallion see **ONION**
SCALLOP 16:1511
illus. 16:1511
Scalp see **HAIR; SKIN MODIFICATIONS**
SCANDIUM 16:1511
Scapula see **SKELETON**
SCAR 16:1511
Wound 19:1882
SCARAB 16:1512
illus.: rhinoceros beetle 16:1512; tumblebug 16:1512; unicorn 16:1512
SCARLET FEVER 16:1512
Scarlet tanager see **TANAGER**
SCAVENGER 13:1247; 16:1512
Scheelite see **TUNGSTEN**
Schist see **ROCKS**
Schizocarp 8:735
Schizomycophyta 18:1739
Schleden, Matthias J. see **SCHWANN, THEODOR**
SCHRIEFFER, JOHN R. 16:1513
SCHULTZE, MAX 16:1513
Schwann, Theodor 16:1513
SCHWANN, THEODOR 16:1513
SCIENCE 16:1513-1514
applied 16:1514
biological 16:1514
definitions 16:1513
future of 16:1514
history 16:1514
physical 16:1514
pure 16:1513-1514
Technology 18:1722
Science and religion 5:434, 446
SCIENTIFIC METHOD 16:1514-1515
Data 5:482
Experiment 7:662
Physics 13:1287-1288
Psychology 14:1380-1381
Research 15:1450-1451
Theory 18:1740
SCLEROSIS 16:1515
SCORPION 16:1515
illus. 16:1515
reproduction 16:1515
SCORPIUS 16:1515-1516
illus. 16:1516
mythology 16:1516
Sagittarius 15:1488-1489
Scotch broom, illus. 7:644
Screech owl see **OWL**
Screw see **MACHINES, SIMPLE**
SCRUB 16:1516
Scuba see **OCEANOGRAPHY**
SCULPIN 16:1516
Scurvy see **VITAMIN DEFICIENCY**
SEA 16:1516
SEA ANEMONE 16:1516
illus. 5:418; 16:1516
SEA COW 16:1516
illus. 16:1516
SEA CUCUMBER 15:1443; 16:1517
circulatory system 16:1517
illus. 6:549; 16:1517
reproduction 16:1517
uses 16:1517
water vascular system 16:1517

Sea fan, illus. 5:419
SEA LEVEL 16:1517
  illus. 16:1517
  mean sea level 16:1517
  Oceanography 12:1190-1195
  Tide 18:1750-1751
SEA LILY 16:1517-1518
  illus. 16:1518
SEA LION 16:1518
  illus. 16:1518
SEA SQUIRT 16:1518
  illus. 16:1518
SEA URCHIN 16:1518
  illus. 6:549; 16:1518
  Sand dollar 15:1493
  Sea cucumber 16:1517
SEA WATER 16:1519-1520
  Currents, ocean 5:467-471
  density 16:1519-1520
  exp. 16:1519
  illus. chart 16:1519
  Natural resources 12:1131-1133
  Ocean 12:1188-1190
  Oceanography 12:1190-1195
  salinity 16:1519
  Sargassum 15:1497
SEABORG, DR. GLENN THEODORE
  16:1520
  Curium 5:466
  Plutonium 14:1340
SEAHORSE 16:1520-1521
  illus. 16:1520
SEAL 16:1521
  illus. 16:1521
  Marine biology 11:1019-1021
  reproduction 16:1521
  Sea lion 16:1517-1518
  varieties 16:1521
  Walrus 19:1828
SEAMOUNT 16:1521
SEAPLANE 16:1521-1522
  illus. 16:1521
  pontoon 16:1521
SEARCH FOR EXTRATERRESTRIAL
  INTELLIGENCE (SETI) 16:1522
  illus. 17:1636
SEASONS 16:1522-1523
  Earth 6:543
  illus. 16:1522
  inclination of earth's axis 16:1522
  Solstice 16:1581
SEAWEED 16:1523
  illus. 16:1523
  Marine biology 11:1019-1021
  Mucilage 12:1117
Sebaceous gland see SKIN
SECRETION 16:1523
SEDATIVE 16:1523
  bromides 16:1523
  tranquilizer 16:1523
SEDIMENT 16:1523
  Peneplain 13:1261
Sedimentary rock see ROCKS
SEDUM 16:1524
  illus. 16:1524
  Plants, succulent 14:1329
Seebeck, Thomas J. see PELTIER,
  JEAN CHARLES ATHANASE;
  THERMOCOUPLE
SEED 16:1524-1525
  exp. 16:1525
  Flower 7:693-694
  Follicle (botanical) 8:709
  Germination 8:774
  illus. 16:1524
  life span 16:1524-1525
  parts 16:1524
  Radicle 15:1416
  Seed dispersal 16:1526

SEED DISPERSAL 16:1526
  carried by wind 16:1526
  Composite flower 5:431
  Cone 5:439
  Follicle (botanical) 8:709
  hitchhiking 16:1526
  illus. 16:1526
  pods 16:1526
  Seed 16:1524-1525
SEEDLING 16:1526
SEGMENT 16:1526
SEGRE, EMILIO 16:1526
SEICHE 16:1526
SEISMOGRAPH 16:1527
  depth of polar icecaps 16:1527
  Depth sounding 5:493-494
  Earthquake 6:547
  earthquake detection 16:1527
  Geology 8:768-769
  illus. 16:1527
  International Geophysical Year:
    the Solid Earth 9:894
  types 16:1527
SELENIUM 16:1527
Selye, Hans 17:1678
Semen see REPRODUCTION,
  SEXUAL; SPERM; TESTIS
Semiautomatic .38, illus. 19:1839
Semiautomatic rifle, illus. 19:1839
Semicircular canal see EAR
Semilunar valve see HEART
SENSE ORGANS 16:1528-1529
  exteroception 16:1528
  illus.: sensory nerves 16:1529;
    taste buds 16:1528
  interoception 16:1528
  Physiology 13:1289-1291
  proprioception 16:1528
  Receptors 15:1438
  Smell 16:1562
  Taste 18:1718-1719
Septum see HEART
Sequoia see REDWOOD
SERPENTINE 16:1529
  antigorite 16:1529
  chrysotile 16:1529
  illus. 16:1529
SERUM 16:1530
  albumin 16:1530
  antibody 16:1530
  Globulin 8:783; 16:1530
  immunity 16:1530
SESAME 16:1530
  illus. 16:1530
SESSILE 16:1530
SEWAGE DISPOSAL 16:1530-1531
  illus. 16:1531
  Sanitation 15:1495
  septic tank 16:1530-1531
SEX 16:1531
  Gamete 8:749
  Puberty 14:1383
Sex determination see HEREDITY
SEX-LINKED CHARACTERISTICS
  16:1531
SHAD 16:1532
SHADOW 16:1532
Shaking palsy 13:1250
SHAMROCK 16:1533
SHARK 16:1533
  body structure 16:1533
  illus. 16:1533
  Pisces (animal) 14:1307-1308
  reproduction 16:1533
  Skate 16:1551
  varieties 16:1533
Shasta daisy see BURBANK, LUTHER
SHEEP 16:1534
  Cashmere 4:347

illus. 16:1534; 19:1880
Lanolin 10:942
varieties 16:1534
Wool 19:1879-1880
SHEEPSHEAD 16:1534
  illus. 16:1534
SHELL 16:1534
SHELLAC 16:1534
Shellfish see MOLLUSCA
SHEPARD, ALAN B. 16:1535
  illus. 16:1535
SHERRINGTON, SIR CHARLES
  SCOTT 16:1535
SHINGLES 16:1535
  causes 16:1535
  symptoms 16:1535
SHIPS 16:1536-1539
  ancient 16:1536
  Boats 3:275-276
  future 16:1539
  illus.: 16:1536, 1537, 1538, 1539
  Navigation 12:1134-1135
  nuclear 16:1538
  steam 16:1537
  Submarine 17:1681
SHIVERING 16:1539
Shoal 10:917
SHOCK 16:1539
  Transfusion 18:1766-1767
SHOCKLEY, WILLIAM 16:1540
Shooting star see METEOR
SHORT CIRCUIT 16:1540
  illus. 16:1540
SHORT WAVE RADIO 16:1540-
  1541
  history 16:1541
  illus. 16:1541
  Marconi, Guglielmo 11:1018
  transmission 16:1541
Shotgun, illus. 19:1840
SHREW 16:1542
  illus. 7:643; 9:884; 16:1542
  Mammalia 11:1011-1012
SHRIKE 16:1542
  illus. 16:1542
SHRIMP 16:1542-1543
  Crustacea 5:459
  illus. 5:459; 16:1543
SHRUB 16:1543-1544
  acid soils 16:1544
  borders and hedges 16:1544
  colorful fruit 16:1544
  fall and winter 16:1544
  flowering 16:1544
  Hydrangea 9:863
  illus.: azalea 16:1545; berberis
    16:1545; callicarpa 16:1545;
    heather 16:1545; hibiscus
    16:1543; ilex 16:1545; ligustrum
    16:1545; mountain laurel
    16:1545; pussy willow 16:1543;
    sophora 16:1545; sumas
    16:1543; viburnum 16:1545;
    wild rose 16:1543
  Laurel 10:945
  rocky areas 16:1544
  Rose-of-Sharon 15:1478
  shade 16:1544
  Snowberry 16:1570
  spring-flowering 16:1544
  summer and late-flowering 16:1544
  Weigela 19:1859
  Witch hazel 19:1878
Shunt see AMMETER
Siamese fighting fish see TROPICAL
  FISH
SICKLE-CELL ANEMIA 16:1545
  Pauling, Linus 13:1255
Sidereal day see EARTH

Siemens-Martin process 13:1210
Sierra Nevadas see **NORTH AMERICA**
Sigma see **STATISTICS**
Sikorsky, Igor 1:31
SILAGE 16:1545
SILICON 16:1545
  Porifera 14:1351-1352
SILICON LIFE 16:1546-1547
  Carbon life 4:341-342
  illus. 16:1546
  life in other worlds 16:1546
  on other planets 16:1546
  resemblance to carbon 16:1546
  Silicon 16:1545
SILICONE 16:1547
Silk see **SILKWORM**
Silk-cotton tree see **KAPOK**
SILKWORM 16:1548
  exp. 16:1548
  habitat 16:1548
  illus. 16:1548
  Rayon 15:1436
  spinneret 16:1548
Silt see **OCEAN; RIVER**
SILVER 16:1549
  illus. 16:1549
  Mineral 11:1065-1067
  properties 16:1549
  uses 16:1549
Silver maple, illus. 7:607
SILVERFISH 16:1549
  illus. 16:1549
SIMMOND'S DISEASE 16:1549
  causes 16:1549
  symptoms 16:1549
  treatment 16:1549
Simple machines see **MACHINES, SIMPLE**
Sinanthropus see **EVOLUTION OF MAN**
SINKHOLE 16:1550
  illus. 16:1550
  Karst topography 10:930
  Lake 10:939-940
SINUS 16:1550
  ethmoids 16:1550
  frontal 16:1550
  functions 16:1550
  illus. 16:1550
  maxillaries 16:1550
  sinusitis 16:1550
Sinusoids 4:335
SIPHON 16:1551
SIRIUS 16:1551
SISAL 16:1551
  Century plant 4:365
SKATE 16:1551
  body structure 16:1551
  illus. 16:1551
  reproduction 16:1551
Skeletal joints see **JOINTS, SKELETAL**
SKELETON 7:679; 16:1552-1555
  Anatomy 1:76
  Animals, classification of 1:94-96
  annelida 16:1552
  Ape 2:121
  Arthritis 2:140
  arthropoda 16:1552
  Bone 3:282-283
  Cartilage tissue 4:346
  coelenterates 16:1552
  Cranium 5:455
  echinodermata 16:1554
  Endoskeleton 7:610
  Extremities 7:664
  human 16:1555

  illus.: arthropoda 16:1552; coel-
    enterates 16:1552; echinodermata
    16:1554; human 16:1553; lower
    chordates 16:1554; mollusca
    16:1554; porifera 16:1552;
    protozoa 16:1552
  Joints, skeletal 10:924-925
  lower chordates 16:1554
  Mammalia 11:1011-1012
  Mandible 11:1013
  mollusca 16:1554
  nemathelminthes 16:1552
  Ossification 13:1228
  Pelvis 13:1260
  platyhelminthes 16:1552
  porifera 16:1552
  protozoa 16:1552
  Sprain 17:1653
  vertebrates 16:1554
SKIN 16:1556-1557
  Anatomy 1:76
  Dermatitis 5:495
  Dermatology 5:495
  dermis 16:1556
  epidermis 16:1556
  exp. 16:1557
  glands 16:1557
  Histology 9:849
  illus. 16:1556-1557
  Impetigo 9:874
  Infection 9:877
  Leather 10:947
  nerve fibrils 16:1557
  Pigment 13:1294
  Sense organs 16:1528-1529
  Skin modification 16:1558
SKIN MODIFICATION 16:1558
  callouses 16:1558
  dermal scales 16:1558
  Histology 9:846-849
  illus. 16:1558
  Leather 10:947
  Nail 12:1129
  Oil gland 12:1197
  Scale, animal 16:1510
  Skin 16:1556-1557
  Sweat glands 18:1710
SKIN TEST 16:1557
Skin-diving see **OCEANOGRAPHY**
Skink see **LIZARD**
Skull see **SKELETON**
SKUNK 16:1559
  illus. 1:84; 16:1559
  odor 16:1559
  protection 1:87
  varieties 16:1559
  Weasel 19:1841-1842
Skunk cabbage see **WILD FLOWERS**
SKY 16:1559
  Air 1:42-44
  Astronomy 2:166-167
  color 16:1559
  illus. 16:1559
Skylab Orbital Workshop 2:164;
  17:1633
Skylark see **LARK**
Skysweeper, illus. 19:1840
SLAG 10:915; 16:1560
Slaked lime see **SOLVAY PROCESS**
Slate see **ROCKS**
SLEEP 16:1560
  aquatic mammals 16:1560
  physiological changes 16:1560
SLEEPING SICKNESS 16:1560
  Koch, Robert 10:936
Sleet see **PRECIPITATION**
SLIDE RULE 16:1560
Sliding friction see **FRICTION**
Slip see **PROPAGATION**

SLOTH 16:1561
  characteristics 16:1561
  habitat 16:1561
  illus. 16:1561
  varieties 16:1561
SLUDGE 16:1561
SLUG 16:1561
  illus. 16:1561
Small intestine 6:511
SMALLPOX 16:1561-1562
  Black Death 3:265
  control 16:1562
  Jenner, Edward 10:921
  Medicine 11:1038-1040
  symptoms 16:1562
  Vaccine 18:1792
SMELL 16:1562
  exp. 16:1562
  olfactory nerve 16:1562
SMELLING SALTS 16:1563
SMELT 16:1563
Smilax see **WILD FLOWERS**
SMOG 9:823; 16:1563
SMOKE 16:1563
  illus. 16:1563
Smut see **CORN; PLANT DISEASES**
SNAIL 16:1564
  body structure 16:1564
  illus.: 11:1020, 1085; 15:1454;
    16:1564
  Marine biology 11:1019
  Mollusca 11:1084-1086
  Periwinkle 13:1267
  reproduction 16:1564
  Whelk 19:1866
Snakeroot see **WILD FLOWERS**
SNAKES 16:1564-1566
  characteristics 16:1564
  exp. as pets 16:1565
  feeding 16:1565
  food 1:86
  illus.: 11:1087; anaconda 16:1567;
    bull snake 16:1567; charts, kinds
    of snakes 16:1566; coach whip
    16:1567; cobra 16:1567; cotton-
    mouth 16:1567; diamondback rat-
    tler 16:1567; European viper
    16:1567; fer-de-lance 16:1567;
    garter snake 16:1567; hog-nosed
    snake 16:1567; indigo racer
    16:1567; prairie rattler 16:1567;
    rat snake 16:1567; rattlesnake
    5:495
  Jungle 10:926
  Mongoose 11:1089
  Poison gland 14:1343
  poisonous 16:1566
  Reptilia 15:1449-1450
  senses 16:1566
  Venom 19:1809
SNAPDRAGON 16:1568
  illus. 16:1568
SNAPPER 16:1568
  illus. 16:1568
Snapping turtle see **TURTLE**
Sneezewart see **WILD FLOWERS**
SNIPE 16:1568
  illus. 16:1568
  Sandpiper 15:1495
Snorkel see **SUBMARINE**
Snow see **PRECIPITATION**
SNOW GAUGE 16:1569
  exp. 16:1569
  Gauge 8:756
SNOWBERRY 16:1570
  illus. 16:1570
SNOWDROP 16:1570
  Stem, underground 17:1668-1669
Snowshoe rabbit, illus. 14:1394

SOAP 16:1570
  Detergent 5:496
  Ester 7:637
SOAPSTONE 16:1570
SOCIOBIOLOGY 16:1570
Sociology 3:253
Soda see **SODIUM BICARBONATE**
SODDY, FREDERICK 16:1570-
  1571
SODIUM 16:1571
  Cesium 4:368
  Davy, Sir Humphry 5:483
  properties 16:1571
  Water 19:1831
SODIUM BICARBONATE 16:1571
Sodium chloride 4:381
Sodium chlorite 3:266
SODIUM PENTOTHAL 16:1571
Sodium perborate 3:266
Soft coal see **COAL**
Soft palate 6:511
Soft water see **WATER**
SOFTWOOD 16:1571-1572
  cedar trees 16:1572
  fir trees 16:1571
  Hardwood 9:820
  illus.: longleaf pine 16:1572;
    redwood 16:1572; western hem-
    lock 16:1572; white fir 16:1572;
    white pine 16:1572
  pines 16:1572
  spruce 16:1572
Soil erosion, illus. 1:40
SOIL TESTING 16:1572
  acidity 16:1572
  nutrients 16:1572
SOIL TYPES 6:543; 16:1573
  alluvium 16:1573
  Clay 4:392
  Decomposition 5:487
  exp. 16:1573
  Geography 8:761-763
  Humus 9:859
  Loam 10:975
  Loess 10:977; 16:1573
  Mulch 12:1118
  Natural resources 12:1131-
    1133
  Paleontology 13:1237-1238
  soil orders 16:1573
  Soil testing 16:1572
  till 16:1573
  Topsoil 18:1760
Solar battery, illus. 10:991
SOLAR CELL 16:1574
  Battery 3:232-233
  illus. 16:1574
Solar day 6:543
Solar eclipse see **ECLIPSE**
Solar energy see **ENERGY; SOLAR
  CELL; SUN**
SOLAR PLEXUS 16:1574
SOLAR SYSTEM 16:1575-1578
  Asteroids 2:152; 16:1575
  Astronomy 2:167
  Comet 5:426; 16:1575
  Earth 6:541-545
  Earth, early development of 6:545-
    547
  exp.: building model planets
    16:1577
  Galaxy 8:745
  illus. 18:1788; ancient astrono-
    mers 16:1578; planets 16:1575,
    1576
  Interstellar communication
    10:907-909
  Jupiter 10:928-929
  Mars 11:1023-1025

  Mercury (planet) 11:1044-
    1046
  Milky Way 11:1062
  Moon 11:1092-1094
  Nebula 12:1136
  Neptune 12:1140
  orbits 16:1576
  Planet 14:1312; 16:1575
  Pluto 14:1338-1339
  Ptolemy 14:1382-1383
  Revolution 15:1456
  Satellite, natural 16:1508
  satellites 16:1575
  Saturn 16:1509-1510
  *Search for Extraterrestrial Intel-
    ligence (SETI)* 16:1522
  Solar system, origin of 16:1579
  sun 16:1578
  theories of origin 16:1578
  Uranus 18:1789-1790
  Venus 19:1810-1811
  Viking Project 19:1814
  Zodiac 19:1893
SOLAR SYSTEM, ORIGIN OF
  16:1579
  illus.: LaPlace theory 16:1579
  nebular contraction 16:1579
  nebular theory 16:1579
  planetesimal theory 16:1579
  tidal theory 16:1579
SOLAR TURBULENCE 16:1580
  chromosphere 16:1580
  corona 16:1580
  illus. 16:1580
  photosphere 16:1580
  sunspots 16:1580
SOLAR WIND 16:1580
SOLDERING 16:1580
SOLE 16:1580
SOLENOID 16:1581
  Electromagnet 6:577
  illus. 16:1581
SOLID 16:1581
  illus. 11:1031
  Molecular theory 11:1083
  Physical states and changes
    13:1286-1287
Solo man see **EVOLUTION OF
  MAN**
SOLSTICE 16:1581
  Saturn 16:1510
  summer 16:1581
  winter 16:1581
SOLUBILITY 16:1582
  Raoult's Law 15:1428-1429
  Supersaturated solutions
    17:1694
SOLUTE 16:1582
SOLUTION 16:1582-1583
  Colloidal state 5:421
  dissolving 16:1583
  Emulsion 7:609
  heterogeneous 16:1582
  homogeneous 16:1582-1583
  illus. 16:1582
  Insoluble 9:884
  Ion 10:911-912
  Mixture 16:1582
  Physical states and changes
    13:1286-1287
  Reagent 15:1437
  Raoult's Law 15:1428-1429
  Saturation 16:1508
  Solvent 16:1582; 1583
  super-saturated 16:1583
SOLVAY PROCESS 1:72; 16:1583
  illus. 16:1583
SOLVENT 16:1582-1583
  Acetic acid 1:19

  Acetone 1:19
  Raoult's Law 15:1428-1429
  Rayon 15:1436
  Solute 16:1582
  Solution 16:1582
  Supersaturated solutions 17:1694
Somatotropin 8:775
SONAR 16:1584
  Acoustic weapons 1:22
  Depth sounding 5:493-494
  illus. 16:1584
  Seismograph 16:1527
  transducer 16:1584
  transmitter 16:1584
Song sparrow see **FINCH**
SONIC BARRIER 16:1584
Sonic boom see **SUPERSONIC**
SONIC DEPTH RECORDER 16:1584
Sonoran Desert 5:496
Sophora, illus. 16:1545
SORE THROAT 16:1584
SORGHUM 16:1584
SOUND 16:1585-1590
  Acoustics 1:22-23; 16:1588-1590
  air column 16:1587-1588
  amplitude 16:1586-1587
  Carrier wave 4:345
  Diffraction 6:509
  Doppler effect 6:525
  Dynamics 6:536
  ears 16:1585
  Echo 6:550
  Electromagnetic spectrum 6:578
  exp. 16:1589
  Filter 7:681
  frequency 16:1586
  illus.: amplitude 16:1587; con-
    struction of a clarinet 16:1587;
    reverberation 16:1590; various
    rates of travel 16:1586; vibra-
    tions 16:1585; vibrations per
    second 16:1586; wave lengths
    16:1588
  Marconi, Guglielmo 11:1018
  Motion pictures 12:1112-1114
  Musical instruments 12:1126
  Noise 12:1155
  noise pollution 16:1590
  Overtones 13:1229-1230
  Physics 13:1287-1288
  Radio 15:1416-1418
  Rocket sled 15:1470
  Short wave radio 16:1540-1541
  Sonar 16:1584
  Sound interference 16:1591
  Supersonic 17:1694-1695
  supersonic boom 16:1590
  Telephone 18:1726-1727
  vibration 16:1585
  Voice 19:1820-1821
  waves 16:1586
SOUND BARRIER 16:1590
  Sound interference 16:1591
  Supersonic 16:1590; 17:1694-
    1695
SOUND INTERFERENCE 16:1591
  illus. 16:1591
  rarefactions 16:1591
  Short wave radio 16:1540-1541
  Spectrum pollution 17:1643-1644
  zone of silence 16:1591
SOUND RECORDING 16:1592
  High fidelity 9:844
  illus. 16:1592
  motion pictures 16:1592
  Sound 16:1585-1590
  speaker systems 16:1592
  stereophonic 16:1592
  Stereophonic sound 17:1670

Sounding see **DEPTH SOUNDING; SONAR**
SOUTH AMERICA 16:1593-1597
Climate 4:394-397; 16:1593-1594
Continent 5:444
evolution 16:1593
Geography 8:761-763
Geology 8:768-769
illus.: animals 16:1596, 1597; native plants 16:1593; rain forest 16:1593
Jungle 10:926-927
land forms 16:1593
map: physical 16:1595; temperature and rain fall 16:1594; vegetation 16:1594
natural resources 12:1131-1133; copper 16:1596; diamonds 16:1596 emeralds 16:1596; gold 16:1596; guana droppings 16:1597; platinum 16:1596; rubber 16:1597
plants: cacao 16:1596; cassava 16:1596; coffee 16:1596; quinine 16:1596; sugar cane 16:1596
rivers and drainage: Amazon 16:1594; Iguassu 16:1594; Magdalena 16:1594; Orinoco 16:1594; Parana 16:1594
South Equatorial Current 5:470
South Equatorial Drift 5:469
South Pole see **POLES, NORTH AND SOUTH**
Sow see **PIG**
SOYBEAN 16:1597
illus. 6:554
SPACE 17:1607-1611
Altimeter 1:66
Altitude 1:66
Astronaut 2:155-156
Atmosphere 2:171
cislunar 17:1608
corpuscular radiation 17:1609-1610
electromagnetic radiation 17:1609
environment 17:1611
gravitation 17:1608
illus.: corona of sun 17:1610; solar flare 17:1609
Interstellar communication 10:907-909
Lunar base 10:980-983
magnetic fields 17:1610
matter 17:1610-1611
Radiation 15:1407-1409
Ray, cosmic 15:1434
Satellite, natural 16:1508
Solar system 16:1575-1578
Space pilot 17:1616-1617
Universe 18:1786-1788
SPACE MEDICINE 17:1611-1616
acceleration 17:1611
air pressure 17:1614
Astronaut 2:155-156
Astronautics 2:157-165
Atmosphere 2:168-171
biodynamics 17:1611
chart: corpuscular radiation data 17:1614
corpuscular radiation 17:1614-1616
Cosmonaut 5:450-451
excessive vibration 17:1613
food 17:1613
gravity 17:1612-1613
illus.: 17:1611, 1612, 1613; clothing 17:1615
Lunar base 10:980-983

oxygen 17:1613
physiological aspects 17:1611-1616
psychological aspects 17:1617
Space 17:1607-1611
Space station 17:1620-1621
temperature control 17:1614
water 16:1613-1614
Weightlessness 19:1861
SPACE PILOT 17:1616-1617
chart of crews 17:1617
illus.: 17:1616, 1617
preflight training 17:1617
SPACE SHUTTLE ORBITER 1:50,53; 2:164; 17:1618-1619; 17:1633
Enterprise 17:1618-1619
illus. 17:1618, 1619, 1632
Jupiter Orbiter Probe 10:929; 17:1619
purposes 17:1619
SPACE STATION 17:1620-1621, 1633
illus. 17:1620, 1621, 1637
living conditions 17:1620
radiation protection 17:1620-1621
Rocket 15:1461-1463
Satellite, man-made 16:1507-1508
Space 17:1611
space flight simulation 17:1621
Space Shuttle Orbiter 17:1618-1619
Space travel 17:1622-1624
Space vehicles 17:1624-1637
Weightlessness 19:1861
SPACE TRAVEL 17:1622-1624
Astronaut 2:155-156
Astronautics 2:157-165
Aviation 2:191-197
Cape Canaveral 4:334
capture period 17:1623-1624
chart of travel times 17:1623
Cosmonaut 5:450-451
G 8:744
illus.: 17:1607, 1609, 1610, 1622; command module, Apollo missions 17:1622
Lunar base 10:980-983
lunar module, Apollo missions 17:1622
Mars 11:1023-1025
Navigation 12:1134-1135
orbit 17:1622-1623
Orbital systems 13:1218-1220
Rocket 15:1461-1463
Space 17:1607-1611
Space pilot 17:1616-1617
Space station 17:1620-1621
Space vehicles 17:1624-1637
speed of transfer 17:1623
Titov, Major Gherman Stepanovich 18:1754
Venus 19:1810-1811
Weightlessness 19:1861
SPACE VEHICLES 17:1624-1637
Astronautics 2:157-165
Aviation 2:191-197
chart: classification of space vehicles 17:1625; descent and landing vehicles 17:1635; earth launch vehicles 17:1628; international space vehicles 17:1634; orbiting space vehicles 17:1629, 1631, 1633
Cosmonaut 5:450-451
Descent and landing vehicles 17:1632
Earth launch vehicle 17:1624-1628

illus.: 17:1624, 1627, 1630, 1632, 1636, 1637; Infrared Astronomical Satellite (IRAS) 17:1624; Jupiter Orbital Probe 17:1636; lunar base 17:1637; Saturn 17:1627; Search for Extraterrestrial Intelligence 17:1636; Space shuttle 17:1632; Space station 17:1637; Viking 17:1636; Viking photo from Mars 17:1630
Interorbital Space Vehicles 17:1631-1632
Lunar base 10:980-983
Missile 11:1071-1075
Orbital systems 13:1218-1220
Orbiting space vehicles 17:1628-1631
Revolution 15:1456
Rocket 15:1461-1463
Rocket engine 15:1463-1467
Rocket propellants 15:1468-1469
Satellite, man-made 16:1507-1508
Space pilot 17:1616-1617
Space Shuttle Orbiter 17:1618-1619
Space station 17:1620-1621
Space travel 17:1622-1624
terms 17:1626
Viking Project 19:1814
Weightlessness 19:1861
SPALLANZANI, LAZZARO 17:1638
Leeuwenhoek, Anton van 10:950
Spontaneous generation 17:1652
SPANISH MOSS 17:1638
illus. 17:1638
SPARK 17:1638
illus. 17:1638
SPARROW 17:1638-1639
Grosbeak 9:807
Sparrow hawk see **HAWK; KESTREL**
SPASM 17:1639
SPAWNING 17:1639
illus. 17:1639
milt 17:1639
oviparous 17:1639
Salmon 15:1491
Smelt 16:1563
SPEARMINT 17:1640
illus. 17:1640
Mint 11:1070
SPECIALIZATION 17:1640
SPECIFIC GRAVITY 17:1640-1641
Archimedes' principle 17:1640
Density 5:493
exp. 17:1641
illus. 17:1640
Mineralogy 11:1068
pycnometer 17:1641
SPECIFIC HEAT 4:326; 17:1641
Specimen see **MICROSCOPE**
SPECTROGRAPH 17:1641-1642
illus. 17:1642
optical 17:1642
Spectroscope 17:1642-1643
SPECTROMETER 17:1642
illus. 17:1642
Spectrograph 17:1641-1642
SPECTROSCOPE 1:16; 17:1642-1643
Absorption of light 1:16
Bunsen, Robert Wilhelm 4:314
Doppler effect 6:525
Herzberg, Gerhard 9:842
Observatory 12:1187
Photography 13:1281-1282
Stars 17:1660-1662
SPECTRUM 1:16; 17:1643
Absorption of light 1:16

classic color triangle 17:1643
Color 5:422
Crux 5:460
Diffraction grating 6:509
Dispersion 6:519
Doppler effect 6:525
electromagnetic 17:1643
Electromagnetic spectrum 6:578
Iridescence 10:912
Light 10:959-963
nanometer 17:1643
Neptune 12:1139
Prism 14:1370
rainbow 17:1643
Sky 16:1559
Spectroscope 17:1642-1643
White light 19:1867
SPECTRUM POLLUTION 17:1643-
1644
causes 17:1644
correction 17:1644
SPEED 17:1644
Machinery 10:989-991
SPEED OF SOUND 17:1644
SPELEOLOGY 17:1644
SPERM 3:207; 17:1644
Menstruation 11:1044
Spallanzani, Lazzaro 17:1638
Testis 18:1736-1737
Sperm whale see **WHALE**
SPERMATOPHYTE 17:1645
Spermatozoa see **SPERM**
SPERRY, ELMER AMBROSE
17:1645
Sphagnum see **MOSS; PEAT**
Sphenophyta 18:1763
Sphere see **GEOMETRY**
Spherical symmetry see **ANIMALS,
CLASSIFICATION OF**
SPHINCTER 17:1645
SPICE 17:1645
Cloves 5:411
cultivation 17:1645
illus.: bay leaf 17:1645; pepper
17:1645; sweet basil 17:1645;
tarragon 17:1645; thyme
17:1645
Paprika 13:1243
Sage 15:1488
Tarragon 18:1718
uses 17:1645
SPICULE 17:1646
Spider mite, illus. 11:1064
SPIDER PLANT 17:1646
Plants, tropical 14:1329-1330
SPIDERS 17:1646-1647
body structure 17:1646
Daddy longlegs 5:475
exp.: preserving a spider web
17:1647
illus.: 5:417; 17:1646
respiratory system 17:1646-1647
varieties 17:1646
webs.17:1647
Spiderwort see **WILD FLOWERS**
SPINACH 17:1647
illus.: 17:1647; 19:1817
SPINAL CORD 17:1648-1649
Autonomic nervous system 2:189-
190
illus. 17:1648
Medulla oblongata 11:1041
Meninges 11:1043
Multiple sclerosis 12:1119
Myelitis 12:1128
Pain 13:1235
Paralysis 13:1245
protection 17:1648
structure 17:1648

SPINY ANTEATER 17:1649
Duckbill 6:531
illus. 17:1649
Monotreme 11:1091
SPIRACLE 17:1649
illus. 17:1649
SPIREA 17:1649
illus. 17:1649
Spirilla see **BACTERIA**
SPIROCHETES 17:1650
illus. 17:1650
Yaws 19:1887
SPIROGYRA 17:1650
illus.: 14:1334; 17:1650
SPLEEN 17:1650-1651
illus. 17:1651
invertebrates 17:1650-1651
Leukemia 10:956
Migratory cells 11:1061
Mononucleosis 11:1090
SPONTANEOUS COMBUSTION
17:1651
Oxygen 13:1233
SPONTANEOUS GENERATION
17:1652
illus. 17:1652
Redi, Francesco 17:1652
Spallanzani, Lazzaro 17:1638
SPOONBILL 17:1652
illus. 17:1652
Sporangium see **MOLD**
SPORE FORMATION 1:58; 17:1652-
1653
Club moss 5:411
Fucus 8:738
Fungus 8:741-742
Horsetail 9:856
illus. 17:1653
Liverworts 10:973-974
Mold 11:1081-1082
Moss 12:1108-1109
Plant 14:1314-1317
Reproduction, asexual 15:1445
Rust 15:1484
Yeast 19:1888-1889
SPOROPHYTE 1:65; 17:1653
Gametophyte 8:749
illus. 17:1653
Moss 12:1108-1109
Spore formation 17:1653
Sporophyte generation, illus. 1:65
SPRAIN 17:1653
SPRING (MECHANICAL) 17:1653
Spring see **RIVER; SEASONS**
SPRUCE 17:1654
Evergreen 7:646
illus. 17:1654
SPURGE 17:1654
illus.: hevea 17:1654; poinsettia
17:1654; snow-on-the-mountain
17:1654
Squab see **PIGEON**
SQUALL LINE 17:1654
jet stream 17:1654
Square see **GEOMETRY**
SQUASH 17:1655
illus. 17:1655
SQUID 17:1655
Chromatophores 4:385
Cuttlefish 5:471
illus. 1:85; 17:1655
Marine biology 11:1019-1021
Octopus 12:1195-1196
protection 1:87
SQUIRREL 17:1655-1656
illus.: 1:84; 7:643; 15:1474;
17:1656; tracks 1:90
Rodent 15:1474-1475
varieties 17:1656

Stability see **COMPOUNDS,
STABILITY OF**
Stabilizer (airplane) see **AIRPLANE;
GYROSCOPE**
STAINING 17:1656
illus. 17:1656
STALAGMITE AND STALACTITE
17:1657
Calcium carbonate 4:323
exp. making formations 17:1657
illus. 17:1657
Speleology 17:1645
STAMEN 17:1657
Dioecious 6:516
Pollination 14:1346-1347
STANDARD PRESSURE 17:1657-
1658
Standard temperature 17:1658
STANDARD TEMPERATURE
17:1658
STANDING WAVE 17:1658
electromagnetic 17:1658
mechanical 17:1658
sound 17:1658
Wave 19:1837
STANLEY, WENDELL M. 17:1658
Stapes 6:539
Staphlococcus see **BACTERIOLOGY**
STAR, DOUBLE 17:1658-1659
Big and Little Dippers 3:250
Doppler effect 6:525-526
illus. 17:1658
Laplace, Pierre Simon, Marquis de
10:942
STAR, VARIABLE 17:1659
Nova 12:1161
STARCH 17:1659
animal digestion 1:86
Arrowroot 2:138
illus. 17:1659
Plastics 14:1332-1334
Protein 14:1376-1377
Sugar 17:1683
STARFISH 17:1659-1660
body structure 17:1659
illus.: 1:85; 6:549; 11:1019;
15:1443, 1454; 17:1660; 19:1834
reproduction 17:1660
Reproduction, asexual 15:1445
respiration 17:1659-1660
Sea urchin 16:1518
Water vascular system 17:1659;
19:1834
STARLING 17:1660
Myna 12:1128
STARS 17:1660-1662
Asteroid 2:152
Astronomy 2:167
Betelgeuse 3:148
Boötes 3:283
Canis Major and Canis Minor
4:333
Centaurus 4:363
Cepheus 4:365
chart 17:1662
Doppler effect 6:525-526
evolution 17:1662
illus.: 11:1008; 17:1661
Interstellar communication
10:907-909
Jupiter 10:928-929
Light 10:959-963
Light year 10:963
Magnitude 11:1008
Milky Way 11:1062; 17:1660
Nova 12:1161
Orion 13:1224
Parallax 13:1245
Perseus 13:1269

Proxima Centauri 17:1661
Pulsars 14:1384
Search for Extraterrestrial Intelligence 16:1522
Sirius 16:1551
Solar system, origin of 16:1579
Spectroscope 17:1642-1643
Star, double 17:1658-1659
Sun 17:1660; 1686-1691
Starvation see **MALNUTRITION**
States of matter see **GAS; LIQUID; PHYSICAL STATES AND CHANGES**
STATIC ELECTRICITY 1:69; 17:1663
creation of 17:1663
dangers 17:1663
Electricity 6:563-572
exp. 8:730
illus. 17:1663
Spark 17:1658
uses 17:1663
Xerography 19:1884
Statics see **DYNAMICS; MECHANICS**
STATISTICS 17:1664-1665
Biometry 3:254
frequency curve 17:1664
frequency distribution 17:1664
illus. 17:1664
mean 17:1664
Median 11:1038; 17:1664-1665
mode 17:1664-1665
Numeral systems 12:1179-1183
Psychology 14:1380-1381
range 17:1665
raw data 17:1664
STEAM 17:1665
automobile 2:184, 189
Engine 7:623
Steam engine see **ENGINE; TRAIN, RAILROAD; TURBINE**
Steamboat see **FULTON, ROBERT**
STEEL 17:1666-1668
Alloy 1:62
Annealing 2:107
Carbonization 4:343
electric furnace process 17:1666
Hematite 9:833
illus. 17:1666-1667
Iron 10:913-915
Manganese 11:1013
Monel metal 11:1088
Open hearth process 13:1210-1212
Ore 13:1221
oxygen-converter process 17:1666-1667
Reduction 15:1439
Rusting 15:1485
Slag 16:1560
types of steel 17:1668
Stegosaurus 6:514
STEIN, WILLIAM HOWARD 17:1668
STELE 17:1668
illus. 17:1668
STELLAR 17:1668
STEM 17:1668
Bulbs 4:314
Cactus 4:321
economic importance 17:1668
Herb 9:836
internal structure 17:1668
Node 12:1155; 17:1668
Runner 15:1484
Tuber 18:1775
STEM, UNDERGROUND 17:1668-1669

bulb 17:1669
corm 17:1669
illus.: external 17:1669; onion 17:1669; potato 17:1669; sweet flag 17:1669
internal 17:1669
Rhizome 15:1457-1458; 17:1669
tuber 17:1669
STENTOR 17:1670
illus. 17:1670
Protozoa 14:1378-1379
STEPPE 17:1670
Climate 4:397
Steradian see **CANDELA**
STEREOPHONIC SOUND 17:1670
illus. 17:1670
STEREOSCOPE 17:1670
STERILITY 17:1670
STERILIZATION 17:1671
Antiseptic 2:118
Food preservation 8:709-710
Sternum see **SKELETON**
STEROID 17:1671
Adrenal glands 1:27-28
androgen 17:1671
cholesterol 17:1671
Cortisone 5:449
ergosterol 17:1671
Estrogen 7:637; 17:1671
Gonad 8:787
illus.: chemical structure 17:1671
progesterone 17:1671
sitosterol 17:1671
STETHOSCOPE 17:1672
illus. 17:1672
Laënnec, Rene 10:939
STICKLEBACK 17:1672
STIGMA 17:1672
Still see **DISTILLATION**
STIMULANT 17:1672-1673
STIMULUS 17:1673
Psychology 14:1380-1381
Stress 17:1678
Sting ray see **RAY**
Stingaree 15:1432
Stinkbug see **BUGS**
Stock see **GRAFTING**
STOICHIOMETRY 17:1673
Stomata see **LEAVES; TRANSPIRATION**
STONE AGE 17:1673
Archeology 2:129-131
chart: Stone age cultures 17:1675
Eolithic Period 17:1674
illus.: artifacts 17:1673, 1674
Mesolithic Period 17:1674
Mineralogy 11:1067-1069
Neolithic Period 17:1674
Paleolithic Period 17:1674
Storage battery see **BATTERY**.
STORK 7:643; 17:1676
illus. 17:1676
STORKS'-BILL 17:1676
illus. 17:1676
STORM 17:1676
Strabismus 13:1217
Strain see **ELASTICITY; STRESS**
STRAIT 17:1676
STRATIFICATION 17:1676
STRATIGRAPHY 2:131; 17:1676-1677
Stratosphere see **ATMOSPHERE**
Stratum see **GEOLOGY; PALEONTOLOGY**
Stratus see **CLOUDS**
STRAWBERRY 17:1677
illus. 17:1677
STRAWFLOWER 17:1677
STREAM 17:1677

Stream, jet see **JET STREAM**
STREAMLINING 17:1677
illus. 1:29
Streptococcus see **BACTERIA**
Streptomycin see **ANTIBIOTICS**
STRESS 17:1677-1678
biological 17:1678
Elasticity 6:562
Homeostasis 9:851
illus. 17:1678
Mechanics 11:1037-1038
Modulus 11:1080
Physiology 13:1289-1291
Rocket sled 15:1470
Selye, Hans 17:1678
Shock 16:1539
Tensile strength 18:1733
Torsion 18:1761
STRIP MINING 13:1212; 17:1678
ecological problems 17:1678
methods 17:1678
STRONTIUM 17:1679
Davy, Sir Humphry 5:483
Structural formulas 4:375
STRYCHNINE 17:1679
Stucco see **PLASTER**
STURGEON 17:1679
Caviar 4:357
SUBLIMATION 17:1680
Dry ice 6:530-531
SUBMARINE 17:1680-1681
buoyancy 17:1680
Deep-sea diving 5:488
illus. 17:1680
military uses 17:1681
nuclear 17:1681
Periscope 13:1266
Subsonic see **SUPERSONIC**
SUBSTANCES, PROPERTIES OF 17:1681-1682
chemical 17:1682
chemical compounds 17:1681
Fluid 7:694
Freezing point 8:728-729
illus. 17:1681
mechanical 17:1682
Mixture 11:1079
nuclear 17:1682
Subtraction see **ARITHMETIC**
Subtropic plants 17:1682
SUCCESSION 4:397; 17:1682-1683
Eutrophication 7:646
illus. 17:1682
primary 17:1682-1683
secondary 17:1683
Swamp 18:1709
terminal 17:1683
Succulent plants see **PLANTS, SUCCULENT**
Sucker see **ECHINODERMATA**
Sucrase 6:512
Sucrose see **CARBOHYDRATES; DIGESTIVE SYSTEM; ENZYMES**
Suez Canal 4:330
Suffocation see **FIRST AID**
SUGAR 17:1683
animal digestion 1:86
Assimilation 2:151
Beet 3:241
Enzymes 7:629-630
illus. 17:1683
Insulin 9:887
lactose 17:1683
maltose 17:1683
Maple 11:1015
Molasses 11:1081
monosaccharides 17:1683
polysaccharides 17:1683
table sugar 17:1683

SULFA DRUGS 17:1684
Domagk, Gerhard 6:525
illus. 17:1684
Infection 9:877-878
SULFIDES 17:1684
SULFUR 17:1684-1685
illus. 17:1685
Insulator 9:887
Protein 14:1376-1377
SULFURIC ACID 17:1685
Hydrochloric acid 9:865
illus.: extraction 17:1685
SUMAC 17:1685
illus.: 14:1343; 17:1685
Sumas, illus. 16:1543
Summer see **SEASONS**
SUN 17:1686-1691
Astronomy 2:166-167
compared with other stars 17:1689-
1691
Corona 6:551
Eclipse 6:551
energy 17:1691
formation of planets 17:1688-
1689
Fuel 8:740
Hydrogen-cloud theory of origin
17:1686-1688
illus.: hydrogen-cloud theory
17:1687, 1688; observing
17:1690; planets 17:1687; size
compared with earth 17:1686;
size compared with other stars
17:1688, 1689; solar spectrum
17:1689
International Geophysical Year:
Atmosphere 9:891-892
Jupiter 10:928-929
Light 10:959-963
Moon 11:1092-1094
Moon, phases of 11:1094
Solar cell 16:1574
Solar system 16:1575-1578
Solar system, origin of 16:1579
Solar turbulence 16:1580
Stars 17:1660-1662
sunspots 17:1691
Universe 18:1786-1788
SUNBURN 17:1691
SUNDEW 17:1691
illus. 17:1691
Plants, insectivorous 14:1328
Venus's flytrap 19:1811
SUNDIAL 17:1692
exp.: construction 17:1692
Egyptian 17:1692
15th century 17:1692
Greek 17:1692
illus. 17:1692
SUNFISH 17:1693
illus. 17:1693
SUNFLOWER 17:1693
illus. 17:1693
Sunset see **TYNDALL EFFECT**
SUNSHINE RECORDER 17:1693-
1694
Campbell-Stokes 17:1693-
1694
Maring-Marvin 17:1694
photoelectric 17:1693
pyroheliometer 17:1694
Sunspot see **SOLAR TURBULENCE**
Sunstroke see **FIRST AID**
SUPERSATURATED SOLUTION
17:1694
SUPERSONIC 17:1694-1695
illus.: sonic boom 17:1695
shock waves 17:1694-1695
Sound barrier 16:1590

SURFACE TENSION 17:1695
Capillarity 4:334
Cohesion 5:420
illus. 17:1695
Liquid 10:968-970
Soap 16:1570
Wetting agent 19:1863
SURGERY 17:1696-1697
anesthetics 1:80; 17:1696-1697
antibiotics 17:1697
antiseptics 17:1697
Atropine 2:174
control of bleeding 17:1696
dissection 17:1696
Harelip 9:821
Hernia 9:841
history 17:1696
illus.: ancient 17:1696, 1697;
modern 17:1697
Ligature 10:958
Lister, Joseph 10:971; 17:1696
Medicine 11:1038-1040
Pare, Ambroise 17:1696
Plastic surgery 14:1332
Sterilization 17:1671
Suture 18:1708
Transplant 18:1770
SURVEYING 18:1707
geodetic 18:1707
illus. 18:1707
topographic 18:1707
types of measurements 18:1707
Surveyor 17:1635
Survival of the fittest 5:482
Suspension see **COLLOIDAL STATE**
Suspension bridge see **BRIDGES**
SUTHERLAND, EARL W. 18:1708
SUTURE 18:1708
SWALLOW 18:1708
Bird houses 3:258
illus. 18:1708
Swallowtail see **BUTTERFLIES**
SWAMMERDAM, JAN 18:1708-
1709
SWAMP 18:1709
illus. 18:1709
SWAN 18:1709
illus. 18:1709
SWEAT GLANDS 18:1710
Glandular tissue 8:780
illus. 18:1710
Skin 16:1556-1557
Sweet alyssum see **ALYSSUM**
SWEET GUM 18:1710
SWEET PEA 18:1710
illus. 7:644; 18:1710
SWEET POTATO 18:1711
illus. 18:1711
Sweet William see **PINKS**
SWEETBREAD 18:1711
SWEETBRIAR 18:1711
SWEETENERS, DIET 18:1711
Cyclamates 5:473
SWIFT 18:1711
Swim bladder see **PISCES**
Swine see **PIG**
SWISS CHARD 18:1711
Beet 3:241
SWITCHES, ELECTRIC 18:1712
illus. 18:1712
knife 18:1712
mercury 18:1712
push button 18:1712
snap 18:1712
Solenoid 16:1581
SWORDFISH 18:1712
illus. 18:1712
SYCAMORE 18:1713
illus. 18:1713

Symbiosis see **BALANCE OF**
NATURE
SYMBOL, CHEMICAL 18:1713
Elements 6:586-589
SYMMETRY 18:1713
bilateral 18:1713
illus.: 1:95; 18:1713
radial 18:1713
SYMPTOM 18:1713
Synapse see **NERVE CELL**
SYNDROME 18:1713
Synergistic 8:775
SYNTHESIS 18:1714
SYNTHETIC FABRIC 18:1714
eutetics 18:1714
man-made 18:1714
molded 18:1714
monomers 18:1714
Nylon 12:1185
Plastics 14:1332-1334
Rayon 15:1436
Textile 18:1737
SYPHILIS 18:1714
causes 18:1714
damaging effects 18:1714
Gonorrhea 8:787
symptoms 18:1714
treatment 18:1714
Venereal disease 19:1809
SYRINGA 18:1714
Lilac 10:964; 18:1714
Syrphus, illus. 11:1064
System see **ANATOMY;**
PHYSIOLOGY
Systole see **HEART**
TACHOMETER 18:1715
illus. 18:1715
TADPOLE 11:1052; 18:1715
illus. 18:1715, 1753
Toad 18:1755
TALC 18:1715
illus. 9:819
TALLOW 18:1715
Fat 7:672
TAMARACK 18:1715
illus. 18:1715
Tamarau see **WATER BUFFALO**
TANAGER 18:1716
Tangerine see **CITRUS FRUIT**
Tank 19:1841
TANNIN 18:1716
Tanning see **LEATHER**
TANTALUM 18:1716
TAPEWORM 18:1716-1717
body structure 18:1717
illus.: 13:1247, 1248; 18:1716
life cycle 18:1716-1717
Parasites 13:1247-1249
Platyhelminthes 14:1336-1337
TAPIR 18:1717
illus. 18:1717
Taproot see **ROOT**
TAR 18:1717
Tarantula see **ARACHNIDA;**
SPIDERS
Tarnish see **RUSTING**
TARO 18:1718
Caladium 4:323
illus. 18:1718
TARPON 18:1718
illus. 18:1718
TARRAGON 18:1718
Tarsier see **PRIMATES**
TASTE 18:1718-1719
illus. 18:1719
link with smell 18:1719
Sense organs 16:1528-1529
taste cells 18:1718
tongue 18:1718-1719

TATUM, EDWARD L. 18:1718
TAURUS 18:1719
  illus. 18:1719
  mythology 18:1719
TAXIDERMY 18:1719-1721
  exp. 18:1720
  illus. 18:1721
  techniques: fish 18:1721; large
    mammals 18:1720-1721; reptiles
    18:1721; small mammals and birds
    18:1719-1720
Taxonomy see **ANATOMY;
  ANIMALS, CLASSIFICATION OF;
  EVOLUTION; PLANTS,
  CLASSIFICATION OF**
TEA 18:1721-1722
  illus. 18:1722
TEAK 18:1722
  Hardwood 9:820
  illus. 18:1722
Teal see **DUCK**
TEARS 18:1722
TECHNETIUM 18:1722
Technicolor see **MOTION PICTURES**
TECHNOLOGY 18:1722
TEETH 18:1723
  aid in digestion 18:1723
  development 18:1723
  human 18:1723
  Hygiene 9:869
  illus. 18:1723
  internal structure 18:1723
  Tooth decay 18:1759-1760
TEKTITES 18:1724
TELEGRAPH 18:1724
  Communication 4:427-429
  exp. 18:1725
  Henry, Joseph 9:835
  illus. 5:427; chart: Morse code
    18:1725
  inventors 18:1724
  Morse, Samuel Finley Breese
    11:1097
  Radio 15:1416-1418
  radiotelegraphy 18:1724
  wire 18:1724
TELEPHONE 18:1726-1727
  Bell, Alexander Graham 3:244
  Cables 4:320
  Coaxial cable 5:415
  Communication 5:429
  dialing system 18:1727
  diaphragm 18:1726
  electromagnets 18:1726
  headset 18:1726
  Henry, Joseph 9:835
  illus. 5:428; 18:1726, 1727
  Radio 15:1416-1418
  switching system 18:1726-1727
TELEPHOTOGRAPHY 18:1727
  illus. 18:1727
TELESCOPE 18:1728-1730
  Binoculars 3:250-251
  exp.: making a refracting tele-
    scope 18:1728
  Hale, George Ellery 9:816-817
  Huygens, Christian 9:816
  illus. 13:1215; 18:1729
  Jupiter 10:928-929
  Lens, man-made 10:952-953
  Magnifying power 11:1007
  Magnitude 11:1008
  Mirror 11:1070
  Moon 11:1092-1094
  Newton, Sir Isaac 12:1147
  Observatory 12:1187
  Optical instruments 13:1214-1215
  Periscope 13:1266
  Photography 13:1281-1282

  Planetaruim 14:1312-1313
  Radio telescope 15:1419
  reflecting 18:1728-1729
  refracting 18:1728
  uses for 18:1729-1730
TELEVISION 18:1730-1732
  Antenna (electronic) 2:114
  Baird, John Logie 3:212-213
  Camera 4:329; 18:1730
  Carrier wave 4:345
  Cathode 4:354
  Cathode ray 4:354
  Cathode-ray tube 4:355
  closed-circuit 18:1732
  color 18:1732
  Condenser 5:438
  DeForest, Lee 5:491
  Electricity 6:571
  Electronics 6:581-585
  illus. 18:1730, 1731, 1732
  Photoelectricity 13:1278-1280
  Printed circuit 14:1364
  receiver 18:1731-1732
  Telephone 18:1726-1727
  transmitter 18:1731
  Vacuum tube 18:1793-1794
  VHF 19:1813
TELLURIUM 18:1732
Telophase see **MITOSIS AND
  MEIOSIS**
TEMPERATURE 18:1733
  Isothermal lines 10:918
  Temperature scales 18:1733
  Thermometer 18:1743-1744
  Thermostat 18:1744-1745
TEMPERATURE SCALES 18:1733
  Absolute zero 1:15
  Centigrade or Celsius 4:363
  Heat 9:826-827
  illus. 18:1733
  Kelvin, William Thompson, Lord
    10:931
  Measurement 11:1033-1036
  Thermometer 18:1743-1744
TEMPERING 18:1733
Tendon see **ANATOMY; FIBROUS
  TISSUE**
TENDON OF ACHILLES 18:1733
TENDRIL 18:1733
  Tennant 3:266
TENSILE STRENGTH 18:1733
TENTACLE 18:1734
  Hydroid colony 9:867
  Jellyfish 10:921
  Man-of-war, Portuguese 11:1014
TERATOLOGY 3:254; 18:1734
TERBIUM 18:1734
TERMITE 18:1734
  colonies 18:1734
  illus. 18:1734
  species 18:1734
TERN 18:1734-1735
  illus. 18:1734
Terramycin see **ANTIBIOTICS**
Terrapin see **TURTLE**
TERRARIUM 18:1735-1736
  exp.: making a terrarium
    18:1735-1736
Tertiary see **CENOZOIC ERA;
  GEOLOGIC TIME TABLE**
Testa see **SEED**
TESTIS 18:1736-1737
  Androgen 1:79
  Endocrine glands 7:610
  Gonad 8:787
  illus. 18:1737
TETANUS 18:1737
  causes 18:1737
  Medicine 11:1038-1040

  Tetracycline 2:116
  Tetrapods 4:385
TEXTILE 18:1737
Thalamus see **BRAIN**
THALLIUM 18:1737
THALLOPHYTES 18:1738-1739
  Chrysophyta 18:1738
  Chlorophyta 18:1739
  Cyanophyta 18:1738
  Embryophyta 7:607
  Euglenophyta 18:1738
  Eumycophyta 18:1739
  Fungus 8:742
  illus.: algae 18:1738; bacteria
    18:1739; diatom 18:1738; fla-
    gella 18:1738; fungus 18:1739;
    lichen 18:1738
  Myxomycophyta 18:1739
  Phaeophyta 18:1739
  Plants, classification of
    14:1322-1327
  Pyrrophyta 18:1738-1739
  Rhodophyta 18:1739
  Schizomycophyta 18:1739
  Seaweed 16:1523
  Spirogyra 17:1650
THAW 18:1740
Theine see **TEA**
THEORY 18:1740
THERAPY 18:1740
THERMAL 18:1740
THERMOCHEMISTRY 18:1740
  Heat 9:826-827
THERMOCOUPLE 6:571; 18:1740-
  1741
  illus. 18:1740
  meters 18:1741
  thermopiles 18:1741
THERMODYNAMICS 18:1741-1742
  entropy 18:1742
  Giauque, William F. 8:775
  Gibbs, Josiah Willard 8:766
  illus.: first law 18:1741; second
    law 18:1742
  Kelvin, William Thompson, Lord
    10:931
  Law of Conservation of Energy
    18:1741
  Law of Degradation of Energy
    18:1741-1742
  second law 13:1268
  Thermoelectricity 18:1743
  Universe 18:1786-1788
THERMOELECTRICITY 18:1742-
  1743
  Electricity 6:563-572
  Heat 9:826-828
  Thermocouple 18:1740-1741
  uses 18:1742-1743
Thermograph see **THERMOMETER**
THERMOMETER 18:1743-1744
  bimetallic 18:1743
  exp.: making an air thermometer
    18:1744
  Fahrenheit 7:669
  illus. 18:1743
  liquid 18:1743
  Mercury (element) 11:1044
  Temperature scales 18:1733
  thermograph 18:1743-1744
  Thermostat 18:1744-1745
THERMONUCLEAR REACTION
  18:1744
Thermos bottle, illus. 9:828
THERMOSTAT 18:1744-1745
  illus. 18:1744
  Thermometer 18:1744
Theory of relativity see **EINSTEIN,
  ALBERT; RELATIVITY**

Thigmotropism see **TROPISM**
THIRST 18:1745
THISTLE 18:1745
  Camomile 4:329
THOMSON, SIR GEORGE PAGET
  18:1745
THORAX 18:1745
THORIUM 18:1745
  Curie, Pierre and Marie 5:466
THORN 18:1745
  illus. 18:1745
Thorn apple see **HAWTHORNE**
THRASHER 18:1746
  illus. 18:1746
Threadworm see **NEMATHEL-
  MINTHES; PINWORM; WORMS**
Thrombin see **BLOOD**
Thromboplastin 3:269
THROMBOSIS 18:1746
  Apoplexy 2:122
  Blood 3:268-269
  Embolism 6:592; 18:1746
  heart attack 18:1746
THRUSH 18:1746
  Nightingale 12:1149
Thrust see **AERODYNAMICS**
THULIUM 18:1747
THUNDER 18:1747
  Lightning 10:963-964
Thundercloud see **WEATHER**
THUNDERSTORM 18:1747
  convectional 18:1747
  frontal 18:1747
  Hail 9:816
  illus. 18:1747
THYME 18:1748
  illus. 18:1748
  Mint 11:1070
THYMUS 18:1748
  Endocrine glands 7:610
  Glandular tissue 8:781
  illus. 18:1748
THYROID 18:1748-1749
  Cretin 5:456; 18:1748
  Endocrine glands 7:610
  Glandular tissue 8:781
  Goiter 8:785; 18:1748
  Histology 9:849
  hyperthyroidism 18:1748
  Metabolism 11:1048
  Midget 11:1059
  Parathyroid 13:1249
THYROID GLAND 18:1749
  illus. 18:1749
Thyroxin see **THYROID**
Tibia see **SKELETON**
TICK 18:1749
  illus. 18:1749
Tick fever see **ANIMAL DISEASES**
TIDAL WAVE 18:1749
  Tsunami 18:1775
TIDE 18:1750-1751
  causes: moon and sun 18:1750;
    oscillation 18:1750; shape of
    local basin and shoreline
    18:1750
  Gravity 8:794-795
  illus. 18:1750, 1751
  importance 18:1751
  Moon 11:1092-1094
  Oceanography 12:1190-1195
  Sea level 16:1517
  tidal bores 18:1751
  Wave 19:1836-1837
Tiger see **CAT FAMILY**
Tiger lily see **LILY**
Tilt wing 1:50
Timber see **ECONOMIC BOTANY;
  FOREST PRODUCTS; FORESTRY**

TIME ZONES 18:1751-1752
  Day and night 5:483
  daylight saving time 18:1752
  exp. 18:1752
  International Date Line 9:889
  Measurement 11:1033-1036
  Meridian 11:1046
  Sundial 17:1692
  Washington Meridian Conference
    18:1751-1752
TIMOTHY 18:1752
TIN 18:1752-1753
  Metal 11:1049-1051
TINBERGEN, NIKOLAAS 18:1753
TINCTURE 18:1753
Tintype see **PHOTOGRAPHY**
Tissue see **ANATOMY; HISTOLOGY**
TISSUE CULTURE 18:1753-1754
  Staining 17:1656
  value 18:1754
TITANIUM 18:1754
TITMOUSE 18:1754
  illus. 18:1754
**TITOV, MAJOR GHERMAN
  STEPANOVICH** 5:450; 18:1754
TITRATION 18:1754
TNT see **EXPLOSIVES**
TOAD 18:1755
  illus. 18:1755
  internal anatomy 18:1755
  reproduction 18:1755
  Tadpole 18:1715
TOADSTOOL 18:1755
TOBACCO 18:1756
  Nicotine 12:1148
  smoking and health 18:1756
TODD, SIR ALEXANDER R. 18:1756
TOMATO 18:1756
  Potato 14:1354
TONGUE 18:1756-1757
  illus. 18:1756
TONSILLITIS 18:1757
TONSILS 18:1757
  Adenoids 1:26
  illus. 18:1757
  Lymphatic system 10:986-987
Tonus see **MUSCLE SYSTEM**
TOOLS 18:1757-1759
  hand 18:1758
  history 18:1757-1758
  illus. 18:1757, 1758
  machine 18:1758-1759
TOOTH DECAY 18:1759
  causes 18:1759-1760
  illus. 18:1759-1760
  infection 18:1760
  prevention 18:1760
  Teeth 18:1723
TOPAZ 18:1760
  illus. 9:819; 18:1760
TOPOGRAPHY 18:1760
TOPSOIL 18:1760
TORNADO 18:1761
  Cyclone 5:473
  Wind 19:1874-1875
Torpedo, illus. 19:1841
Torpedo ray, illus. 15:1432
TORQUE 18:1761
  Dynamometer 6:537
  illus. 18:1761
  moment of force 18:1761
  torque rule 18:1761
  Torsion 18:1761
Torricelli, Evangelista see
  BAROMETER
Torrid zone 6:543
TORSION 18:1761
  Mass 11:1027
  Torque 18:1761

Tortoise see **TURTLE**
TOUCH 18:1762
  illus. 18:1762
  tactile corpuscles 18:1762
TOUCH-ME-NOT 18:1762
  illus. 18:1762
TOURMALINE 18:1762
  illus. 11:1067
Tourniquet see **FIRST AID**
Toxin see **POISON; VACCINE**
Tracer see **NUCLEAR SCIENCE
  GLOSSARY**
Trachea see **RESPIRATORY
  SYSTEM**
TRACHEOPHYTES 18:1763
  Angiosperm 1:81-82
  Embryophyta 7:608
  Horsetail 9:856
  illus.: club moss 18:1763; corn
    18:1763; cycad 18:1763;
    fern 18:1763; horsetails 18:1763;
    peony 18:1763; pine 18:1763;
    psilotum 18:1763
  Lycophyta 18:1763
  Psilophyta 18:1763
  Pterophyta 18:1763
  Sphenophyta 18:1763
Tracheostomy 10:915
Trachodon 6:515
TRADE WINDS 18:1764
  Currents, ocean 5:468-469
  Doldrums 6:524; 18:1764
  horse latitudes 18:1764
TRAILING ARBUTUS 18:1764
TRAIN, RAILROAD 18:1764-1765
  cars 18:1765
  illus. 18:1765
  locomotives 18:1764-1765
  Monorail 11:1091
  passenger traffic 18:1765
Trajectory see **ASTRONAUTICS**
TRANQUILIZER 18:1766
TRANSFORMER 18:1766
  Electricity 6:571
  illus. 18:1766
  Solenoid 16:1581
  Volt 19:1823-1824
TRANSFUSION 18:1766-1767
  Blood 3:268-269
  Blood types 3:271
  Intravenous 10:909
  method 18:1767
  plasma 18:1767
TRANSISTOR 18:1767-1768
  circuit 18:1768
  Electricity 6:570
  Electronics 6:585
  illus. 18:1767-1768
  Indium 9:876
  junction: n-p-n 18:1767; p-n-p
    18:1767
  Photoelectricity 12:1278-1280
  signal amplifier 18:1768
  uses 18:1768
  Vacuum tube 18:1793-1794
TRANSLUCENT 18:1769
  Opaque 13:1210
  Porcelain 14:1350
Transmission see **AUTOMOBILE**
Transonic see **SUPERSONIC**
TRANSPARENT 18:1769
TRANSPIRATION 18:1769
  exp. 18:1769
  Expiration 7:663
  Homeostasis 9:851
  Leaves 10:949
  Plant 14:1314-1317
  Plants, succulent 14:1329
  Tropism 18:1774

TRANSPLANT 18:1770
Death 5:485
Heart 9:823-825; 18:1770
kidneys 18:1770
rejection 18:1770
Surgery 17:1696-1697
TRANSPLANTING 18:1770
Ageratum 1:37
Root 15:1476-1477
TRANSURANIUM ELEMENTS
18:1770
TREE OF HEAVEN 18:1771
TREE-RING DATING 18:1771
illus. 18:1771
TRENCH, DEEP-OCEAN 18:1771
TRENCH MOUTH 18:1771
Triangle see **GEOMETRY**
Triassic see **MESOZOIC ERA;
GEOLOGIC TIME TABLE**
Triceratops 6:515
TRICHINA 18:1771-1772
Nemathelminthes 12:1137-1138
Parasites 13:1247-1249
Trichinosis see **TRICHINA**
TRICHOCYST 18:1772
Trigonometry see **MATHEMATICS**
Trillium see **WILD FLOWERS**
TRILOBITE 18:1772
Fossils 8:723
Paleontology 13:1237-1238
Triplets see **MULTIPLE BIRTHS**
Tritium see **HYDROGEN**
Trochophore 6:943
Tropic of Cancer 4:330; 6:543
Tropic of Capricorn 6:543
Tropical climate see **CLIMATE**
TROPICAL FISH 18:1772-1773
Aquarium 2:125
bubble-nest builders 18:1773
cichlids 18:1773
egg-layers 18:1772-1773
Goldfish 8:787
Guppy 9:811
habitat 18:1772
illus.: angel fish 18:1773;
bloodfins 18:1773; neon tetras
18:1773; platy 18:1773; sword-
tail 18:1773; tropical catfish
18:1773
live-bearers 18:1773
Protective coloration 14:1375-
1376
Seahorse 16:1520-1521
Tropical plants see **PLANTS,
TROPICAL**
Tropics see **CANCER (CONSTEL-
LATION); CAPRICORNUS; EARTH**
TROPISM 18:1774
exp. 18:1774
illus. 18:1774
Troposphere see **ATMOSPHERE**
TROUT 18:1774-1775
illus. 18:1775
Trypsin 6:512
Trypsinogen 6:512
TSUNAMI 18:1775
Tidal wave 18:1749
Tube-nosed swimmers 1:55
Tube worm, illus. 19:1881
TUBER 18:1775
Caladium 4:323
Corm 5:448
Gardening 8:751-753
illus. 18:1775
Perennial 13:1264
Stem, underground 17:1668-1669
TUBERCULOSIS 18:1775-1776
causes 18:1775-1776
Koch, Robert 10:936

Lung 10:983-984
Pleurisy 14:1337
Skin test 16:1558
treatment 18:1776
vaccine 18:1776
TUBEROSE 18:1776
Tuberous begonia see **BEGONIA**
Tufted titmouse see **TITMOUSE**
Tularemia see **ANIMAL DISEASES**
TULIP 18:1776
illus.: 7:644; 18:1776
Stem underground 17:1668-
1669
TULIP TREE 18:1776-1777
illus. 18:1777
Tumblebug see **SCARABS**
TUMBLEWEED 18:1777
TUMOR 18:1777
benign 18:1777
malignant 18:1777
TUNA 18:1777-1778
illus. 18:1777
Mackerel 10:995
Marine biology 11:1019-1021
TUNDRA 18:1778
Arctic 2:133
Asia 2:149
Climate 4:397
illus. 18:1778
Mammoth 11:1013
TUNGSTEN 18:1778
Argon 2:134
Tunicate see **CHORDATA**
Tuning fork see **SOUND;
OVERTONES**
Turbellaria see **PLANARIA**
TURBINE 18:1778-1779
Automobile 2:189
Electricity 6:569
Engine 7:619
gas 18:1779
Hydroelectric power 9:865-866
illus. 18:1779
impulse 18:1779
pressure 18:1779
steam 18:1779
water wheels 18:1779
Turbojet see **ENGINE; JET
PROPULSION**
Turboprop see **JET PROPULSION**
TURKEY 18:1780
Fowl 8:724
illus. 18:1780
mating 18:1780
varieties 18:1780
TURMERIC 18:1780
illus. 18:1780
TURNIP 18:1780
illus. 18:1780
TURPENTINE 18:1781
Essential oils 7:637
TURQUOISE 18:1781
illus. 18:1781
TURTLE 18:1781-1782
Animals, life span 1:97
hatching 18:1782
illus.: 1:25; 15:1449, 1450,
18:1781; Australian snake-
necked turtle 18:1782; box
turtle 18:1782; common snapping
turtle 18:1782; common spotted
turtle 18:1782; diamondback
terrapin 18:1782; giant
tortoise 18:1782; South
American land turtles 18:1782;
warm water green turtle 18:1782
Marine Biology 11:1019-1021
Reptilia 15:1449-1450
shell 18:1781

Turtledove see **DOVE**
TUSKS 18:1783
illus. 18:1783
Tweeter see **HIGH FIDELITY**
TWILIGHT 18:1783
TWILIGHT SLEEP 18:1783
Twins see **MULTIPLE BIRTHS**
Tympanic membrane see **EAR**
TYNDALL EFFECT 18:1783
Colloidal state 5:421
Sky 16:1559
Type see **PRINTING**
TYPHOID FEVER 18:1784
Antiseptic 2:118
Infection 9:878
Peritoneum 13:1267
Sanitation 15:1495
symptoms 18:1784
vaccine 18:1784
TYPHUS FEVER 18:1784
Typhoid fever 18:1784
vaccine 18:1784
Typography see **PRINTING**
Tyrannosaurus see **DINOSAUR**
ULCER 18:1785
cause 18:1785
treatment 18:1785
Ulna see **SKELETON**
Ultraviolet ray see **RAY,
ULTRAVIOLET**
Umbilical cord see **EMBRYOLOGY**
UMBRA 18:1785
Underground stems see **STEM,
UNDERGROUND**
Underwing moth 14:1375
Undulant fever see **ANIMAL
DISEASES**
UNGULATA 18:1785
Buffalo 4:310
Hoof 9:852
illus. 18:1785
Unicellular organism see
PROTOZOA
UNIDENTIFIED FLYING OBJECT
18:1786
Operation Blue Book 18:1786
sightings 18:1786
U.S. Atomic Energy Commission
12:1175
UNIVERSE 18:1786-1788
Cosmology 5:450
Earth, early development of
6:545-547
evolutionary theories 18:1786-
1787
Galaxy 8:745
historical studies 18:1786
illus.: elements 18:1787; theories
18:1786; solar system 18:1788
Infrared Astronomical Satellite
9:879
Milky Way 11:1062
steady-state theory 18:1788
Ural Mountains see **ASIA**
URANIUM 18:1788-1789
Carnotite 4:345
Curie, Pierre and Marie 5:465-
466
Hahn, Otto 9:815
illus. 18:1788
Metal 11:1049-1051
Nuclear reactor 12:1166-1168
Pitchblende 14:1309
Plutonium 14:1340
Radioactive elements 15:1420
Ray, beta 15:1433

URANUS 18:1789-1790
  characteristics 18:1789-1790
  discovery 18:1789
  Herschel, William 9:842
  illus.: orbit 18:1789
  Neptune 12:1139
  Pluto 15:1338-1340
  ring system 18:1790
  rotation 18:1789
UREA 18:1790
  Woehler, Friedrich 19:1878
  Urea cycle 10:937
Ureter see **EXCRETORY SYSTEM; KIDNEY**
Urethra see **EXCRETORY SYSTEM; KIDNEY**
UREY, HAROLD CLAYTON
  18:1790-1791
  illus. 18:1790
URIC ACID 18:1791
URINE 18:1791
  Diabetes 5:497
URSA MAJOR AND MINOR 18:1791
  Big and Little Dippers 3:250
  Draco 6:526-527
  illus. 18:1791
  mythology 18:1791
  Polaris 14:1344
  Star, double 17:1658-1659
  Ursidae 3:236
Uterus see **PREGNANCY**
Uvula see **VOICE**
VACCINE 18:1792-1793
  illus. 18:1792
  Jenner, Edward 10:922
  modified bacteria 18:1792
  passive immunity 18:1792-1793
  Poliomyelitis 14:1346
  Virus 19:1816-1817
  Salk, Jonas Edward 15:1490-1491
  Serum 16:1530
  Smallpox 16:1561-1562
  toxins 18:1792
VACUOLE 18:1793
VACUUM 18:1793
VACUUM TUBE 18:1793-1794
  beam-power tube 18:1794
  cathode 18:1793
  DeForest, Lee 5:491
  Electroencephalograph 6:574-575
  Electricity 6:570
  electrode 18:1793
  Electronics 6:581-585
  illus. 5:491; 18:1793, 1794
  Photoelectricity 13:1278-1280
  Radio 15:1416-1418
  triode 18:1794
Vagus nerve see **NERVOUS SYSTEM**
VALANCE 18:1795
  Electron 6:579
  Halogen 9:818
VALLEY 18:1795
  illus. 18:1795
VALVES, CIRCULATORY 18:1795
Vampire see **BAT**
Van Allen belts see **ATMOSPHERE**
Van de Graaf see **ACCELERATOR**
VANADIUM 18:1796
Vane see **WIND VANE**
VANILLA 18:1796
  illus. 18:1796
  Orchid 13:1221
VAPOR 18:1796
Vapor lamp see **BULB, ELECTRIC**
VAPOR PRESSURE
  Liquid 10:968-970
  Raoult's Law 15:1428-1429
Vapor pressure see **BOYLE'S LAW; CHARLES' LAW; GAS**

Vaporization see **EVAPORATION; HEAT OF VAPORIZATION**
Variable 1:60
Variable geometry 1:50
Variable star see **STAR, VARIABLE**
VARICOSE VEINS 18:1796
VARNISH 18:1796-1797
  Paint 13:1236
  Shellac 16:1534
VASCULAR BUNDLE 18:1797
  Angiosperm 1:81
  illus. 18:1797
  Leaves 10:948-949
VASCULAR TISSUE
  Annual rings 2:109
  illus. 9:847
Vaso presin 9:872
VECTOR 18:1797
  illus. 18:1797
  Velocity 19:1809
VEGETABLE 19:1807
  categories 19:1807
  exp. flowers 19:1808
  Horticulture 9:856
  illus. 19:1807
  nutritional value 19:1807
  uses other than eating 19:1807
  See also individual vegetable names
VEGETATION 19:1808
VEGETATIVE REPRODUCTION
  19:808
VEIN 19:1808
  Artery 2:139
  Capillary 4:335
  cellular structure 19:808
  Circulatory system 4:387
  Heart 9:824
  Histology 9:846-849
  illus. 19:1808
  vena cava 19:1808
VELOCITY 19:1809
  Acceleration 1:17
  Light year 10:963
  Momentum 11:1088
  Motion 12:1111-1112
  Spectrum pollution 17:1643-1644
  Wave 19:1837
Vena cava see **CIRCULATORY SYSTEM**
Venation see **LEAVES**
VENEER 19:1809
  Forest products 8:712
VENEREAL DISEASE 19:1809
  Antibiotics 2:116
  Gonorrhea 8:787
  Syphilis 18:1714
VENOM 19:1809
VENT 19:1809
VENTRAL 19:1809
Ventricle see **HEART**
Venules 4:335
VENUS 19:1810-1811
  atmosphere 19:1811
  diameter 19:1810
  illus. 19:1810-1811
  Jupiter 10:928-929
  orbit 19:1810
  phases 19:1810
  Planet 14:1312
  spacecraft 19:1810
  surface 19:1810-1811
VENUS'S FLYTRAP 19:1811
  illus. 14:1328
  Plants, insectivorous 14:1328
VERBENA 19:1812
  illus. 19:1812
VERMICULITE 19:1812
Vernal equinox 6:543

VERTEBRATE 19:1812
  Chordata 4:383
  Larynx 10:944
  Pineal gland 13:1296
  Respiratory system 15:1453-1455
  Skeleton 16:1552-1555
Vertical take-off and landing see **AIRCRAFT**
VERTIGO 19:1812
  causes 19:1812
  symptoms 19:1812
VESALIUS, ANDREAS 19:1812-1813
Vesta see **ASTEROID**
VETERINARY MEDICINE 19:1813
  Animal diseases 1:89
  Animal husbandry 1:89-90
  Biology 3:254
  illus.: veterinarian 19:1813
VHF 19:1813
VIBRATION 19:1813
  Viburnum, illus. 16:1545
Viceroy see **BUTTERFLIES**
Vicuna see **LLAMA**
VIGNEAUD, VINCENT DU 19:1813-1814
Viking Landers 17:1635
VIKING PROJECT 19:1814
  Search for Extraterrestial Intelligence (SETI) 16:1522
  Viking Spacecraft 17:1634
Villi see **DIGESTION; PREGNANCY**
VINCA 19:1814
Vinci see **LEONARDO DA VINCI**
VINE 19:1814
  Gardening 8:752
  Grape 8:791
  illus. 19:1814
Vinegar see **ACIDS AND BASES**
VINYL 19:1815
VIOLET 19:1815
  illus.: 19:1815; 13:1264; African 8:797
  Pansy 13:1241
Violet ray see **RAY, ULTRAVIOLET**
Viper fish, illus. 11:1021
Viper see **SNAKES**
VIRCHOW, RUDOLPH 19:1815, 13:1254
VIREO 19:1815
  illus. 19:1815
Virginia deer, illus. 5:489
VIRGO 19:1816
  illus. 19:1816
  mythology 19:1816
Virilism see **ADRENAL GLANDS**
Virtual image see **LENS, MAN-MADE**
VIRUS 19:1816-1817
  causes of disease 19:1816-1817
  characteristics 19:1816
  Chicken pox 4:378
  Germ theory 8:773
  illus. 19:1816
  Infection 9:877
  Influenza 9:879
  Meningitis 11:1043-1044
  Microbe 11:1054
  Parasites 13:1247-1249
  Porosity 14:1352
  Shingles 16:1535
  Smallpox 16:1561-1562
  Vaccine 18:1792-1793
  Yellow fever 19:1889
VISCERA 19:1817
Viscose process 15:1436
VISCOSITY 19:1817
  methods of measuring 19:1817
Vision see **EYE; SENSE ORGANS**

VITAMIN 19:1817-1818
  Biochemistry 3:251
  Citrus fruits 4:390-391
  Dairy products 5:476-477
  Digestive system 6:513
  Elements in the human body 6:590
  Hygiene 9:869
  Liver 10:972
  Metabolism 11:1048
  Nutrition 12:1184
  sources 19:1817-1818
  synthesis by body 19:1818
  Vegetable 19:1807
  Yolk 19:1889-1890
VITAMIN DEFICIENCY 19:1818
  chart 19:1819
  Hygiene 9:869
  Nutrition 12:1184
  pellagra 19:1818
  rickets 19:1818
  scurvy 19:1818
  sprue 19:1818
VIVIPAROUS 19:1818
Vixen see **FOX**
Vocal chords see **VOICE**
VOICE 19:1820-1821
  illus. 19:1820-1821
  Larynx 10:944
  Musical instruments 12:1124-1126
  problems 19:1821
  qualities of a good voice 19:1820
  Sound 16:1585-1590
  Telephone 18:1726-1727
  Tongue 18:1756-1757
  voice production: articulators 19:1821; resonators 19:1821; respiratory system 19:1820; trachea 19:1821; vocal chords 19:1821
VOLCANO 19:1822-1823
  Cave 4:357
  Crater 5:456
  damage 19:1822-1823
  exp. 19:1823
  formation 19:1822
  Galapagos Islands 8:745
  Geology 8:768
  illus. 19:1822
  Island 10:917
  island formation 10:917
  Lava 10:945
  Magma 10:995; 19:1822
  Paricutin Volcano 13:1249
  Vent 19:1809
VOLE 19:1823
  illus. 19:1823
VOLT 10:1823-1824
  alternating current 19:1824
  Ampere 1:72-73
  battery 19:1823
  electromotive force 19:1823
  Volta, Alessandro 19:1824
  Voltmeter 19:1824-1825
VOLTA, ALESSANDRO 19:1824
  Electrochemistry 6:573
  Galvani, Luigi 8:748
  illus. 19:1824
VOLTMETER 19:1824-1825
  alternating current 19:1825
  direct currents 19:1824-1825
  Electricity 6:566
  illus. 19:1825
  Thermocouple 18:1740-1741
  vacuum tube 19:1825
VOLUME 19:1825
Voluntary muscles see **MUSCLE TISSUE**

VOLVOX 19:1825-1826
  illus. 19:1826
  Protozoa 14:1378-1379
VOMIT 19:1826
Von Baer see **BAER, KARL ERNST VON**
Von Braun see **BRAUN, WERNER VON**
VORTEX 19:1826
  illus. 19:1826
VORTICELLA 19:1826
  illus. 19:1826
Vote recorder, illus. 6:557
VTOL (Vertical take-off and landing) see **AIRCRAFT**
Vulcan, illus. 19:1840
VULCANIZATION 19:1826
Vulture see **BIRDS OF PREY**
WALKING STICK 19:1827
  illus. 11:1064; 14:1375; 19:1827
WALLABY 19:1827
  Australia 2:181
  illus. 19:1827
  Marsupial 11:1026
Wallace, Albert Russell see **DARWIN, CHARLES ROBERT**
Walleyed pike see **PERCH**
WALNUT 19:1828
  illus. 19:1828
WALRUS 19:1828
  illus. 1:85; 19:1828
  Mammalia 11:1011-1012
  varieties 19:1828
WALTON, ERNEST THOMAS S. 19:1828
Wapiti see **DEER FAMILY**
WARBLER 19:1829
  Chat 4:371
WARBURG, OTTO H. 19:1829
Warm front see **WEATHER FORECASTING**
Warmhouses 8:797
WART 19:1829
Wart hog see **PIG**
Washington Meridian Conference 18:1751-1752
WASP 19:1829-1830
  illus. 19:1829
  nest 19:1829
WATER 19:1830-1831
  chemical formula 19:1830
  exp.: boiling water after cooling it 19:1830
  hard 19:1831
  Hydroelectric power 9:865-866
  Hydrogen bond 9:867
  Ice 9:873
  illus. 19:1830
  in protoplasm 19:1830
  International Hydrological Decade 9:894-895
  Mineral water 11:1065-1067
  Natural resources 12:1131-1133
  Purification 14:1387
  testing 19:1831
WATER BEARER 19:1831
Water beetle see **BEETLE**
WATER BUFFALO 19:1831-1832
  illus. 19:1831
Water bug see **BUGS**
WATER CYCLE 19:1832-1833
  Clouds 5:409-410
  condensation 19:1832-1833
  Evaporation 7:646; 19:1832
  Groundwater 9:807-808
  illus. 19:1832
  International Hydrological Decade 9:894-895
  Water vapor 19:1834

WATER DESALINIZATION 19:1833
  condensation 19:1833
  electrodialysis 19:1833
Water flea see **DAPHNIA**
Water, heavy, see **HEAVY WATER**
WATER LILY 19:1833
  Plants, tropical 14:1329-1331
Water moccasin see **SNAKES**
Water power see **DAM; ENERGY; HYDROELECTRIC POWER**
WATER TABLE 19:1833-1834
  illus. 19:1833
  Well 19:1862
WATER VAPOR 19:1834
  Condensation 5:437
  Dew 5:497
WATER VASCULAR SYSTEM 19:1834
  Echinodermata 6:550
  Hydra 9:862
  illus. 6:550; 19:1834
  Sea cucumber 16:1517
  Starfish 17:1659
Water wheel, illus. 10:991
WATERCRESS 19:1832
  illus. 19:1832
WATERFALL 19:1834-1835
  illus. 19:1835
  River 15:1459-1460
Watermelon see **MELON**
WATERSHED 19:1835
  River 15:1459-1460
WATERSPOUT 19:1835
WATSON, JAMES D. 19:1835
WATT 19:1835
  Electricity 6:568
WATT, JAMES 19:1836
  Automation 2:182
WATT-HOUR METER 19:1836
  illus. 19:1836
  Kilowatt hour 10:933
WAVE 19:1836-1837
  electromagnetic 19:1837
  illus. 19:1837
  mechanical 19:1836
  Oceanography 12:1190-1195
  Sea level 16:1517
  sound 19:1836
  Tidal wave 18:1749
  Tide 18:1750-1751
  velocity 19:1837
  VHF 19:1813
  Vibration 19:1813
WAX 19:1837
WAXWING, CEDAR 19:1837
  illus. 19:1837
WEAPONS 19:1838-1841
  aerial bombs 19:1841
  Ballistics 3:221
  cannons 19:1838, 1840-1845
  Explosives 7:663
  Gunpowder 9:811; 19:1838
  illus.: automatic rifle 19:1839; Colt patent 19:1839; Derringer 19:1839; flame thrower 19:1841; Gatling gun 19:1840, guided missile 19:1841; mine 19:1841; mobile cannon 19:1840; semiautomatic .38 19:1839; semiautomatic rifle 19:1839; shotgun 19:1840; tank 19:1841; torpedo 19:1841; Vulcan 19:1840
  machine gun 19:1840
  medieval 19:1838
  Munitions 12:1119
  pistol 19:1839
  prehistoric 19:1838
  rifle 19:1838

Roman and Greek 19:1838
shotgun 19:1840
Skysweeper 19:1840
Submarine 17:1681
tank 19:1841
WEASEL 7:643,19:1841-1842
characteristics 19:1838-
1841
illus. 14:1375; 19:1842
marten 19:1842
Otter 13:1228
varieties: ermine 19:1841-1842;
mink 19:1842; sable 19:1842;
stoat 19:1842
WEATHER 19:1843-1846
Air 1:42-44
atmosphere 19:1843
Beaufort scale 3:238
Climate 4:394-397
clouds 19:1845-1846
Fog 8:708
Gale 8:745
Hail 9:816
Horse latitudes 9:855
humidity 19:1844
Hurricane 9:859-860
illus.: clouds 19:1845; divisions
of atmosphere 19:1844; effect of
revolution of earth 19:1844;
lightning 19:1843; snow-covered
mountains 19:1846; water vapor
19:1844
Lightning 10:963-964
Low-pressure center 10:979
Mistral 11:1075
Ocean 12:1188-1190
Polar easterlies 14:1343-1344
precipitation 19:1846
Precipitation (weather) 14:1358
Pressure 14:1361
Rain making 15:1426-1427
Snow gauge 16:1569
stratosphere 19:1844
Thermal 18:1740
Thunderstorm 18:1747
Tornado 18:1761
Trade winds 18:1764
troposphere 19:1844
Water cycle 19:1833
Weather forecasting 19:1847-1853
Westerlies 19:1863
wind 19:1844
Wind 19:1874-1875
WEATHER BUREAU 19:1846-1847
illus.: satellite 19:1846
local 19:1846-1847
national 19:1846
Weather station 19:1856-1858
WEATHER FORECASTING 19:1847-
1852; 19:1856-1858
Air masses 1:46
analysis of data 19:1849
anemometer 1:79-80
Clouds 5:409-410
collection of observations
19:1848-1849
forecasting 19:1849-1852
Gale 8:745
High-pressure center 9:844
Humidity 9:859
Hurricane 9:859-860
illus.: cold front 19:1852; eye
of a hurricane 19:1849; International Geophysical Year 19:1847;
rain and snow gauges 19:1848;
snow storm 19:1850; use of computer 19:1851; warm front
19:1852; weather map 19:1850
Isothermal lines 10:918

Lightning 10:963-964
Low-pressure center 10:979
observations 19:1847-1848
Radiosonde 15:1424
Snow gauge 16:1569
Thunderstorm 18:1747
Weather Bureau 19:1846-
1847
Weather map 19:1854-1855
WEATHER LORE 19:1853
illus. 19:1853
WEATHER MAP 19:1854-1855
air masses 19:1854
illus.: 19:1850, 1855; symbols
- 19:1854
Isothermal lines 10:918
Millibar 11:1062
steps for studying 19:1854
Squall line 17:1654
teleprinter machines 19:1854
Weather forecasting 19:1852
Weather station 19:1858
weather symbols 19:1854
WEATHER STATION 19:1856-1857
Balloon 3:222
ESSA satellites 19:1857
exp. making a weather station
19:1857
Hurricane 9:860
Hygrometer 9:870-871
illus.: 19:1856, 1857; photograph
taken from satellite 19:1858
instruments: barometer 19:1856;
thermograph 19:1856; thermome-
ters 19:1856; wind vane 19:1856
radar 19:1865
radiosondes 19:1856
Snow gauge 16:1569
Sunshine recorder 17:1693-1694
Weather forecasting 19:1848-1852
Wind vane 19:1875
Weather symbol see **WEATHER
FORECASTING; WEATHER MAP**
Weather vane see **WIND VANE**
WEATHERING 19:1858
Erosion 7:635
Leaching 10:947
Web see **SPIDERS**
Weber-Fechner Law of Loudness
5:486
Wedge see **MACHINES, SIMPLE**
WEED 19:1858
WEED CONTROL 19:1858-1859
effect on balance of nature
19:1859
illus. 19:1859
Ragweed 15:1425
Weevil see **BEETLES; PLANT
PESTS**
WEIGELA 19:1859
illus. 19:1859
Weighing machine see **BALANCE**
WEIGHT 19:1860
exp.: making scales 19:1860
Gravity 8:795; 19:1860
Mass 11:1027
Weight arm see **MACHINES, SIMPLE**
WEIGHTLESSNESS 19:1861
G 8:744
Mass 11:1027
problems in space 19:1861
Space travel 17:1622-1624
Space vehicles 17:1624-1637
WEISMANN, AUGUST 19:1861
Welding see **ARC; ENGINEERING**
WELL 19:1862
illus. 19:1862
Pump 14:1385
Water table 19:1833-1834

WELLER, THOMAS H. 19:1862
WERNER, ALFRED 19:1862
WEST WIND DRIFT 19:1863
Currents, ocean 5:467-471
illus. 19:1863
WESTERLIES 19:1863
Polar easterlies 14:1343-
1344
Wet bulb see **HYGROMETER**
Wet cell see **BATTERY**
WETTING AGENT 19:1863
Soap 16:1570
Surface tension 17:1695
WHALE 19:1864-1865
Cetacea 4:368
endangered species 19:1865
illus.: 4:368; baleen 19:1864;
toothed 19:1865
Mammalia 11:1011-1012
Marine biology 11:1019-1021
Porpoise 14:1352
varieties 19:1864-1865
WHEAT 19:1866
Cereal grains 4:366
Gluten 8:783
illus. 6:554; 19:1866
Wheel and axle see **MACHINES,
SIMPLE**
WHELK 19:1866
illus. 11:1085; 19:1866
Mollusca 11:1084-1086
WHIPPOORWILL 19:1867
illus. 19:1867
WHIRLPOOL 19:1867
illus. 19:1867
Whirlybird see **HELICOPTER**
White birch, illus. 7:644
WHITE DAMP 19:1867
White-footed mouse, illus.
12:1117
WHITE LAMP 19:1867
WHITE MICE 19:1867-1868
as pets 19:1868
breeding 19:1867-1868
illus. 19:1868
Mouse 12:1117
Rat 15:1430-1431
White oak, illus. 9:820
White wax see **PARAFFIN**
WHITEFISH 19:1868
illus. 19:1868
WHITNEY, ELI 19:1869
Automation 2:182
cotton gin 19:1869
illus. 19:1869
mass production 19:1869
WHOOPING COUGH 19:1869
cause 19:1869
importance of immunization
19:1869
symptoms 19:1869
Whooping crane see **CRANE**
Wild boar, illus. 7:643
Wild carrot, illus. 1:81
WILD FLOWER 19:1870-1871
bitterroot 3:264
Buttercup 4:317
comparison with wild animals
19:1870
disappearance 19:1870
exp. collecting wild flowers
19:1871
grouping by locality 19:1870
illus.: common wild flowers
19:1872-1873; goldenrod
19:1870
seed and fruit dispersal 19:1870
Thistle 18:1745
Weed control 19:1858-1859

Wild lily, illus. 1:81
Wild onion, illus. 1:81
Wild rose, illus. 16:1543
Wildcat see **CAT FAMILY**
Wildebeest see **GNU**
WILDERNESS 19:1871-1874
WILLET 19:1874
 illus. 19:1874
WILLOW 19:1874
WILSON, CHARLES THOMSON REES 19:1874
 Cloud chamber 5:408
WIND 19:1874-1875
 Anemometer 1:79-80
 Jet stream 10:924
 Mistral 11:1075
 Trade winds 18:1764
 Water cycle 19:1833
 Waterspout 19:1835
WIND SOCK 19:1875
 exp. 19:1874
WIND TUNNEL 19:1875
WIND VANE 19:1875
 Beaufort scale 3:238
 exp. 19:1875
 Gale 8:745
WINDBREAK 19:1876
 illus. 19:1876
WINDLASS 19:1876
 illus. 19:1876
WINDMILL 19:1876-1877
 Dutch-type 19:1876-1877
 energy source 19:1877
 illus. 19:1877; 10:991
 Machinery 10:989-991
 multi-bladed 19:1876
 propeller-type 19:1877
Windpipe see **RESPIRATORY SYSTEM**
Winter see **SEASONS**
Winter sleep see **HIBERNATION**
Wire recorder see **SOUND RECORDING**
Wireless see **RADIO**
WISTERIA 19:1877
 illus. 19:1877
WITCH HAZEL 19:1878
 illus. 19:1878
Withdrawal symptoms 1:26
WOEHLER, FRIEDRICH 19:1878
 Aluminum 1:68
WOLF 19:1878
 characteristics 19:1878
 danger of extinction 19:1878
 Dog 6:521
 habitat 19:1878
 illus.: 7:643; 6:521; 19:1878
Wolfram see **TUNGSTEN**
WOLVERINE 19:1879
 illus. 19:1879
Womb see **PREGNANCY**
WOMBAT 19:1879
 illus. 19:1879
Wood duck see **DUCKS**
Wood see **FOREST PRODUCTS; FORESTRY; LUMBER**
Wood pulp see **PAPER**
Wood rat see **RODENTIA**
Wooden rose 14:1330-1331
WOODPECKER 19:1879
 illus.: 19:1879; 1:84
WOOL 19:1879-1880
 Alpaca 1:64
 illus. 19:1880
Wool fat see **LANOLIN**

WORK 19:1880
 Energy 7:612-617
 Foot-pound 8:710
 illus. 19:1880
 Joule 10:925
 Machinery 10:989-991
 Machines, simple 10:992-994
 overcoming resistance 19:1880
 Torque 18:1761
 work formula 19:1880
WORM 19:1881-1882
 acorn 19:1882
 arrow 19:1881-1882
 Earthworm 6:548
 exp. making a wormery 19:1882
 horsehair 19:1881
 illus.: clamworm 19:1881; marine nematode 19:1881; nemertean ribbon worm 19:1881; tube worm 19:1881
 ribbon 19:1881
 spiny-headed 19:1881
WOUND 19:1882
WREN 19:1882
 Bird houses 3:258
 illus. 19:1882
Wright Brothers' aircraft, 1903; illus. 1:30
WRIGHT, ORVILLE AND WILBUR 19:1883
 Aerodynamics 1:29
 Aeronautics 1:30
 Aviation 2:191-192
 first heavier-than-air-craft 1:48
 illus. 19:1883
Wrought iron see **IRON**
X-RAYS 19:1884-1886
 Electron 6:579
 Fluoroscope 7:696
 illus. 19:1885
 Moseley, Henry Gwyn-Jeffreys 11:1097
 Photography 13:1281-1282
 Ray, gamma 15:1434
 Roentgen, Wilhelm Konrad 15:1476
XANTHOPHYLL 19:1884
XENON 19:1884
XEROGRAPHY 19:1884
XY chromosomes see **HEREDITY**
XYLEM 19:1886
 Absorption, physiological 1:15
 Annual rings 2:109
 Bark 3:225
 Cambium 4:326
 Heartwood 9:826
 illus. 19:1886
YAK 19:1887
 illus. 19:1887
 Oxen 13:1231
YAM 19:1887
 illus. 19:1887
YAWN 19:1887
YAWS 19:1887
Year see **CALENDAR; EARTH**
YEAST 19:1888-1889
 exp. 19:1888
 Fermentation 7:675
 illus. 19:1888
 Meningitis 11:1043
 reproduction 19:1888
YELLOW FEVER 19:1889
 Mosquito 12:1107
 Reed, Walter 15:1440
Yellow jacket see **WASP**
Yellow River see **ASIA**

YEW 19:1889
 illus. 19:1889
YOLK 19:1889-1890
 illus. 19:1889
YUCCA 19:1890
 illus. 19:1890; 1:81
 Joshua 10:925
 Plants, succulent 14:1329
 reproduction 19:1890
YTTERBIUM 19:1890
 Lutetium 10:985
YTTRIUM 19:1890
ZEBRA 4:329, 19:1891
 characteristics 19:1891
 illus.: 14:1375; 19:1894; 19:1891; 1:34
 varieties 19:1891
ZENITH 19:1891
 illus. 19:1891
 Nadir 12:1129
Zeppelin see **AIRSHIP; DIRIGIBLE**
ZERO 19:1891-1892
ZINC 19:1892
 Calamine 4:323
 Metal 11:1049-1051
 Mineral 11:1065-1067
Zinjanthropus see **EVOLUTION OF MAN**
ZINNIA 19:1892
 illus. 19:1892
ZIRCON 19:1892
 illus. 19:1892
ZIRCONIUM 19:1893
ZODIAC 19:1893
 Aries 2:134
 Astrology 2:154
 Cancer (constellation) 4:330-331
 Capricornus 4:336
 illus. 19:1893
 Gemini 8:760
 Leo 10:954
 Libra 10:956-957
 Pisces (constellation) 14:1307-1308
 Scorpius 16:1515-1516
 Taurus 18:1719
 Virgo 19:1816
ZOO 19:1894
 contributions 19:1894
 illus.: zoo animals 19:1894
ZOOLOGY 19:1895-1896, 1897
 Biology 3:253-254
 disadvantages of rigid classification 19:1896
 experimental 19:1896
 illus. 19:1895-1897
 Mendel, Gregor Johann 11:1042
 morphology 19:1895
 Oral 13:1217
 physiology 19:1895
 Salamander 15:1489-1490
 specialized fields 19:1896
 systematic 19:1895
 Zoo 19:1894
ZOOPHYTE 19:1896
ZYGOTE 3:207; 19:1896
 Alternation of generations 1:65
 Cleavage 4:393
 Embryology 6:594
 Heredity 9:838
 illus. 15:1446; 19:1896
 Reproduction, sexual 15:1446-1447
 Sperm 17:1644
 Spore formation 17:1653

INDEX OF THINGS TO DO

ABSORPTION OF LIGHT 1:16
ACIDS AND BASES 1:20
ACOUSTICS 1:23
AIR 1:43
AIR PRESSURE 1:47
AIRPLANE 1:53
ANEMOMETER 1:80
ANIMAL CAGES 1:88
ANIMAL TRACKS 1:91
ANNUAL RINGS 2:109
ANTISEPTIC
  bacteria culture 2:118
ANT COLONIES 2:119
ARACHNIDA
  as pets 2:127
ARCHIMEDES' PRINCIPLE 2:132; 133
AUTONOMIC NERVOUS SYSTEM 2:189
BACTERIA
  growing colonies 3:211
BAROMETER
  aneroid 3:228
  mercurial 3:227
BATTERY
  making a storage battery 3:233
BEETLES
  growing 3:242
BERNOULLI'S PRINCIPLE 3:245
BLUEPRINT 3:274
BOILING POINT
  effect of air pressure 3:278
BOYLE'S LAW 3:287
BULB, ELECTRIC 4:313
BULBS
  presence of sugar 4:314
BUOYANCY 4:315
BUTTERFLIES 4:318
CAMERA
  construction 4:328
  how a camera works 4:328
CAPILLARITY 4:335
CARBON
  collecting carbon from oxidation 4:338
CARBON DIOXIDE
  production 4:340
CATALYST 4:353
CENTRIFUGAL OR CENTRIPETAL FORCES 4:364
CHARCOAL
  making charcoal 4:370
CHEMICAL CHANGE 4:371
CHICKEN
  embryo development 6:596
CHLOROPHYLL 4:382
CIRCULATORY SYSTEM
  dissection of heart 4:388
CLOUDS 5:409
COAL TAR 5:414
COLOR
  in a beam of sunlight 5:422
  mixing colored lights 5:423
  white 5:422

COMPASS
  making a compass 5:430
CONDENSATION 5:437
CONVECTION 5:445
CRYSTAL 5:461
CRYSTAL RADIO SET 5:462
CURRENTS, OCEAN 5:468
DAY AND NIGHT 5:484
DIFFUSION 6:509
DIGESTIVE SYSTEM
  effect of saliva 6:510
  peristalsis 6:512
DRY ICE
  effect on burning candle 6:531
  use in freezing 6:531
DYE 6:534
EAR 6:540
ECHO 6:550
ELECTRICITY
  battery 6:570, 571
  conductors 6:565
  magnetism 6:568
ELECTROLYSIS
  electrolyte solutions 6:576
ELECTROMAGNET 6:577
EMBRYOLOGY
  watching chicks develop 6:596
EMULSION 7:609
ENZYMES 7:629
EQUILIBRIUM 7:633
EVAPORATION 7:646
EXPANSION
  gases 7:661
  liquids 7:662
  solids 7:662
EYE
  blind spot 7:666
  iris 7:666
  right and left 7:666
  rods and cones 7:667
FAT 7:672
FERNS 7:677
FIRE EXTINGUISHER
  construction of 7:684
FOG 8:708
FOREST PRODUCTS
  planting trees 8:712
FOSSILS
  how fossils are formed 8:722
FREEZING POINT 8:729
FRICTION 8:730
  measuring 8:731
FROG
  hatching 8:732
FROST 8:733
FRUIT FLY
  breeding 8:737
FUSE
  breaking a circuit 8:743
GALVANOMETER 8:749
GAS 8:754
GERMINATION 8:774
GRAVITY
  center of gravity in human body 8:794
  rate of descent 8:795
GUPPY
  raising guppies 9:811
HARDNESS SCALE 9:819
HEART 9:823
HEAT
  conductors 9:827
HIBERNATION
  frog 9:843
HISTOLOGY
  making tissue slides 9:848
HYDRA
  attacking food 9:863
HYDROPONICS 9:868

HYGROMETER 9:870
ICE
  effect of salt 9:873
INCUBATOR
  hatching baby chicks 9:875
INK 9:880
INSECTA
  collecting 9:882
JET PROPULSION 10:923
LEAVES
  making leaf guide 10:949
LIGHT
  direction light travels 10:960
  preventing total reflection of light 10:960
  reflections, how others see you 10:959
LIGHTNING
  measuring distance of thunderstorm 10:964
MACHINES, SIMPLE
  inclined plane 10:992
  pulley 10:994
  wheel and axle 10:994
METALS
  salts 11:1051
MICROSCOPE
  making slides 11:1056
MILLIKAN'S ELECTRONIC CHARGE 11:1063
MINERAL
  determining true color 11:1066
  in animals 11:1066
MOLD
  growing 11:1082
MOLLUSCA
  observing marine life 11:1086
MOMENTUM 11:1088
MOON, PHASES OF 11:1094
MOSS
  reproduction 12:1108
MOTOR 12:1115
MUSHROOMS
  growing 12:1123
MUSICAL INSTRUMENTS
  constructing a rhythm band 12:1126
NERVOUS SYSTEM
  nerve endings on skin 12:1142
OSMOSIS 12:1127
OXIDATION 13:1231
PAINT
  homemade 13:1236
PARACHUTE 13:1244
PARAMECIUM 13:1246
PERISCOPE 13:1266
PHOTOGRAPHY
  taking pictures through a microscope 13:1281
PHOTOSYNTHESIS 13:1285
PIGMENT 13:1294
PLANARIA 14:1311
PLANETARIUM 14:1313
POLLEN
  growing 14:1346
PORIFERA
  growing sponges 14:1351
PRECIPITATION (CHEMICAL) 14:1357
PROTEIN 14:1376
PROTOZOA 14:1378
PURIFICATION
  filtering plant 14:1387
RAIN GAUGE 15:1426
RAINBOW 15:1427
REAGENT 15:1437
REGENERATION 15:1442
RESONANCE 15:1453

RESPIRATORY SYSTEM
  constructing a respiratory model
    15:1455
RUSTING
  prevention 15:1485
SALAMANDER
  caring for 15:1490
SALT
  as a conductor of electricity
    15:1492
SEA WATER 16:1519
SEED 16:1525
SILKWORM 16:1548
SKELETON 16:1555
SKIN 16:1557
SMELL 16:1562
SNAKES
  as pets 16:1565
SNOW GAUGE 16:1569
SOIL TYPES 16:1573
SOLAR SYSTEM
  building model planets 16:1577
SOUND 16:1589
SPECIFIC GRAVITY 17:1641
SPIDERS
  preserving a spider web 17:1647
STALAGMITE AND STALACTITE
  making formations 17:1657
STATIC ELECTRICITY 8:730
SUNDIAL
  construction 17:1692
TAXIDERMY 18:1720
TELEGRAPH 18:1725
TELESCOPE
  making a refracting telescope
    18:1728
TERRARIUMS
  making a terrarium 18:1735-1736
THERMOMETER
  making an air thermometer
    18:1744
TIME ZONES 18:1752
TRANSPIRATION 18:1769
TROPISM 18:1774
VEGETABLE
  flowers 19:1808
VOLCANO 19:1823
WATER
  boiling water after cooling it
    19:1830
WEATHER STATION 19:1857
WEIGHT
  making scales 19:1860
WILD FLOWER 19:1871
WIND SOCK 19:1874
WIND VANE 19:1875
WORM
  making a wormery 19:1882
YEAST 19:1888